Missing
Witches

Missing Witches

RECOVERING TRUE HISTORIES OF FEMINIST MAGIC

RISA DICKENS AND **AMY TOROK**
FOREWORD BY AMANDA YATES GARCIA

North Atlantic Books
Berkeley, California

Published by
North Atlantic Books
Berkeley, California

Cover design by Jasmine Hromjak
Cover art © gettyimages.com/Arina-Ulyasheva
Interior design by Happenstance Type-O-Rama
Interior illustrations by Amy Torok
Printed in the United States of America

Missing Witches: Recovering True Histories of Feminist Magic is sponsored and published by North Atlantic Books, an educational nonprofit based in Berkeley, California, that collaborates with partners to develop cross-cultural perspectives, nurture holistic views of art, science, the humanities, and healing, and seed personal and global transformation by publishing work on the relationship of body, spirit, and nature.

North Atlantic Books' publications are distributed to the US trade and internationally by Penguin Random House Publishers Services. For further information, visit our website at www.northatlanticbooks.com.

Library of Congress Cataloging-in-Publication Data
Names: Dickens, Risa, 1980- author. | Torok, Amy, 1977- author.
Title: Missing witches : recovering true histories of feminist magic / Risa
    Dickens and Amy Torok ; foreword by Amanda Yates Garcia.
Description: Berkeley, California : North Atlantic Books, [2021] | Includes
    bibliographical references and index. | Summary: "A guide to
    invocations, rituals, and histories at the intersection of magic and
    feminism, as informed by history's witches—and the sociopolitical
    culture that gave rise to them"—Provided by publisher.
Identifiers: LCCN 2020032805 (print) | LCCN 2020032806 (ebook) | ISBN
    9781623175726 (paperback) | ISBN 9781623175733 (ebook)
Subjects: LCSH: Wicca. | Witches—Biography. | Witchcraft. | Feminism. |
    Magic.
Classification: LCC BP605.W53 D43 2021 (print) | LCC BP605.W53 (ebook) |
    DDC 299/.94—dc23
LC record available at https://lccn.loc.gov/2020032805
LC ebook record available at https://lccn.loc.gov/2020032806

3 4 5 6 7 8 9 KPC 26 25 24 23 22 21

North Atlantic Books is committed to the protection of our environment. We print on recycled paper whenever possible and partner with printers who strive to use environmentally responsible practices.

This book is dedicated to the
Witches within. To our ancestors,
parents and stepparents, our families,
chosen families, our partners,
helpers, teachers, and loves. To
May Marigold, a magical future, and
to all those who go looking.

ACKNOWLEDGMENTS

We thank Lily Miller and Gillian Hamel of North Atlantic Books.

We thank every one of the Witches we've had the honor to interview and learn from.

We thank Amanda and Sandra for offering their words to this circle.

We thank our podcast listeners and patrons, the Missing Witches Coven, who make us feel like what we have to say is worth hearing. This magic book would not exist without you.

CONTENTS

Foreword   xi
Notes from an Educator   xv
Introduction   1

1
Yule: *Monica Sjöö and Doreen Valiente*   11

2
Imbolc: *Zora Neale Hurston and Faith Ringgold*   47

3
Ostara: *Paula de Eguiluz and María Sabina*   79

4
Beltane: *Mama Lola*   107

5
Litha: *Marija Gimbutas and Z. Budapest*   139

6
Lughnasadh: *Ipsita Roy Chakraverti and Lal Ded*   171

7
Mabon: *Enheduanna*   201

8
Samhain: *Pamela "Pixie" Colman Smith and H. P. Blavatsky*   231

Notes   259
Bibliography   277
Index   287
About the Authors   293

FOREWORD

A WITCH RECOGNIZES ANOTHER WITCH. That conspiratorial glance across the boardroom; the student with the snake ring who always gives the feminist critique; the jogger who stops to clear the trash tangled in the mugwort leaves. We Witches see each other. A spark passes between us, neurons firing, DNA lighting up, spiraling back through our lineages, back to the first Witches who danced in the woods and spoke their spells into their boiling cauldrons. Even if we don't know their names, we can feel them, our kinfolk. Even when, as with many contemporary Witches, our cauldrons are cups of to-go coffee that we grab on our way to work, or baby formula heated on an electric stove, or the ceramic cup on our dresser—an altar so subtle we are the only ones who know. This world can be a hostile place for a Witch, and in our most desperate moments, when we start to lose our faith in the goodness of the world or our gumption to change it, catching the eye of another Witch can restore our power and help us remember that we're not alone. Yet when we read this book in our hands, we're not just catching the eye of other Witches, we're dancing with them, we're flying with them through the night and across time, wing to wing. In this book, we meet our Witch ancestors. Our sisters, our cousins. Here in *Missing Witches,* even if we already have them (but especially if we don't), we meet the Witch friends we always wanted and find the coven we always wish we had.

The work of Witches is ancestral work. This book is an ancestral book. Many of us have been told that Witches don't exist, even though we knew in our hearts we were one. It's a special kind of erasure to be told that the thing you know you are does not exist. But Witches are real. We exist, and this book shows that we come from a long and powerful tradition. Here we meet a refreshingly diverse coterie of witches, drawing from the powerful magic of women from Sweden to Colombia, from the deserts of Mexico to the brownstones of Harlem. María Sabina, Zora Neale Hurston, Monica Sjöö. The authors include themselves in this brew, mixing their stories with the stories of our Witch grandmothers, showing us how all our stories combine. "We make medicine from poison, Art out of grief, grab calm from inside a storm," the authors say. This work is devotional work. Amy and Risa assembled scraps of heirloom fabric into quilts, pored over documents in libraries, sifted through the graveyard dirt, and reeled and recovered from their own Witch wounds to bring us this book. In it they speak about their anxiety, their broken hearts, the births and deaths, and everything in between—because this book is about the human experience of being a Witch. One of the things I love best about Witches is that they are magical and human at the same time. Witches are magic living in this world in human form.

And here's something else I love: the authors' commitment to telling the truth and their willingness to embrace ambiguity. We don't have to pretend that all our Witch ancestors were saints (though a few might have been burned by them). We commit, the authors say, to telling "true stories, and where we don't know, to resist wrapping up our stories in nice bows. When we reach ambiguous spaces, let's keep what we can from the warrior Witches who kept seeds, preserved languages, fought for land and soil and body and soul and equality and justice, but let's not neglect to face the ugly stuff." In this book, we get to gaze into the faces of our Witch ancestors, to see all the holy mess of who they were, and . . . the holy mess of who WE are, and come to love ourselves, warts and all.

Remembering that to love is also to be humble. To be willing to be vulnerable and face our flaws. I appreciate the authors' willingness to unpack their own biases and blind spots here, to look at racism and internalized sexism and colonialism and continue the work of unsettling. Because Witch work is anti-racist work. And anti-racist work is anti-capitalist work. And in a way, the inquisitors of Old Europe were right: Witches want to bring this whole monstrous system down. We won't stop until we do. And part of that work of unsettling and dismantling is recognizing what is ours and what is not. We should not take what is not ours. Simultaneously, we need to honor the work and practices of Witches from all cultures and backgrounds.

The authors don't give us easy answers for how to move forward—or any answers—but they do help us ask the right questions about what belongs to us and what doesn't, and how to honor our histories without pretending problems don't exist. *Missing Witches* helps us understand our own traditions and catch the torches of our ancestors as they lead us through the underworld. By the end of the book, we find the torches in our hands, and we feel encouraged to carry those fires forward and create new rituals and rites that meet the needs of everyone. *Missing Witches* helps us understand that magic is real in that it is something we can touch and feel, it is something we can create. Magic, the ability to transform reality according to our will, is available to us, right now. We are not at the mercy of hostile forces. Today, in order to thrive, we need to remember we have power. Then, we have to use it.

Witches work with the elements, with Nature. We open portholes, we work for justice against the authoritarian powers that try to claim it for themselves. Witches are resistors, lovers, fighters, magic makers, and Nature worshippers. We tend to the sick and travel between the worlds, casting spells for love and fertility. We are the death doulas and the women who said no.

I've been thinking a lot lately about how Witchcraft is about deciding. Seeing what is and then making choices about how we want to "work with change," as Octavia Butler said. To work our magic means to gather our raw materials, to work with them, to carve them and dance with them, to sing over them, to activate them, and to coax them to grow in a healthy direction. As the world grows hotter and the ice caps melt, as fascism rises and Black and Indigenous people of color throughout the world are on the front line, facing the most brutal consequences, we Witches have to take a stand. The fires of the Inquisition flamed outward to engulf the entire world, a rapacious "rationalism" fueled by colonialism, capitalism, racism, and greed. As I write this, I can smell the fires burning: unrest, disquiet, strife. We Witches need to remember who we are and where we come from. The world needs Witches now: people who are comfortable in the mess and storm, who can call the winds and the rain. The Witch is one who has always stood outside the status quo, one who was born in the flames of resistance. Now, we Witches must use our breath to calm ourselves, to speak, to inspire, to chant, and to add our voices to the chorus around the world, invoking the spirit of Justice.

"Wait, what?" the authors ask. In order to hear the voices, we have to stop and listen. This book makes us do that. And as we slow down and pay attention, we realize that, in fact, the Witches were never missing—we just couldn't see them. As we slow down and pay attention, we see that we live in a magical world. An enchanted world calling out for our recognition, rituals, and our care.

I end these words with a blessing. May everyone who reads this book feel the love of our Witch ancestors. May every Witch who reads this feel empowered to weave her own thread into our historic tapestry. May this be the first of many books for the authors; may its reach be wide and may it be praised and celebrated as it so richly deserves. May the stories of all its readers come together, drops into the ocean, drawn by the powers of the Moon, alive with the mysteries of healing and rebirth. May this book help us remember that the Witch we've been missing has been inside of us all along, inside our own hearts and bodies. May we hear her voice and know . . . she's been with us from the beginning, she'll be there at the end . . . and now, she calls us forward.

Amanda Yates Garcia is the Oracle of Los Angeles, author of *Initiated: Memoir of a Witch,* and host of the *Between the Worlds* podcast.

NOTES FROM AN EDUCATOR

Sandra Huber uses the Missing Witches
*podcast as a teaching aid for her class Anthropology
of Magic, Religion, Science and Ideology, so we asked
her to help us open this book. She wrote:*

WHO ARE THE ANCESTORS OF THE WITCHES? To find out, we look
for the stories we've been missing. We know these stories by how hard
they are to find: not located in thick history books, but in whispered
voices around a kitchen table, or the veiny pages of a hidden spell book,
or an unannounced gathering in a forest clearing. To find the Missing
Witches, the authors of this book cast the net wide, revealing a crooked
and expansive path that reaches from India to Haiti, from Harlem
to Mexico to the Moon Temple of Ur. In doing so, they reopen the
question—who is the Witch? And what does she do? A Witch is one
who carries the Saturnian forms of bones and blood and oaths as much
as the Venusian forces of ecstasy and bewitchment. But the Witch is also
she who, like Doreen Valiente, knows when the best way to make oneself useful is just to wash the dishes. And who, like Backxwash, knows
that part of the Witch's craft is learning to take up space—especially
in a society that treats your body, your race, your gender as deviant. In
finding the Witches, this book shows that perhaps they are no longer
missing, but they are always renegade.

In the present era, we are looking for a new Witchcraft, one that is the most ancient Witchcraft of them all. It is rarer these days to seek out a hierarchical mystery school than to go in search of messier methods—the murmurs, webs, and riddles that have always been reserved for the dedicated and daring. We seek out our Witchy ancestors by celebrating the turning of the seasons—Yule, Imbolc, Ostara, Beltane, Litha, Lughnasadh, Mabon, Samhain—whether in the heart of the woods or the electric eye of the city. We retrace their steps by learning their rhythms. We emphasize their voices by picking up a red pen and a blue pen, as Risa and Amy suggest, and building our will around the power of the mark, connecting ourselves to our most ancient ancestor of alphabets, the spider.

As the Earth is rocked by pandemic and disease, by systemic oppression, by borders and barriers that are longing to break open, to purge, we must ask: what is the work we are being called to do right now? How do we continue invoking the Witch in a way that honors her heritage of risk-taking, of aligning with the dispossessed and disenfranchised, of listening to the dead? In the pages that follow, Witchcraft is alive and lively. It is encapsulated as much in ritual song as in the shadow work of facing ourselves every morning in the shower; in the meconium of birthing and in the shape-shifting power of donning a magical garment. Just as the authors do not shy away from including the more controversial Witches in our pantheon (Z. Budapest, I'm looking at you), they reach further into a wider, shared pantheon of sacred women to include a poet, a *curandera,* an anthropologist, a filmmaker—Enheduanna, María Sabina, Zora Neale Hurston, Maya Deren. The Witch is one who speaks what they truly desire into the dark night. The Witch uncoils their will to the stars and watches it unfold like a fern, a shore, a lure.

The first time I tuned in to the *Missing Witches* podcast—it was their third episode, on the ever-beloved Ipsita Roy Chakraverti—I was enchanted by Amy's music, Risa's voice and storytelling, I had the feeling of being led down into the cellar of an abandoned house and I was more than willing to go. I knew that, once there, I would meet someone I had known maybe for a very long time. Amy's drawings have a similar sonorous beckon: encountering them is like looking through a keyhole into a portal, like peering into the faces of the tarot. This book is a collection of doorways, as the authors write, but I would add that through these doorways you'll find a collection of memories, deep in your bones. I believe it is for those who need to remember what once was forgotten—or be forcefully admonished—that this book is written. The seemingly smallest acts of the Witch are the ones that are the most insurgent—attunement, attention, and the revolutionary choice to truly listen, to follow the whisper of yes, further, that beckons you down the winding way.

Listening—which includes reading, remembering—is how the Witch finds her missing ancestors, and how the ancestors find where we've been missing all along. Between the two is the place between the worlds, I've heard, where a clearing is made for the Witches to enter and regather us, the future ancestors, into the weaving of the song.

Sandra Huber (she/her) is a doctoral candidate at the Centre for Inter-disciplinary Studies in Society and Culture, Humanities Department, at Concordia University, Montréal, Québec/Tio'tia:ke.

INTRODUCTION

WE WENT LOOKING FOR THE WITCHES WE'D BEEN MISSING.
It's fair to ask why.

We are otherwise sane people in our early forties. We worked in arts and tech and teaching and eldercare. We had organized bizarre, inter-disciplinary live shows for years in Montréal before we ever met. We met playing music and kept on playing music together, and between songs we'd talk about community, art and transformation, philosophy, politics, and science.

Neither of us remember the precise moment we started talking to each other about Witchcraft. We had both practiced in one way or another for our whole lives, but when we started talking, things started happening. We were given a pile of books on Witchcraft rescued by a friend from the burn bin at the Salvation Army. We took this as a sign and started to craft in a small circle of women, learning together that words are spells. The most powerful thing we remember from that time was hearing ourselves say out loud what we really, truly, secretly wanted. We made a space for our real voices, opened a circle for honesty and vulnerability. The full Moon shone on our laughter and was reflected in our tears. Then a friend died suddenly, someone we both knew and admired who had made an impact on both our lives, though it's unlikely she really knew it. We didn't feel we had the means to mourn in a way that worked for us, so we took a few cues from our burn-bin books and improvised a ritual. It helped somehow. We lit candles and sang and spoke and cried. Things got better and then harder and then better again, and in that cycle we began to own the label Witch.

We started the Missing Witches project because we wanted an ongoing excuse to talk to other Witches and continue to do the research we were doing anyway. For years we've been passing notes back and forth between us as we went looking for role models and a history of women who had known magic. We want to find out what story can be told by piecing together these voices: the magical, excluded, and demeaned.

This history is harder to access than you might think. We went looking for true stories of Witches and magical people, and what we mostly found at first were histories of the European and American Witch hunts told as cautionary tales about hysteria; stories of female anthropologists debunked; and stories of white men like Gerald Gardner and Aleister Crowley giving birth to the craft.

Eventually we found Barbara Ehrenreich, who (with Deirdre English) wrote *Witches, Midwives, and Nurses: A History of Women Healers,* as well as *Nickel and Dimed: On (Not) Getting By in America;* and Silvia Federici, who wrote *Witches, Witch-Hunting, and Women* and *Re-enchanting the World: Feminism and the Politics of the Commons.* These feminist historians helped us start to read Witch hunting into a global context of power and domination over both women and colonial subjects. We started to trace routes from the magic we were guessing at to something much bigger. We saw the lessons we met in these Witches echoed in what we were learning from Nature itself.

This book is a collection of the doorways to that story we have found so far.

With this book we hope to reach out into the wider web of all those who feel drawn to be a Witch. People who, like us, want a way to connect with Nature and each other, but who find themselves alienated by dogma, cynical of New Age spiritualism, or left out and insulted by the unexpected thorns of misogyny, commodifying racism, nationalism, transphobia, anti-science, and more that can appear in modern mainstream paganism.

Our beliefs are much more deeply rooted in research than in blind faith, but we still get funny looks from time to time when we call ourselves Witch—which we do at our discretion and only if and when we please. Dismissed as flaky or demeaned as illogical, we come to those encounters armed with the words of researcher, scientist, and author Migene González-Wippler, who said in her book *The Complete Book of Spells, Ceremonies & Magic,* "I don't believe in the supernatural. I believe in nature and all things natural. Everything that happens in this world always happens through natural channels and in accordance with immutable cosmic laws. All things—both real and surreal—are part of the cosmos, where everything has a place and a reason for being."[1]

The Wheel of the Year we offer here is old and new. It combines a simple, ancient celebration of seasons—solstices and equinoxes and the cross-quarter days between them—with the common contemporary pagan mix of Celtic-derived and Germanic-derived names popularized by British Wiccans of the 1960s.

Most importantly for us, we mark our time around the Wheel with real histories, telling stories from Witches—and Witch hunts—in Brazil, India, Haiti, Northern Europe, and beyond.

Artist and activist Marisa de la Peña[2] told us that it is the job of the descendants of colonizers, of settlers, to UNsettle their colonial thinking. That's what we are attempting here. To go beneath and beyond the trappings of New Age trends to retrieve the real and true history of magic makers from all over the world, listening to their voices to unsettle ourselves and our own understanding of the mystical and the intersectional.

We're just willing to try. We're trying to write what we see from where we are as we go looking. We are not gurus on mountaintops or preachers up in pulpits. We are in the trenches alongside you, looking for a world of metaphor and meaning-making beyond the all-pervasive discourses of dominance and war, and sharing what we've learned. We asked a lot of modern Witches what their message to the world would be, and by far, the most common answer we got was to listen. Everyone needs to listen to people whose experience is different from their own.

As we try to wrap our heads around esoteric teachings from many cultures, Indigenous philosophies, and world religions that have hundreds and thousands of years of history and complex thought, we always feel like we're slipping on piles of books, getting tangled up in translations, trying to keep our eye to a small keyhole through which we can barely start to understand something. We hope you'll read all this as the ongoing crafting of people attempting to educate themselves, to follow the gaping holes we can see in our knowledge, to explore and share these incredible vistas that keep opening up, endless, in front of us.

This is our offering; we only hope we haven't fucked it up too much.

"Missing Witches" for us doesn't just mean missing as in they aren't there but as in the French meaning of "missing." Instead of saying "I miss you," we say *tu me manques,* which translates directly as "you are missing from me." You are a piece of myself that I lack. Maybe you too are seeking voices that resonate, a community. Maybe the Witch you've been missing is You.

We made the decision to include people who did not self-identify as Witches. It's something we've wrestled with, since to be called a Witch is and has been dangerous. But to leave words to be defined by oppressors heightens the danger for us all. So we insist on making a big tent of the word "Witch." "Show me your Witches and I'll show you your feelings about women."[3] And as Ipsita Roy Chakraverti iconically put it, "Every strong woman is a Witch, and she is always hunted."[4]

Whether some of these people thought of themselves as Witches or not, they have all shaped our ideas about what it means for us to be Witches today. They belong in the canon of the craft.

It is imperative that we learn from these powerful ancestors. Under the pressures of capitalism, the phenomenon of Witch hunting is spreading. There are reports of murders of Witches in Nepal, Papua New Guinea, and Saudi Arabia, to name but a few places. In Witch camps in northern Ghana, hundreds of women have taken refuge from their communities. North America and Europe play out their own versions of gendered violence, demonization, and desecration, especially of Black and Indigenous bodies, under the extreme conditions imposed by this era of late-stage capital, climate crisis, and pandemic.

Silvia Federici wrote, "The very sense that we are living at the edge of the volcano makes it even more crucial to recognize that, in the midst of destruction, another world is growing, like the grass in the urban pavement, challenging the hegemony of capital and the state and affirming our interdependence and capacity for cooperation. . . . This is the horizon that the discourse and the politics of the commons opens for us today, not the promise of an impossible return to the past but the possibility of recovering the power of collectively deciding our fate on this earth. This is what I call re-enchanting the world."[5]

We dedicate this book, and our love and labor in creating it, to these Missing Witches who have been flourishing at the edge of the volcano, affirming amid violence that another world is possible. Here you'll meet poets and archaeologists, scientists and priestesses, travelers, artists, philosophers, and the thread that connects them all. We offer the wisdom we have found in their lives and the rituals they have inspired for us as touchstones for eight times of taking stock each year. We want to add our work to the common craft of healing, empowering, reimagining, and re-enchanting.

Amanda Yates Garcia reminded us that "it matters whose stories get told; it matters how we tell them. Imagination matters. Our connections to one another matter, as does the pleasure we take in our experience. Witches stand in solidarity with those already doing this work. Because people have been doing this work since humans first appeared on the surface of the earth. Now we listen to them, we participate, we use techniques of the healer, the poet, the artist, the scholar, the cunning folk to re-enchant the world."[6]

We also dedicate this book to the Wheel of the Year and the eight Sabbats that mark the passage of time and the changing of the natural world. We offer you these Missing Witches, the wisdom we have found in their lives, and the rituals they have inspired, as sparks to light your way along the eight stately steps of each year as the Earth spins. We want to offer you a new pantheon of real people for the pagan Sabbats. Because whether you are pagan, Christian, Jewish, Muslim, atheist, Hindu, Buddhist, or Satanic, or you make up your own belief system as you go along, the winter solstice will be the longest night of your year. If you are spinning in the Northern Hemisphere, you'll celebrate in December. In the Southern Hemisphere you will mark this Sabbat in June. Either way, one thing is sure: you will be bathed in dark to the degree that you are angled between the blue Earth and the Sun. If you are standing along the equator on an equinox, then you will watch our star trace a perfect line across the sky.

Straight lines, dividing time. Whatever you believe, you can't deny that the Moon has a cycle from new to full. Or that the seasons change from winter to summer, or from rainy to dry. We think that this rooted-ness is a good starting point and a good metaphor for our approach to craft. Nature gives instructions if you listen. Magic is real. It is happening in rhythms and waves whether we know it or not, and a Witch is someone who listens, who notices. Who is uplifted by the swirling dance of the world to become one of the choreographers.

Nature, in its complex chaos and perfect organic order, is complete. Different systems working together. Growth and rot. Root and bloom. It is happening all around at all times, and it all occurs without scorn, judgment, or shame. The tree doesn't tell the river to be still. They exist side by side in all their perfect differences. There is no hierarchy, no line of ascension, only a circle. A wheel that keeps turning.

Some see the solar festivals as signs of the patriarchy; they mark a turning away from lunar goddess ritual in many cultures. But for us— ritual improvisers, story chasers—we think that together they can offer a completeness. Celebrated with a focus on history and ritual, maybe this waltz of days can bring us toward a balance of the energies we call male and female. Maybe we can spiral together toward whatever it is that will be post patriarchy.

We hope that by marking our time around the Wheel with real histories—and in sanctifying our swings between binaries with empowering ritual—we can continue the work of our elders to open safe spaces for the full, glorious spectrum of beings to find peace and come into power.

We're both city girls who moved to the woods. Out here, navigating the changing of the seasons means processing the changing of our world. Our homes are surrounded by deep snow in the winter and a riot of greens in the summer. We feel the turning of the Wheel in the air we breathe, bearing witness to the sprouting of buds, the return of birds, the quiet labor of bugs turning soil under our feet. This change is the only constant. We have taken lessons from the Witches we have found and from Nature itself, because the story of a seed doesn't just apply to a farmer. When we think of a seed as an idea, we can transfer these lessons from Nature into our modern lives, giving ourselves time to plant, nurture, and harvest, celebrating each step. The Moon becomes a role model for the phases of change. Plants and animals, clouds and leaves become messengers, a method of communication to and from the Earth. Patterns become stories. Stories become teachers.

Artist and scientist WhiteFeather Hunter says: magic is inherently anti-capitalist.[7] She believes in process over product. Magic isn't an end goal, and it's certainly not a product—it is a way of seeing and being in the world that echoes with Nature. In this magical philosophy, agency and personal power are balanced and deeply integrated with community care. This book is anchored in the stories of real people who've had human struggles, failures, disappointments but have still risen to make magic, disrupt the dominant system, and make a mark on the world.

Paula Gunn Allen wrote that the root of oppression is loss of memory.[8] Our project—with all its probable errors and missteps—has at its heart a hopeful act of memory. It is, at best, a grimoire of histories and ideas that can give power to our lives and to our resistance.

Alongside these histories we take (frequent) detours to tell you our own stories. Because the personal is still political. Every Witch who we have read about, met, or interviewed has added a thread to the tapestry of our understanding. We include our own subjective and stumbling experiences because we're trying to be honest about how our perspectives and privileges situate our offering. We think this is a crucial strategy of feminist history: to make feminism not just the subject matter but the methodology as well. Feminism, like magic, is a practice, not a product. A means of being in the world that believes it can change it.

As we go around the Wheel and around the world in this book, sanctifying our swings around the Sun with true stories and empowering ritual, the main thing we hope you'll find is just real people from real places, who had real struggles but managed to be magic nonetheless. Just like you.

Calling the Corners

We call the corners to acknowledge what we are made of and surrounded by. This can be as simple as stating the directions and elements: North, South, East, West, Earth, Air, Fire, Water. Or it can be a complex ritual in itself, with salt, candles, odes. As with everything you'll learn in this book, where you go with it is really up to you. Whether you are minimalist or flamboyant in your practice, the calling of the corners is meant to ground and center you in this moment. In this place. Empowered and humbled by your connection to space and time, this earth and this sky, calling the corners quiets the mind, awakens the spirit, and plugs you into the flow of life's great electricity.

We're placing the calling of corners in the introduction because we think it's a great first step for every ritual and for every day. It is an acknowledgment that difference is good, that vastness is empowering; it reminds us of what is truly essential. Calling the corners reminds us to inform ourselves about the experience of others, full in the knowledge that we are all made of the same stuff. The Elements and the Directions honor distance and closeness, the gigantic and microbial. Physical, spiritual, intellectual, and emotional. North, South, East, West, Earth, Air, Fire, Water. Oneness. Wholeness. Difference. Equality.

1

Yule

This circle is led by Risa

THE WINTER SOLSTICE IS ABOUT BIRTH, AND IT'S ABOUT FIRE. It is the stillness right before a blaze of light.

Fierce and gentle reader, you can enter this book anywhere you like. If you decide to begin it here at the winter solstice, may I suggest you tie your breath to the breath the world takes before the Sun rises out of the dark and frozen sky. Breathe in deep, then let it fly.

Amy and I have a longstanding tradition of getting together during the holiday season. We play music, like we do most times we are together. Amy does her human radio bit, pulling the chords for any song you can think of out of her fingers and shaking the rafters with her pipes. I learned how to sing by trying to be loud enough to sing along with Amy. After walking out on an eleven-year relationship, I kept showing up at her house. I couldn't really talk about it, so we would play guitars and ukuleles and sing. And then, one minute I was whispering tight throated, and the next my voice came cracking and tumbling out. My real voice.

Singing—brokenly, happily, badly, bravely—led me out of a frozen place. I cracked and fell toward a life so much more vibrantly alive, it was like being born. So we get together around Yule and we holler punk versions of Christmas carols, or we harmonize, conjuring our best Mom-at-church voices. Like any good chosen family, we have incanted new possibilities into each other's lives just by being there, just by singing together.

The Roman festival of Sol Invictus (the "unconquerable Sun") was celebrated on December 25, as was the birth of Mithra in the male-only Roman mystery cult Mithraism, loosely inspired by the Zoroastrians.

But it is Mother's Night, December 20, that begins the twelve nights of Yule. This is a time to draw closer to your maternal ancestors. Mother's Night begins this season in the dark, tied with our breath and our voices to all the possibilities inherent in that space before and between. We keep the Yule log burning to keep us on this side of life, to stay warm and survive until tomorrow. This moment is a dangerous encounter with death, just like the labor of childbirth has been for most of human history. And in this way this moment is, by its very nature, dangerous to patriarchy.

In some traditions the women and girls of a village would craft a life-size doll out of wheat, reeds, and flowers. Holding hands with this figure of the snow queen, they went walking her through town, singing songs at the doorways where girls lived. They walked her to the river, and they drowned her. In other traditions they burned the snow queen and warmed their hands by her fire, to call forth the end of winter with her death and to celebrate her rebirth as the goddess of spring.[1]

The winter goddess of death, of frozen fear and storms and raging, is also the Spring Queen bursting through the other side, adorned with flowers, steeled by the soul of the ancestors who walk with her from the dark. She has been through the underworld and has known fear and, as the Wiccan axiom whispers to us, where there is fear, there is power.

On the longest night of the year, we sit at the crux with the crone. We are with her in the underworld as we burn the Yule log, and we are the Yule log burning. We bake up the last of our stores and huddle together singing, hoping to make it through to the other side.

And we are with you, huddled together. If you live in a place where you see racism, sexism, poverty, injustice, fascism, prejudice, and disease encroaching on you, we want to whisper to you: Witches are with you. Working alongside you in the fertile dark, even on the coldest nights.

The Cailleach is the personification of winter in Gaelic mythology. She herds deer, she fights spring, and her staff freezes the ground.

"The Dark Mother, Cailleach, was the source of inspiration and visions. At the time of the waning moon in November, the crone or hag Goddess retreated into Her mountain fastness or into Her tombs . . . where she becomes the womb of death and birth . . . The daughter and the ancient Mother are one and the same, and this is the mystery."[2] Cailleach and Brìghde are two faces of the same power, the same great goddess, the same queen of Earth and weather. Sometimes she is a great bird. Sometimes she is multiple, The Storm Hags, the voice of windstorms, the fury behind great waves. Sometimes she is the stone the storm beats herself against.

Where Amy and I live—each with our good men, all constantly rebuilding our houses as the forest tries constantly to reclaim them out in the mountains, north of Montréal—we spend the winter under a coat of thick, white snow. By Yule, the trees hang heavy and our usual paths are cluttered with downed branches. Ravaged trees hang caught in the forest's arms, breathing danger over our heads in the seemingly peaceful quiet.

On our walks we see spiders in the snow. They are still there, though everything seems frozen; they are stitching webs across the paths, walking slowly. Spiders can create a kind of antifreeze in their small bodies and go on weaving their way deep down within the snow, in the subnivean zone. The coat of silent, white death is an illusion. There is an underworld right there below a foot of hard ice, cupped against the warm black earth where small animals tunnel, hiding out from hungry foxes and birds of prey. Hiding from us.

The spider is the keeper of language and alphabet, the writer of stories, the weaver of worlds. She spins the first material of the universe. She holds the thread of life. The spider is also a traditional Yule guide: in Ukraine and Poland, spider decorations adorn Christmas trees. She is the weaver of the web of dreams and reality, and a symbol of how we can live our lives on the spinning spokes of the Wheel of the Year.

She is a symbol of what Donna Haraway calls "worlding." "Worlding, bodying, everything-ing. The layers are inherited from other layers, temporalities, scales of time and space, which don't nest neatly but have oddly configured geometries. Nothing starts from scratch. But the play—I think the concept of play is incredibly important in all of this—proposes something new, whether it's the play of a couple of dogs or the play of scientists in the field."[3]

When we begin to create our rituals, let's play.

Let us holler brokenly and just for fun until our real voices crack out, run our fingers through the scraps and tapestries inherited from other times and places; let's dance along the lines of oddly configured geometries to make the world more like how spiders and Witches want and need it to be.

Because while this act of calling ourselves Witches—of looking for a history and philosophy that make more sense than the bloody ones we've inherited—is a political act, it's also a creative one. We craft to rediscover what might be sacred, encoded in the subtle and the mundane, hidden in games and dances, songs and dreams.

As Indigenous musician, poet, scholar, educator, and community organizer Lyla June wrote in "Reclaiming Our Indigenous European Roots":

> *I have been called a half breed. I have been called a mutt. Impure. I have been told my mixed blood is my bane. That I'm cursed to have an Indian for a mother and a cowboy for a father.*
>
> *But one day, as I sat in the ceremonial house of my mother's people, a wondrous revelation landed delicately inside of my soul. It sang within me a song I can still hear today. This song was woven from the voices of my European grandmothers and grandfathers. Their songs were made of love.*
>
> *They sang to me of their life before the Witch trials and before the crusades. They spoke to me of a time before serfdoms and before Roman tithes. They spoke to me of a time before the plague; before the Medici; before the guillotine; a time before their people were extinguished or enslaved by dark forces. They spoke to me of a time before the English language existed. A time most of us have forgotten.*
>
> *These grandmothers and grandfathers set the ancient medicine of Welsh blue stone upon my aching heart. Their chants danced like the flickering light of Tuscan cave-fires. Their joyous laughter echoed on and on like Baltic waves against Scandinavian shores. They blew worlds through my mind like windswept snow over Alpine mountain crests. They showed to me the vast and beautiful world of Indigenous Europe. This precious world can scarcely be found in any literature, but lives quietly within us like a dream we can't quite remember.*[4]

My own ancestry is Irish, Scottish, British, Danish, and—six generations back—Iroquois. I was raised with little to no culture from any of these. My lived experience is mostly that of a descendant of Canadian farmers, engineers, teachers: settlers. Beyond them is just "the dream we can't quite remember."

This chapter—and this whole book—is devoted to the Witches who lead us looking for these ancestors.

In particular, here at the beginning, we want to honor the Witches who researched and rebirthed a form of nature religion and goddess[5] worship. And magic.

In this first chapter we honor Doreen Valiente, a mother of modern Witchcraft. The spy who worshipped the Moon and never quite came in from the cold. The historian and sharp researcher who spotted forgeries and accidentally helped create a religion, though she thought organized religion was a curse to humanity. The Wiccan author who was a founding practitioner in the most influential early Wiccan covens, and who wrote beautiful books of poems and spells about how to find your own magic alone with the Moon.

While we were drawn to stories of the mothers of the modern Witch movement in the '50s, '60s, and '70s, we also had this sense that there was a lot of racism and misogyny in the "New Age" that emerged at that time and a lot of profiteering. We were looking for a Witch who spoke to our hope as well as our anger. We need icons of resistance as well as of optimism.

We need the art, writing, and activism of Monica Sjöö.

Monica painted women channeled from "the unknown country." Goddesses, ancestors, cosmic mothers. She also coauthored an overwhelming tome of goddess history, *The Great Cosmic Mother;* walked through live munitions testing from Silbury mound to Stonehenge; and had her iconic paintings threatened with gross-indecency charges. In the wake of a terrifying birth experience, followed by the life-shattering sickness and death of her children, Monica ventured deeply into the New Age world of the 1970s and 1980s. In response to what she found there, she wrote a scathing takedown in *New Age and Armageddon*. She wrote of the gatekeeping, patriarchy, Earth-betrayal, and reckless appropriation of Indigenous spiritualities in the New Age movement.

We offer the stories of these two Witches we'd been missing as ancestors for your Yule.

Women whose powerful and painful lives can help us draw down the magic and power of birth in its different manifestations: birth of a movement, of a wave that moves across the Earth and through our lives; and birth of a single human life that is the birth of yet another death. Birth as it always stands rooted in the impossible, one foot in the eternal stillness before birth, in between and heavy with magic.

For Mother's Night, in celebration of Yule and the winter solstice, let's find our way—through play or song or dreams or history—to a place where everything and nothing are both present, and we are all portal, all potential. "I am the Soul of Nature, who giveth life to the universe; from me all things proceed, and unto me must all things return; and before my face, beloved of gods and mortals, thine inmost divine self shall be unfolded in the rapture of infinite joy . . . I have been with thee from the beginning . . . and I await thee now."[6]

Doreen's most important contribution, the writing that became a touchstone for a re-emergent pagan faith, and core to Wiccan liturgy, is "The Charge of the Goddess."

So let's call it out to this circle as we begin. Because we are a circle, you and you and you and I, joined in the dark, words and their magic looping us together.

Take your mind's eye out to the wild. We go together, below a full Moon, by the woods, by the sea.

We are there with Doreen.

And ye shall be free from slavery; and as a sign that ye are really free, ye shall be naked in your rites; and ye shall dance, sing, feast, make music and love, all in my praise.

For mine is the ecstasy of the spirit and mine also is joy on earth; for my Law is Love unto all Beings.

Keep pure your highest ideal; strive ever toward it; let naught stop you or turn you aside.

For mine is the secret door which opens upon the Land of Youth; and mine is the Cup of the Wine of Life, and the Cauldron of Cerridwen, which is the Holy Grail of Immortality.

I am the Gracious Goddess, who gives the gift of joy unto the heart. Upon earth, I give the knowledge of the spirit eternal; and

beyond death, I give peace, and freedom, and reunion with those
who have gone before. Nor do I demand sacrifice, for behold I am the
Mother of All Living, and my love is poured out upon the earth.[7]

Where did this liturgy come from? We know it was created in response to a challenge presented to Doreen by Gerald. We also know it came from her own decades of research, her own poetic skill, and her lifelong deep intuition and connection with the Moon and what she saw behind it: "Something that was real and very potent. I saw the world of force behind the world of form."[8]

Before Doreen joined a coven and began to transmute her childhood talent for improvised spellwork into the role of a priestess writing a liturgy, she was gathering books, gathering magical friends, gathering her powers. And before that, Doreen was a codebreaker and World War II spy alongside the other math Witch women of Bletchley Park. She was smart, serious, and aware that there are layers of hidden knowledge in the world . . . and excellent at keeping secrets.

Bletchley Park was the central site for British codebreaking during World War II. The work done there and the names of the men and the many more women who did it were closely guarded secrets, still protected by layers of black ink. During the war, Bletchley Park unstitched the secret communications of the German Enigma and Lorenz cipher systems. Intelligence from Bletchley shortened the war by years and was crucial in tipping its outcome toward peace. In January 1945, at the peak of codebreaking efforts, over 10,000 personnel were working at Bletchley and outstations. About three-quarters of these were women. Many held degrees in mathematics, physics, and engineering. Most were not—could not be—recognized for their exceptional contributions when the war was over.

Not much is known of Doreen's time at Bletchley Park, or if she continued to do work for the British secret service after ostensibly leaving the service. We know for certain that she was there at all only because friends of hers insisted she had known insider details about the first computer and the Enigma machine. Following these stories, biographer Philip Heselton checked records at Bletchley Park that had only recently been declassified and discovered her name inscribed under "Foreign Office Civilian Temporary Senior Assistant Officer."[9]

She was a translator, gifted in languages, working on the heart of secrets that were destined to either save the world, or collapse it into genocide and fascism.

She was a hero, and we don't know to what degree.

Some choices she made later in life seem inconsistent with the rest of her ethics.

In "The Mother of Modern Witchcraft Was Also a Pro-Choice Spy," Sarah Waldron wrote,

> *Valiente was pro-contraception, pro-choice, interested in feminism and sexual liberation and was anti-racism and anti-homophobia long before that was common, so it's a surprise to learn that she joined the ultra-right-wing National Front in 1973. She was briefly involved with the Northern League, a neo-Nazi group whose ideology was utterly at odds with her strongly held beliefs. Valiente had spent a world war fighting against fascists. After 18 months, she let her membership lapse.*[10]

Theories abound. Doreen was a natural pragmatist, adept at negotiating dodgy dealings and had a head for meticulous research. She wasn't a fascist. One accepted theory was that she thought that these groups, still in relative infancy, might legitimize paganism through patriotism. Another theory was that she was still working for the government, spying on fascists who were unlikely to suspect a middle-aged woman.[11]

Maybe she was a spy. Or maybe she tried on nationalist thought for a while, like many pagans slipping into racism before her and since.

For the solstice, when we decide what to shed and what to keep, let's commit to telling true stories, and where we don't know, to resist wrapping up our stories in nice bows. When we reach ambiguous spaces, let's keep what we can from the warrior Witches who kept seeds, preserved languages, fought for land and soil and body and soul and equality and justice, but let's not neglect to face the ugly stuff.

We can't gloss over the dangers in our midst with love and light. A philosophy of reverence for land and ancestors runs the risk of tipping toward racist nationalism on the one hand—"our people and traditions are the pure and good"—and of consuming and commodifying Indigenous cultures on the other—"nature-based spirituality is so widespread, it's OK if we cut and paste it." Both rely on a lie.

For the idea of Witchcraft and all the power inherent in it to be useful to us today, we need to do better.

The etymology of this word "Wicca" is tangled. Mythologist Jacob Grimm[12] connected *wikkōn* with the Gothic word *weihs,* or "sacred." Proto-Indo-European has *weik,* as in "to separate, to divide"—which may have referred to early practices of cleromancy, that is, the drawing of lots and reading of signs, as in the reading of the *I Ching* or in the Ifa tradition of divination by "pounding ikin"—sacred palm or kola nuts. Grimm also considered *weik* as in "to curve, bend," which became "wicken," tied to dancing, and *weg'h,* "to move" or "to make mysterious gestures."[13] In a translation of Exodus from circa 1250, the word for Witches is used for the Egyptian midwives who save the newborn sons of the Hebrews.[14] Masters of sacred gestures, reading signs, studying plants, students of the wind and birds, and Egyptian midwives are the Witches' ancestors.

British Wiccans of the 1960s who took up this term sometimes claimed to have access to a pure and secret line of magical ancestry; but the more interesting history is one of research, of studying traditions, and then dancing their way to new expressions of reverence not just of the divine but of the Earth and of each other.

In the early years after World War II, Doreen was reading and collecting material on magic and Witchcraft when she stumbled onto news of Gerald's coven.

In 1952 Doreen read an article in the weekly magazine *Illustrated,* "Witchcraft in Britain," which mentioned a southern coven of British Witches. These were the now notorious practitioners who had invoked the cone of power and had done magical workings in the New Forest in 1940 to help stop the threatened invasion of Britain. Doreen contacted the author of the article and asked to be put in touch with the "Witch cult." Her letter was passed on to Gerald.

Gerald invited Doreen to tea at a friend's house near the New Forest. This friend was the same person who had introduced Gerald to the New Forest coven in the autumn of 1939. This woman used "Dafo" as a pseudonym and denied her involvement in the craft to three different covens who went asking for confirmation of Gerald's well-publicized version of the witch cult. It had been only a year since the Witchcraft Act of 1735 was repealed.[15] To be a Witch in public could be dangerous then. It still can be today.

At this first meeting in Dafo's home, Gerald—of whom Doreen said "one felt he had seen far horizons and encountered strange things"[16]—presented Doreen with a copy of his book *High Magic's Aid*. Apparently, a typical test for potential initiates was to gauge their reactions to ritual nudity and scourging. A year later, in 1953, Doreen received her first-degree initiation into the craft; that evening, Doreen was reborn as "Ameth" to members of her circle.

During the initiation, Gerald used his own *Book of Shadows* containing, as he claimed, remnants of rites taken from an Old Religion passed down to the New Forest coven. He read a passage Doreen instantly recognized. It didn't come from an Old Religion but from a more contemporary source, *The Gnostic Mass,* by Aleister Crowley[17] in 1913. Doreen said, "I told Gerald afterwards, I think he was none too pleased at my recognition of his source."[18]

Gerald gave Doreen free access to his *Book of Shadows* and other materials he had collected. He still claimed most had been passed down to him from the old coven, but he also recognized Doreen's gift for language and research. Doreen began to rewrite his *Book of Shadows*, and this revised version was the basis for what was to become known as Gardnerian Wicca, one of the most influential and dominant traditions of contemporary Witchcraft.

By 1957, however, a rift was opening between Gerald, Doreen (now his High Priestess), and the rest of his coven. Gerald claimed a right to naked nights with the high priestess of "his" coven. Apparently, Doreen found these "embarrassing."[19] And over time, she found more of his behavior difficult to deal with. Gerald repeatedly sought publicity, and though she was open to having their story told in certain ways, Doreen challenged his tactics. Following one of these challenges to his leadership, he produced a surprising new section from his "secret source" of craft law. Doreen was already skeptical about the source of Gerald's updates to the ancient texts he claimed to work from, but the latest addition announced: "The greatest virtue of the High Priestess is that she recognizes that youth is necessary to the representative of the Goddess, so that she will retire gracefully in favour of a younger woman."[20] The obvious manipulation pushed her and other coven members to concede that he had been making up the laws for some time, and a wider rift was opened in an already unraveling coven.

In 1964 Doreen's mother, Edith, and Gerald both died, and Doreen decided to turn her study and practice to another tradition. She was initiated into the Clan of Tubal Cain, a coven led by Robert Cochrane. Robert claimed to be a hereditary Witch and was the founder of the tradition now referred to as the 1734 tradition, a tradition allegedly handed down through his family.

Over time, Doreen became disillusioned with Robert as well, and she was disappointed when he was openly contemptuous of Gardnerian Witches. Whatever her private reservations, she had both respect and fondness for and loyalty to her allies and coven mates. She left the Tubal Cain clan.

Robert died in 1966 by ritual suicide. He ingested a mixture of belladonna leaves, or deadly nightshade, and pharmaceuticals, and left a suicide note saying that he was of sound mind.

She began to devote much of her time to writing. Her first book was *An ABC of Witchcraft* (1973), followed by *Natural Magic* (in 1975) and *Witchcraft for Tomorrow* (in 1978). These three books established Doreen as an authority on Witchcraft. Authors, researchers, and pagans began to beat a steady path to Doreen's small apartment. She shared stories and personal memories, and gave trusted seekers access to her private library.

One of Doreen's magical powers was that she was a genius editor, weaving together the through lines she could see in scattered stories and whispered rituals. Another was that she was a lifelong researcher and archivist. As early as 1951, she kept clippings filed away in her packed-but-meticulously organized home-turned-library on everything from Witchcraft to sexual liberation, UFOs, psychic phenomena, and more.

Her flat "was limited to a single room where she had her bed, a small, but ancient, rented television, her word processor (not even a computer, really), and one armchair. Unfortunately there was little room for anything else, as the rest of the 15 ft. x 15 ft. apartment was taken up with racks of metal shelving with over 2,000 books on the shelves that she had collected over the years and which formed the basis of her research. The books were often stacked three deep, and the rather deep shelving bowed in the middle with the weight."[21]

Doreen could pick a reference book out of that overwhelming stack without blinking a heavily bespectacled eye. She was a force. In the 1970s the British government attempted to pass new legislation against Witchcraft. They hadn't expected Doreen. She succeeded in lobbying Parliament, and in the end the attempt to enact the new laws was abandoned.

I love this description of how she would lead circles with the last, great inspiring love of her life, Ron Cooke.

> *Doreen and her High Priest Ron Cooke would arrive in Ron's three-wheeled Reliant Robin, valiantly chugging along at 30 miles an hour until it reached its destination; with Doreen and Ron stopping every few miles to drink strong tea from a thermos flask. It was wonderful for we young coven leaders in our glamorous black velvet robes to see Doreen casting a circle skyclad, save for a woolen cloak, Witchy regalia, and rubber boots. "Neither clothed nor naked" took on a whole new meaning. But Doreen's outfit epitomized her attitude; at once at one with nature, loving "Witchiness," but ever practical, and never pretentious.*[22]

Ever practical, never pretentious.

And I love that at age sixty-two, Doreen decided to try to learn how to drive. It didn't really work out for her, but I relate to that too. And I love that she tried. And mostly, I love how she would improvise. "They worked in the dark, so everything was unscripted: you couldn't read in the dark, you had to act from your spirit and connect to the power of the land, or on a seashore to the power of the ocean. ..."[23]

This is the kind of magic that makes sense to me: a practice deeply rooted in research and a critical open mind, and then emerges joyfully in response to the living Earth, the sacred flickering present, the ancestors singing silently around us, our own hearts in the dark.

In 1995 she became a Patron of the Centre for Pagan Studies, founded by John Belham-Payne. John would become her last High Priest and working partner, and it was to the Centre for Pagan Studies that Doreen made her last public speech.

In her last address to the National Conference of the Pagan Federation, held at Fairfield Halls in Croydon, London, on November 22, 1997, she addressed and outright rejected some of Gerald Gardner's invention.

> At first I did not question anything Gerald told me about what he claimed to be the traditional teachings of the Old Religion. Eventually however, I did begin to question, and began to ask how much was traditional and how much was simply Gerald's prejudices.
>
> For instance, he was very much against people of the same sex working together, especially if they were gay. In fact he went so far as to describe gay people as being "cursed by the Goddess." Well I see no good reason to believe this. In every period of history, in every country in the world there have been gay people, both men and women. So why shouldn't Mother Nature have known what she was doing when she made people this way? I don't agree with this prejudice against gay people, either inside the craft of the wise or outside it . . .
>
> Another teaching of Gerald's which I have come to question is the belief known popularly as "the Law of Three." This tells us that whatever you send out in Witchcraft you get back threefold, for good or ill.

Well, I don't believe it! Why should we believe that there is a special Law of Karma that applies only to Witches? For Goddess' sake do we really kid ourselves that we are that important?

Yet I am told, many people, especially in the USA, take this as an article of faith. I have never seen it in any of the old books of magic, and I think Gerald invented it.[24]

She took apart an architecture of prejudice and superstition. She also brought a tongue-in-cheek adoption of the language of Crowley's *The Gnostic Mass* into her own fiction/history of the Old Religion, and in doing so she gave us something so much more profound and beautiful: a vision of us all together radiant and holy. "The initiates of the ancient pagan Mysteries were taught to say, 'I am the child of earth and Starry Heaven and there is no part of me that is not of the Gods.' If we in our own day believe this, then we will not only see it as true of ourselves, but of other people also."[25]

She saw the Gods in every part of us. She wrote the words of the goddess: "All acts of love and pleasure are my rituals." She was a Word Witch who helped birth the world.

John Belham-Payne described how shy he felt when he met Doreen. He didn't know what to say besides something like "AHHH! I have all your books!" and Doreen, in turn, hoping to contribute a little, offered to wash the dishes, if they could find her a stool to perch on. Practical and unpretentious, this is maybe what we love most of all about Doreen. Witches know that the mundane stuff needs to get done and we are ready to roll up our sleeves.

Instead of designating her to the dishes, John asked her to give a public talk. She sat in a small armchair on an empty stage.

Doreen asked, "We talk about means of raising power, but what exactly is the Witch power that is raised . . . perhaps today when people's minds are more open, we may begin to study this realm of subtle energies more closely, and perhaps rediscover what really happens when Witches gather to raise the cone of power." She talked about the very nature of fertility in the context of Witchcraft as a fertility cult. "The idea of fertility is something that goes much deeper than the hope for good crops and increase of livestock, and I am sure that it always did. There is a spiritual as well as a material fertility. There is the need for people to be alive and vital and creative. Life is here to be enjoyed, not just endured."[26]

Witchcraft is a fertility cult, but as Doreen taught us, this is fertility in the largest, most world-building sense. Amy said to me once when we were talking about all the death and birth that had piled around us that season: everything from here on out is ancestor work. All our work is ancestor work now as we give birth to our children, to our hopes for the future, to our communities, to our traditions, to the next spins of our spiral dance, and, crucially, to ourselves.

When Doreen finished her final public talk the 2,000+ attendees stood with thunderous applause.

On the winter solstice, honor yourself as a child of starry heaven, and honor yourself—whatever your gender or sexuality—as mother, future ancestor, pregnant with possibility, ready to be born.

All acts of love and pleasure are your rituals.

Doreen described meeting Monica in her book *The Rebirth of Witchcraft*.

She called her "a true priestess of the great goddess."

Monica's pictures are full of strong and potent images of the Goddess which are very different from the rather airy-fairy representations one used to see in earlier books about modern paganism. Living as she does in the West Country, Monica often includes in her pictures the image of the great mound of Silbury Hill, believed by some to symbolize the pregnant womb of the Earth-Mother. My own favourite among her pictures shows Silbury Hill surrounded as it used to be by a moat of water, which reflected the light of the moon. Upon its summit a priestess raises her arms to the orb of the full moon, while below a group of women stand with linked hands. Within the great bulk of the hill appears the form of the unborn Divine Child. Above this simple, yet tremendously meaningful image are written the words: You can't kill Spirit. She is like a mountain.[27]

Monica has been called one of the last great religious painters in Western art.[28] Born in Sweden, she was the child of two painters. But Monica's father would turn her mother's paintings to face the wall. Her mother and father separated, and Monica moved with her mother to Stockholm. "My mother, although she was physically powerful & was an artist, lived in near total isolation with me during my childhood, in one room & a kitchen in a block of flats . . . my own childhood was entirely clouded because of my knowledge of her loneliness & terrible economic poverty . . . She died from pure misery & frustration not having been able to paint for years."[29] Monica was on her own then by the age of sixteen, with twenty pounds in her pocket.

Her fury—at what happened to her mother and at the whole racist misogynist weight of the world—fueled her work. She was determined to paint and write and act for the complete dismantling of patriarchy. She kept her roots sunk in wild and sacred places. She put her body on protest lines and added her voice and art to the fight again and again till the very end of her life. She spoke at anarchist camps and club nights, she traveled with a Goddess tour, she took part in collective environmental actions, and she held up a sign that read "the beginning of the end of patriarchy" at the San Francisco Dyke March in 1996.

She identified as bisexual and in 1980 wrote:

Didn't turn on sexually to men . . . was made to feel guilty. Blamed myself . . . I had been refused a legal abortion & spent an entirely miserable summer unwillingly pregnant . . . Made to feel that I had to get an abortion . . . Humiliations with the gynecologist, psychologist etc. Refused. Feeling the most terrible rage . . . & frustration. After working for years in the Women's movement . . . on abortion, with unsupported mothers etc I announced at one general meeting that I & Dale wanted to start a Gay women's group. Stunned silence and women I had trusted & worked with for years almost visibly edged away . . . I wanted something for myself this time: support from other women, for who I am also.

Many times facing danger. Walking down the road holding a woman's hand, in pubs harassed by men, men screaming abuse. Fear. Trying through all this to hang onto & care for my children . . . Perhaps for the moment my life is relatively easier through living with a man. I don't deny this is so . . . I have certainly discovered that the oppression of us is even more insidious than I had ever conceived of."[30]

To live alone, to raise children, to love and take support from a person of your same sex, to see the divine as a member of your own sex, to slip between binaries into the bright bands of light and dark and brilliant color that exist there—all of this is dangerous and exhausting. Whatever your identity, these acts are part of the great wave of feminist resistance, asserting a space to flourish beyond what seems possible to the poverty mentality of patriarchy.

Monica was the main author of *Towards a Revolutionary Feminist Art* (1971), one of the first, and most militant, feminist art manifestos. Monica said her feminism originated in the experience of giving birth to her second son in her home. Her most iconic and infamous painting, *God Giving Birth,*

was based on the natural home birth of my second son, Toivo in 1961, a birth that I experienced as a first initiation to the Great Mother who is both immanent and transcendent, both dark and light . . . I had given birth to my first son in a hospital in Stockholm and it had been a disaster for both of us. This home-birth, without medical and technical interventions, opened me up to the powers of the Great Mother . . . For the first time I experienced the enormous power of my woman's body, both painful and cosmic and I "saw" in my mind's eye great luminous masses of blackness and masses of radiant light coming and going. The Goddess of the Universe in her pure energy body. This birth changed my life and set me questioning the patriarchal culture we live in and its religions that deny the life-creating powers of the mothers and of the Greater Mother.[31]

28

I was pregnant the year we started to write what would become this book. In preparation for labor, I took a class where we would practice long, loud vowel sounds. We were not only told that these would be useful; but also whether we liked them or not, they would come out of us. Sounds would come howling and droning out on their own as our souls stretched to usher in a new one. This proved to be correct. When I was lost in the waves of pain, my baby stuck between the band of light and dark, death and life, I saw the "great luminous masses of blackness and masses of radiant light coming and going," and they came out of me as sounds, and these sounds were the only thing that kept me anchored to the Earth.

I first read *The Great Cosmic Mother* and *New Age and Armageddon* while I traveled across Canada seven and eight months pregnant, camping in national parks, in forest reserves, and at folk festivals. Then I had my daughter on October 10, 2018, back home in Montréal. The experience of labor was traumatic and enormous.

The possibility of getting pregnant at all had been a shocking change from the years before. Time had been ticking into my late thirties with the chances dwindling for my body to be able to pull this magic off. The men I had allowed into my life were somehow less and less fit to be parents: the addict, the weirdly cruel, the straight up con man. Followed by the rising fury at myself for getting conned, for getting hurt, for wasting time. The years it took to make a reasonable living and the haunting vast majority who don't. The daily terror of a whole world gone mad selling our only original life-giver down the oily jaws of profits for a sociopathic few. How to be a mother here? Even if I could?

Then suddenly, a good man. The best possible person to believe in things with, to camp across the country pregnant with, to move to the woods together. To imagine that the dream of family, our own small sprouted world, a flare of hope in the dark, could be real. To make plans.

And we tried and got pregnant, another shot of crazy luck.

My sister Megan would be our doula. I wanted the full hippie, Earth mother, goddess birth in the heart of a great hospital, just in case. I am a modern science-loving Witch with a healthy dose of modern neurosis and staunch respect for all the layers of care and giving in the medical professions, despite its many misogynistic and racist histories.[32]

At forty-one weeks, one full week past my due date, at 10 a.m., October 9, 2018, we had an ultrasound appointment. The plan was to check on the amniotic fluid levels to see if we could keep waiting for baby May to come on her own. But by bedtime the night before this appointment, the contractions had started. They stayed between five to twenty minutes apart all night, and that morning before we left, they ramped up to every three minutes. We skipped the ultrasound and went straight to intake.

On examination they determined that I was 3 centimeters dilated, that the outer membrane was broken, and that there was meconium in the liquid. The meconium is a baby's first poo and generally it comes after birth; if it comes before, it can enter their mouth or lungs and cause complications. When they took her heart rate, it was a little too slow, but it picked up when I drank some juice. May was already in some distress, but no one seemed to be freaking out. They did decide to admit us immediately. We waited as they prepared our room, as Megan arrived, and the tide of contractions kept coming.

The next twelve hours were intense but beautiful.

We stood outside for a while, riding contractions in the Sun. I took off my shoes and dug feet in the grass, and my grandmother's favorite bird, a cardinal, watched us in the strangely hot October Sun. Later the nurses told us it wasn't safe to go outside.

Megan led us in swaying walks up and down the hallways. Megan and Marc improvised a dance routine to make me laugh. The intensity of the pain grew, but we moaned and hummed and droned together and held hands. I thought we were doing it, I thought it was happening just like it was supposed to. But after twelve hours in the hospital, we were still at only 3 centimeters dilated. And there was the concern about her heart rate. Too slow, but then fine, but then too slow again.

It had been twenty-four hours since contractions had started for me at home the night before, and the doctor was worried about my energy for the next stages, and the baby's. She had let us delay several times, but now we needed to choose: either break the inner membrane with the knitting-needle-shaped hook or start a low level of Pitocin—a chemical that triggers contractions—which might be enough to prompt the body to dilate and break the inner waters on its own.

The doctor said frankly she normally would recommend breaking the membrane, but these days she was increasingly convinced that a low level of Pitocin was a more "natural" option.

I was already blurry. I couldn't remember the recommendations from the books I'd read about this decision point. And I didn't remember that starting the Pitocin meant being on an IV drip from now on, the Pitocin doubling every thirty minutes, and being on permanent heart and contraction monitoring, both combining to mean that I couldn't move much anymore. The pain and intensity of the contractions would augment chemically from here on out, and the dancing, the hot baths, even rolling on my side were pretty much off the table. I also didn't know how much more painful it would be to get an IV rather than a blood sample taken. Especially if the nurse is out of practice and she misses again and again into the bone of your wrists.

I sobbed at this point for the first time in my labor. Both hands aching and things feeling like they're slipping out of reach. I wrestled with feeling like a failure and feeling like I was way out into the waters, beyond where I like to imagine I live with some kind of control.

I felt like a failure for needing medical intervention. So guilty I was almost apologizing to the doctor ten hours later, telling her how long I'd tried without taking any pain relief, when she told me: you don't need to justify this to me.

I'd like to say more about why I felt this guilt, but I don't really understand it myself. I know it affected me enough that I stayed on Pitocin without an epidural for six hours. Increasing amounts pumping into me every thirty minutes, making my contractions stronger and stronger. For the last two hours I was at a point of constant contraction. I couldn't see, and I thought I would die, or should die. I thought I had already.

Only then did I ask for an epidural and sobbed again.

When the anesthesiologist came, he spoke with my sister about her work in Uganda and Burkina Faso and Haiti, and told her he was going to Rwanda the next week to repair fistulas. Marc whispered to me: he's a good person, this is a good idea, you're going to be OK. The doctor asked my sister if she knew a Jack Someone. I couldn't follow the conversation, but Jack was my grandfather's name so I held onto it. I'd had chronic back pain for ten years, I was terrified of a needle in my spine, I'd watched a video of an epidural during a birthing class and had a panic attack . . . but this was a good idea. I was going to be OK.

As the waves of the epidural started to come, the anesthesiologist asked me what was my pain level at when I asked for the epidural? I said ten, it's been ten for two hours. And he looked at me so kindly and so sad. No one in that time had asked me what pain level I was at. I had lived with chronic pain, I have a high pain threshold, I seemed coherent, no one thought to ask.

For the next two hours I lay in the dark and shook violently. Marc covered me with blankets and then with all my sweaters. Slowly, the shaking calmed and the medicine in my spine took the pain away. The IV pumped the contractions ever higher beyond the fog.

I curled into the afghan my great-grandmother Evelyn May had knit, and I heard her wild cackle. Megan and Marc tried to get some sleep.

Later, when the epidural had brought me some rest and a blissful fuzz, my mother came to see me. She'd been sitting outside the room with my sister Brianna and my grandma. She cried and said she was happy I'd finally taken the epidural. She told me she didn't know what to do but be there. She said her mother had cried out in the waiting room, remembering when Mom had me, and Grandma hadn't come. Grandma didn't know why she hadn't come to be there for my mom when she lived through a labor much like mine—the best predictor of what your labor will be like is your mom's with you—except that no one had ever come for her. Grandma was by herself for all three children, and she was a tiny lady and very much afraid. Her husband didn't even come in the room. Why was this normal? How did we get so broken from each other? Why did we leave each other alone at the threshold of birth and death?

After almost a day of the baby's heart in distress and meconium in her system, Pitocin pumping her little house at ever more shattering levels, and my system at constant contraction, I was finally dilated enough to push. My sister held one foot of mine and Marc the other, and all the beautiful strong women of the hospital team surrounded me, and I curled and brought every muscle in my entire body to its absolute utmost and pictured my daughter inside me choosing this moment. And we were amazing. We were a perfect team. I was a power, I would show them, and they were cheering. Again. And again I did it and they cheered. Again and again. And then they got a little quiet. The smallest look on their faces to show . . . this isn't working. The little baby is trying to cross over and getting pulled backward. I am fighting the riptide of all of life and death, and everything I have isn't enough. This goes on for ninety minutes. Push again. One More. You're amazing. Try again. It isn't enough.

The doctor says: "I want to make a cut, this is too long and too much distress. There is no time to choose." It's the right choice and she says I'm going to cut and you're going to push her out on the next contraction. I feel the cut, vertical, episiotomy, and the wave comes. I have to see the ripping in my mind's eye and I have to choose it. And she comes.

They had hoped to clean the meconium from her mouth when she was just part way out, but then she is all the way out and the umbilical cord is around her neck.

I can't see, I think the relief of her coming will be followed by the joy of her on me, but they take her to the side where I can't see and tell me about the cord on her neck. I see the specialist over her. She doesn't make much noise. They show her to me briefly, she is white blue and quiet. I expect them to place her on me, this is the end of the movie, I will hold her, this is the light at the end but instead, she's gone. She leaves with Marc and the specialists, and I can't hear or see clearly after that. It's just loss and void. Emptiness and terror and weeping. They ask me to push out the placenta. The young doctor learns a new sewing technique on me. I just keep asking when she'll be back. They keep saying we'll get you stitched up and ready to be moved and you can go to her. This does not compute. I can't go to her, I am split open, she has to be OK and come lie here with me. She and Marc are gone.

I think, not for the first time, that if she doesn't make it I will never be able to look at or talk to anyone I have ever known ever again.

I will have to be alone forever.

Later I tell Marc about this thought and he says there was a moment during labor where he thought that if he lost us he would walk into the woods with an axe and never come back.

People lose children and find a way to face the day, and those are the bravest, rawest, most beautiful people, balanced between worlds forever I think. That world with the outline of a child in it that they can almost see and then this one. Both must exist for them, and they are here with us. They make toast and work in the garden. I can't imagine the strength of their hearts.

I wait for news of May in the blur of the aftermath of the utmost effort, the most intense pressure on and in my body and my terrified nervous system. My sister is leaning over me, but I can't see her clearly. I'm full of a glowing rage and sorrow. I have been aware the whole of these hours of all the pain and joy of the mothers and children Megan carries with her from her time in rural Uganda, Haiti, Panama, Burkina Faso. I am full of incoherent fury at the whole imbalanced world. Megan told me once of women on the floor, no one with them from their families, waiting to give birth in Uganda, dying from complications that we could have healed here as a matter of course. I see them like spirits with her now, so gentle with me and in such enormous judgment of the broken world system, and I am sobbing and sobbing in fear for May and at all the loss and injustice of everything. Everything is layers of loss and hope. A blur, not gray but the most painfully brilliant light and dark.

And then Marc comes back holding May high like a torch. The specialist behind him pumps her fists in the air and says, "*Elle est championne!*" I am holding her and crying, crying harder than I ever have as though now, officially, I've been broken all the way and turned inside out completely, and here is my inside breathing and looking at me.

I wrote so much of this chapter in the early days, holding her. May Marigold at five days, eleven days, twenty-one days old. I gradually looked less beat up, and she kept growing. She is every platitude accurately, and none of them are adequate: a miracle, the love of my life, my sudden purpose. She grunts and squeaks like a perfect mammal. I tell Amy that May lies on my belly like she's listening, and Amy says she's listening to the sounds of her hometown, and we both get hit with a wave of the enormity of that. I cry missing her and thinking about how I can never take her back to that first home. And I cry, so happy I get to see her face now. Postpregnancy brain chemistry is a wild rewiring.

I had a week of radical highs and lows after she was born. I needed to cry and tell this story more than once. I'm not sorry if it seems over-dramatic, though I struggle with feeling allowed to take up space with this story when so many are so much worse. Good luck and bad—a predictor of life as a mother. Labor has happened to women for hundreds of millions of generations, and I walked around near them and had no idea how every ancient story about a descent into hell was a retelling of this journey.

In ancient matrifocal cultures during the Neolithic, women gave birth in the sacred precincts of the Great Goddess where they were attended by shaman priestesses who were midwives, herbal healers and astrologers. Birth was a sacrament and Vicki Noble once wrote that the original shaman is the birthing woman as she flies between the worlds bringing the spirits of the ancestors back into this realm, risking their own lives whilst doing so. We are spirit embodied.[33]

Monica introduced me to the idea that woman is the original shaman. That each mother faces death to bring life back from the other side. This is a most common terrifying miracle, and this is high Witchcraft. Two people come into a room and three come out. Every act of self-creation, world-making, art has its origin here in the mind-shattering fact that we were all born. Our light and vision came and will go. The new is possible, mundane even, constantly coming and slipping past.

I needed to get my version of being the portal out onto paper, and into the river with the rest, to be able to move on.

I needed to sleep holding her in the Sun. I needed to sleep as my mother and grandmother took turns holding her and talked, as my sisters rocked her and made me strong tea, and Marc made meal after meal, and cried looking into her sweet face and whispered: you are my family.

Monica's friends will know much better than we can poring over her paintings, essays, and books. But looking at them from this distance, I wonder if after a traumatic birth, and then a life-changing home birth, and then the deaths of her children, if she ever did find a safe place to land.

In 1985 her youngest son, Leify, was killed in front of her. Hit by an oncoming car at age fifteen. "The horror when I put my hand under his head & felt a hole behind his ear, blood all over my sleeve, my son's precious life blood." That same year her eldest son, Sean, was diagnosed with non-Hodgkin's lymphoma and died two years later at age twenty-eight.

> *We lived together during the two years he had left to live and during that time we explored spiritualism and sought out healing and meditation circles and attended the Bristol Cancer Help Centre. My son got involved with Rebirthers, a New Age therapy with an extreme patriarchal and right-wing ideology. My son died on a full moon in July 1987 and after he died I made a thorough study of the New Age movement and wrote a book, since updated and re-published under the title "Return of the Dark/Light Mother or New Age Armageddon."[34]*

New Age and Armageddon is fueled by personal despair and frustration. When her son became sick, she went deep into alternative health and New Age schools looking for healing. Her sense of betrayal is palpable, and I relate to this rage too: at seeing something sacred get broken, distorted, and used to make rich men richer and to profit yet again from the bodies of our elders.

I watched my grandfather, dying of cancer, buy a mountain of expensive oils and vitamins, and then get taken in by the Iraqi currency scam. One day hoping he could buy a miracle cure, the next dreaming he could turn his small savings into millions so he might leave us something. Something more, I guess, than all our memories of his great gentleness and optimism. Ultimately those two scams were the same. Patriarchy stripped him of the right to a self-loving identity beyond that of provider, and his wound made him a mark to the con men of the New Age.

36

New Age thinking is full of such dishonest, smug, self-righteous and right-wing double-think paraded as "spirituality." New Agers such as rebirthers can then claim that they deserve to be rich and even physically immortal. Money flows towards those who have plenty of "prosperity consciousness" and make the proper affirmations. They don't have to think about living in a world rampant with Western imperialism . . . In the New Age Movement, there is no recognition that women were the creators of the most ancient cultures and that the original mother of humanity and ancestor Goddess was African and black. Hers is the luminous darkness that creates life. There is no recognition of women's shamanistic death and rebirth every month when we bleed, that women are the guardians of the twilight zones between life and death as we risk our lives giving birth, bringing spirits from the otherworld womb into the Earth plane. Women are always the communicators with the great unknown.[35]

Here is one secret of why they burn Witches: Witchcraft and activism are one. With our acts, words, and rituals, we summon a better world, and we fight inequality. Yes, we summon it for ourselves. Personal healing, joy, and fulfillment, all acts of love and pleasure are our world-changing rituals. Finding our own peace and safety, a room of one's own, honors the fight that came before and gives us strength to press forward again, to take the knowledge of our luck and strength and beauty with us into the next entanglement for justice. Individual healing from trauma helps set a piece of the pattern of the universe into a new (ancient) rhythm of resounding care. Care deviates the drumbeat of trauma on repeat. "Caring for myself is not self-indulgence. It is self-preservation, and that is an act of political warfare."[36]

Self-care, changing the world for ourselves, is only half of the work of a Witch. This is low tide, a drawing in of breath, a rest, a gathering of strength, a necessary withdrawal. After low comes high tide. We gather our power to challenge the violently empowered and to act for the source of all power. As Monica makes clear over and over again in her writing and research, magic comes from the Earth. She wrote: "I believe that we are conscious and alive only because She is. Earth is our great planetary Mother Spirit."[37]

We have to spiral from self-love, nesting and nurturing, to the work of resistance, and of remaking and re-enchanting the world. We are called to add our energy to the waves, and together to make change; to find and support each other's work, to learn about the Earth and each other; to protect the seeds and preserve the grassroots. "I am convinced that the Magic of old worked . . . The Earth was gloriously alive and She has a magnetic Astral Mind that we are a part of (our Lunar mind), and that we must hear if we want to survive. The working with this mind is what the 'craft' of the Old Religion was and is about."[38]

Monica's writing is fitful, furious, seeking, inspired. She was an activist and historian on fire to galvanize the world. But then there is the luminous quiet, that liminal place she gave us, and crucially gave herself, in her paintings. In her paintings, she became the spiritual conduit, tied to the ancestors and to the children on the other side.

Her groundbreaking work tied her to the ancestors and eventually to a vast community of feminists, queer activists, and artists, but it also isolated her and left her out too far ahead, alone.

I wanted to create a painting that would express my emerging religious belief in the Great Mother as the Matrix of cosmic creation. I didn't want Her to be a white woman. As a result of this work I was nearly taken to Court and my painting was censured many times during the '70s and '80s. It was considered "ugly," "obscene" and "blasphemous." A modern-day Witch-hunt was carried out against me and my work. It was racist also. I didn't know at the time I did the painting that the entire human race is thought to have originated from one or a handful of African women in the mists of time. This has been traced through the mitochondrial DNA which is only carried through the mothers/women. In 1968 there was also no women's arts movement or a Goddess movement and I felt totally alone. I had a sense though that ancient women, who coincide with us in another time-space, were communicating with and through me. I was their medium and gateway into this world.[39]

The paintings are beautiful. They are sometimes stark with hard whites and blues like stones, cairns, great birds at night, the gray scale of a world lit by the Moon. They most often depict women, often many races together, with a gentleness and strength and an iconic simplicity as if they are carvings or etchings or essential outlines just at the edge of your eyes, just a sketch in time. Keeping the lonely painter company.

Maybe the loneliness is something I only imagine I hear in her writing. After all, she had no lack of collaborators. By 1976 she was in close contact with the editors of *WomanSpirit* magazine—a lovingly and beautifully produced magazine of feminist spirituality, a time capsule of 1970s feminist art and thinking. You can still buy back issues if you send a letter and a check in the mail. Then she was coauthoring *The Great Cosmic Mother* with incredibly devoted researcher and writer Barbara Mor, traveling and practicing with Starhawk and Z. Budapest, reading essays by Adrienne Rich and Andrea Dworkin that finally began to conjure the new world and politics she had envisioned. She was exchanging loving letters with Doreen Valiente, Marija Gimbutas, Judy Chicago, and Alice Walker. She's been described as "a bridge between Radical and Spiritual Feminism and British Wiccans during the 1970s–1980s."[40] She poked holes and stitched links, and repeatedly put her own body on the line against the all-consuming status quo.

In *The Great Cosmic Mother*, her research tome of women's spiritual history coauthored with the brilliant and self-described Bag Lady Barbara Mor, Monica and Barbara Mor anchor feminist Witch history in a missing context of women's power.

Women's creation of human culture, our epic struggle to imaginatively survive and transform the world to which we gave birth: our collective story, amazes, enrages, energizes us. Individual lives are illumined and empowered by it. Women, and men, are returned to themselves . . . Female spirit, the goddess in us, is not fragile or new; not an invention of privileged women or an escapist New Age elite. We are tough and ancient: tried by a million years of ice and fire. On enormous and minute wheels of pain and beauty we have turned. The spinning wills of Witches transmute our experience into worlds.[41]

In *The Great Cosmic Mother* and even more so in *New Age and Armageddon*, Monica is howling and raging against violence done to the Earth, to true history, to women's bodies and spirits, and she is furious and an activist against the slippery ways she sees patriarchy taking what it wants from ancient knowledge to sell it to us all again and keep us docile and afraid.

In her obituary in the *Guardian* in 2005, Monica was described as "a writer, feminist, formidable networker and activist, eco-Witch, anarchist, founder member, in 1969, of Bristol Women's Liberation and inspiration behind Amu Mawu, a Bristol women's spirituality group. In the 1980s, with a hundred Greenham women, she walked across prohibited land to celebrate on the sarcen stones at Stonehenge at the full moon's eclipse."[42]

On that Beltane, Monica and a circle of powerful Witches reclaimed the ancient breast and belly of Silbury Hill from its use as a bloody punching bag—a site of munitions testing—by melding Witchcraft with activism. "Starhawk led a grounding meditation to center ourselves and then we took the decision to walk through the fences irrespective of the firing. In the meantime, women were facing the barbed wire fences whilst singing 'Earth is our Mother'. I had joined them for a while but was overwhelmed with tears and grief at the sight of those so-beautiful women and the thought of the patriarchal wasteland of destruction and barrenness that lay in front of us once we had entered the Plain."[43]

"We had been dreaming our land. Many pagans and people of the Craft have a love for the land and reverence for the Earth, but many too do not realise that this is not enough and that one must also take political direct action against those that ill-treat and exploit Her. It was this understanding that fired our women and our work."[44]

At Yule, the land itself is dreaming.

Here in the North we are deep under the snow. So let's take wisdom from these Witches, take shelter and dream, act, and encant for a better tomorrow. Follow the brilliant and brave Witches who came before us with their work and art and activism to cast the spell of our own courage for the necessary actions to come. With a determination for love and life and joy, the darkest days become the brightest, and that is the message and power in Yule.

A life mythologized is a kind of spell, continuing to shape what's possible. Today at the winter solstice, as we weave these Witches' stories together, we can begin to craft ourselves a history.

The *Guardian* obituary continued: "[Monica] and others, from End Patriarchy Now, interrupted a Bristol Cathedral service to demonstrate against the non-recognition of female spirituality by the Church of England. The dean joined hands with them, to sing to the goddess in front of the altar."

Monica's own telling of what happened that day is less storybook. We can keep the messy truth and the idealized mythology both, if we like. Here is how Monica remembered it:

> *The bishop and his assistants had to stop what they were doing and he zoomed in on me because as the oldest of the women he thought I was "the leader." I had placed myself in the centre as I was carrying the placard and I wanted it to be seen. Considering that during the early ['70s] I was several times nearly taken to court for "obscenity and blasphemy" for "God giving Birth" (always initiated by right-wing Christians) it was very significant to me that I confronted the bishop with that painting . . . of the Goddess who gives birth to the universe out of Her dark and bleeding womb. He attempted to take it from me and informed me that he was holding a service and that the cathedral is his, at which I answered that the cathedrals are built on ancient sacred sites of the Goddess and that we were holding a service of our own . . . There we were in this great light, congregation in the darkness, candles burning, men in white frocks . . . singing all the verses of "Burning Times" . . . I have amazing visual images of us there . . . the butterfly wings painted around Rachel's eyes fluttering & taking off . . . leaning on the pulpit declaring the glad tidings of the End of Patriarchy to the congregation. . . .*
>
> *Something had happened of cosmic proportions. When we returned to the conference women were drumming ecstatically for hours & we were dancing. . . . [45]*

And we are dancing still.

Amy and I were invited to speak at the Apostolic Johannite Church gnostic conclave in 2019 set to take place in a church. With Monica's story fresh in our minds, we chose the theme of Dance and walked up the aisle singing "The Burning Times," invoking the Goddesses, chanting in song their chorus of names, Isis, Astarte, Diana, Hecate, Demeter, Kali, Inanna, and Yemaya, with Amy on guitar. The theme of that year's conference was "The Divine Feminine," so we invited trans and nonbinary Witches to the pulpit to help us dissect notions of both the Feminine and the Divine. We told some of the stories you read here and we thought together about the magic curled up in our bodies, unleashed in dance, and at the end, we passed the gilded collection plate and passed that collection on to the Native Women's Shelter of Montréal. By the end, the priests were dancing too. We hope we made Monica proud.

Ritual

Find somewhere safe where you can send up a long, slow vowel sound.

Make your throat a hollow cave the wind moans through.

Surrender like the Pythia, the original oracles at Delphi, howling with pure Spirit.

Make a plate of fruit, especially pomegranates. Pour some wine or tea.

Put out some paper and pen, put boughs in vases. We use evergreens, but use whatever is close and bountiful where you are.

Light your Yule log or candles and then turn out all the lights in the house. See the horned goddess in the shadows that the fire makes through the boughs.

Make this shadow sister offerings and sing to her, drone the deep vowel tones that connect our bellies to the caves and bellies of the Earth.

Eat the fruit and think of Persephone, raped in the underworld, who saw the infinite universes in a pomegranate and remembered who she was. She birthed herself from beyond death. Sit in the dark and remember who you are when you are between worlds.

Write in the dark without worrying about the shapes. Scratch what you want to leave behind and what you want to bring to light this year.

Put the papers in a safe cauldron (or in the sink), then burn them. Drink your libations in the dark.

Sing again, to accompany Persephone out of the dark.

Sing the "Solstice Carol" Amy wrote below, or sing anything that comes to you. Or just drone deep vowel sounds in resonance with the mothers who are all around you—who carry the vibration of labor always in them—in resonance with the children all around you who in their deepest memories recognize the sound of their original home-town. For this great celebration of your birth, child of Earth and Starry Heaven, find your own harmony with the ancestor spirit mother who is you, humming to new life through you, no matter who you are.

Of her experiences having and losing children, Monica wrote: "I have been given another overwhelming insight into light and space and love but also into the most unbearable pain and grief. It is in Birth and Death after all that the pathways between this Earth realm and the Spirit-world are open . . . this is what the Ancient Religion and Shamanism has always been about . . . to be able to cross the barriers between worlds. ..."[46]

To all who are out there singing along the webs, holding in your hearts the great power of the longest nights, and of the coming morning, to all of you gathering your stories, gathering your people, gathering the wind about you, gathering your strength, and to the darkness itself: We love you, we are with you. We'll see you on the other side.

INCANTATION

Isis, Astarte, Diana, Hecate, Demeter, Kali, Inanna, Yemaya
All Acts of Love and Pleasure Are My Rituals
Isis, Astarte, Diana, Hecate, Demeter, Kali, Inanna, Yemaya
We Have Been Dreaming Our Land
Isis, Astarte, Diana, Hecate, Demeter, Kali, Inanna, Yemaya
Activism Is Witchcraft
Isis, Astarte, Diana, Hecate, Demeter, Kali, Inanna, Yemaya
We Are Dancing Still
And We Are Dancing Still

SOLSTICE CAROL

C
Oh Yuletide,

G
Oh Solstice

F   Fm
Oh longest night of the Year

C   G   F   Fm
We gather together to share our hope and our fear

C   Am   C   Am
'Cuz we are Witches in the Night

C   Am   F   Fm
We are Witches. We bring our own light to the

C   G   F   Fm
Solstice, at Yuletide on the longest night of the Year

C   G   F   Fm
Please bring us together to share our warmth and our cheer

C   Am   C   Am
'Cuz we are Witches of the Night

C   Am   F   Fm
We are Witches. We make our own light

REPEAT AS NECESSARY

You can listen to a recording of this Solstice Carol on missingwitches.com.

2

Imbolc

This circle is led by Amy

IMBOLC MARKS THE HALFWAY POINT BETWEEN THE WINTER SOL-STICE AND THE SPRING EQUINOX: FEBRUARY 2. It is *not* the new and glorious world of a budding spring but rather the *promise* of a new world. Past the point of longest nights, we are still here. We are awakening. Opening and adjusting our eyes. Inspecting our shrinking shadows. Preparing. Scratching at the dirt, collecting and gathering, building a foundation out of what remnants we can find, fueled by our faith that a new dawn is possible. Anticipating the coming melt, we carve paths of least resistance in the snow. We direct the flow.

Like most of our pagan Sabbats, Imbolc has a modern counterpart: Groundhog Day. This is another one of those magics that goes slipping by unnoticed until you stop for a moment to ask: wait, what? Like blowing out the candles on a birthday cake, certain things we do in modern society make no sense other than as magic-making Witchcraft. These rituals that mark the passage of time contain symbols that are so ingrained in our lives yet so divorced from their origins that they appear both perfectly normal and comically absurd. When Christianity took hold of the narrative, Imbolc became Candlemas, when candles were lit, and a feast was held for Jesus. But even these early Christian European traditions gave a hint of the groundhog's climate-forecasting future. It was thought that shadows cast by a shining Sun on this day foretold another month of winter weather. Eighteenth-century German immigrants brought this magic to Pennsylvania, and the celebration was formalized in the town of Punxsutawney in 1887. In the pageantry of the modern Groundhog Day, members of an occult-sounding group known as the Inner Circle wear top hats and claim to speak "Groundhogese" to interpret the divination.

I have to laugh. Some people will roll their eyes when I say I give gratitude to the Moon and Sun, but they will happily accept, one day a year, that a marmot can both tell the future and communicate its prediction to a human. That is HIGH MAGIC. And I love it for its surreal disruption of the status quo and because it's a great metaphor for Imbolc. It's a time to awaken and thoroughly assess yourself and your surroundings before moving forward. Like the groundhog and the Fool of the tarot, we must balance our curiosity with critical thinking. And approaching the end of hibernation with our reserves dwindling, we must begin to plan for the future. Using critical awareness and hindsight to make preparations is a major theme for Imbolc, as well as a major theme for the two Witches you'll meet in this chapter who sought out the past to inform their futures.

Imbolc is a time to recognize that what we keep from last year we will carry into the next. At Imbolc, Witches take stock both literally and metaphorically. So check in with yourself. Be honest about what you have and what you lack. The groundhog doesn't come out of his hole with his prediction for the future in tow. He emerges. He looks for tangible evidence, makes his evaluation, and only then does he decide what he thinks the future will be. So are you tired? Are you hungry? Unfulfilled? If we never really ask ourselves what we need, we'll never get what we need. It sounds so simple, but in the daily grind of stress and constant distractions, we often forget to ask ourselves who we are.

Here's the naked truth. The first panic attack I remember having was when I was seven years old and walking through a parking lot, heading into a facility for a school placement. I remember my stomach churning. I remember sweat forming, my muscles tightening, and a primal fear washing from my brain down to my feet and rolling back up into my throat. I told my mother I felt sick. She asked if I wanted to go home and I croaked out a feeble "no." This was my first taste of what would, by necessity, become my motto: be scared and do it anyway. Because I have a wonky thyroid and a wacky amygdala (a part of our brains linked to emotions like fear and pleasure responses), I feel scared most of the time. As if every morning I'm taking a test I haven't studied for.

Fear can be a good thing. You see a tiger, you run away. But for me, imaginary tigers lurk around every corner, waiting to pounce. I can feel their teeth and claws and hot breath on my neck. If I were a groundhog, I would always see my shadow and run back into my hole. I admit that sometimes the anxiety is tougher than I am, and the shadow sends me back underground for six more weeks of winter. With a lot of trial and error (so much error), I've come to a place where I can get back out from the underground in a couple days. I've been brainwashed by capitalism, like we all have, to believe that my productivity determines my value, determines my worth. So when I'm too tired or too scared to take on the day, I become not only sick but also a failure. Anxiety can be a snowball that gains weight, girth, and speed as it rolls through the snow. Your essay is a day late, but you're too anxious to work on it, and your greedy anxiety happily expands because now your essay is two days late.

Sometimes my anxiety is useful and produces great results. Things run smoothly because my mind has spent months coming up with every possible thing that could go wrong and solving these problems before they have a chance to happen. People say I seem so confident. I tell them, "That's because you didn't see me throwing up in the shower this morning." I've gotten very good at pretending not to be scared. At being scared and doing it anyway.

Sometimes I wake up not feeling well, so I take the day off work. I tell myself I need rest. I tell myself it's OK. Then I spend the next sixteen hours beating myself up. I feel worthless, unproductive, and lazy, and my day becomes just that. I'm too busy berating myself to get the rest I promised myself so I could rationalize calling in sick. So there are two possible conclusions: I should have just sucked it up and gone to work; or I should have given myself the break I said I needed and allowed myself to see that rest as a productive use of my time. Either way, beating myself up is not useful or productive. Witches must choose to rest or act, and this decision must be made with honesty and without self-loathing. As Audre Lorde wrote in her 1988 book of essays, *A Burst of Light,* "Caring for myself is not self-indulgence, it is self-preservation, and that is an act of political warfare."[1]

Sometimes the groundhog sees his shadow and goes back underground to sleep through six more weeks of winter. Sometimes he sees no shadow and is ready to hit the ground running. We have to honestly take stock and make an honest appraisal. Am I exhausted or am I just afraid? This is where shadow work comes in. Shadow work is about acknowledging our "dark side" without judgment. It's about finding those parts of ourselves that we can't see or won't admit to, even to ourselves, and countering society's message that POSITIVITY equals GOODNESS. When someone starts crying, the first thing they usually hear is "don't cry." But sometimes, crying is the best and most appropriate response. Some biological studies published over the years have shown that crying expels stress hormones through tears and creates mood-enhancing oxytocin and endorphins. But somewhere, sometime, someone (hello, patriarchy) decided that crying was bad and, therefore, inappropriate, shameful even. And we were cut off from this amazing, universal stress reliever. Sometimes Witches cry. But not for long. Because we can thank our tears and then turn our eyes forward to our own agency and capacity to make change.

I have to question and be honest with myself every day. Is the tiger real or imaginary? Is what I'm feeling useful? Am I sick or just scared? Am I exhausted and truly in need of rest, or do I just not want to deal with today? Did my choices yesterday affect how I'm feeling today? What's working in my life and what isn't? This is the message of Imbolc: Get real. Be honest.

What received too much of our energy? What didn't get enough? We analyze so that eventually we can poke our little groundhog heads out of our groundhog holes and greet whatever awaits us, shadow or none, with acceptance and without fear.

Use Imbolc as a reminder to refocus on your own goals. Seek out your shadows as a reminder of work that must still be done. Make a realistic plan based on a realistic assessment of your real self. If you don't like what you find, you can make changes. Small, achievable baby steps or grand, world-changing schemes. You can be like Jimmy, the Wisconsin groundhog who, in 2015, bit the town mayor on the ear in what I interpret as an act of defiant postcapitalist rage. I assume Jimmy the Groundhog took an honest stock of his situation and decided to protest. Jimmy would not be exploited and neither will you.

The bottom line is this: Imbolc is the time to face reality. Director Harold Ramis really nailed this with his film *Groundhog Day* in which Bill Murray is doomed to repeat the same day over and over and over again. That's what Imbolc is telling you. Whatever you keep now, whatever you put off now is staying in the baggage that you'll lug into spring. The choice is yours: Will you repeat last year's mistakes, or recognize them, confront them, and leave them behind? Hindsight is essential to move forward in preparation. Questioning is essential. Curiosity is essential. In a bet with God, curiosity and answer-seeking kept Zora Neale Hurston alive.

So let's travel to Harlem, a hotbed of fresh ideas and awakenings, and home to two seemingly fearless women who wove stories out of shadows and scraps, using the bits and pieces they found to change the world: Zora Neale Hurston and Faith Ringgold.

Zora and Faith navigated their lives with eyes wide open, making these artists the perfect role models for an Imbolc awakening. In her autobiography *Dust Tracks on a Road*, Zora wrote, "Like the dead-seeming, cold rocks, I have memories within that came out of the material that went to make me. Time and place have had their say. So you will have to know something about the time and place where I came from, in order that you may interpret the incidents and directions of my life."[2]

At Imbolc, Witches seek a truer picture than the one our mind invents out of fear or anxiety, a fuller picture than what appears on the surface. Time and place will have their say. So in writing about Zora, it's tempting to just reprint her autobiography for you, here and now, in its entirety. The way her use of language and sense of humor wind their way around her life story brings life, depth, and movement to every detail. It's the same spirit she brings to her research on Caribbean and African American religion and folklore, anthropologically teasing out the spirits within words and deeds. With the curiosity of a thousand groundhogs, Zora brings a new light to the story of Witchcraft by noticing what was missing.

She remains a controversial figure and prolific, continuing to publish "new" books almost sixty years after her death in 1960. *Barracoon: The Story of the Last "Black Cargo,"* published in 2018, is based on her 1927 interviews with Cudjo Lewis, a former enslaved man who was the last survivor of the Middle Passage Atlantic slave trade. The book is a testament to the power of gathering and telling stories. Keeping those stories alive. She said, "I want to collect like a new broom"[3]—brings a whole new meaning to a Witch's flight, right?

Zora called herself Pagan and rewrote the tale of Moses from a rural Black American perspective. She threw around the N-word with a deliberate and near joyful irony. She claimed and reclaimed, felt proud and entitled, and was not humble. But perhaps her most defining characteristic was her curiosity. Zora wrote, "Research is formalized curiosity. It is poking and prying with a purpose. It is a seeking that he who wishes may know the cosmic secrets of the world and they that dwell therein."[4] I mean . . . Those three sentences could easily have been our motto for this book, and they are certainly a clear instruction for Imbolc.

Zora wrote, "I was full of curiosity like many other children . . . I was always asking and making myself a crow in a pigeon's nest. . . . I got few answers from other people, but I kept right on asking, because I couldn't do anything else with my feelings. . . . But no matter whether my probings made me happier or sadder, I kept on probing to know."[5]

In her book *Zora Neale Hurston's Final Decade,* Virginia Lynn Moylan described the front porch of Joe Clarke's general store, which was the center of spinning tales and adult gossip. Children were not allowed to hang about the stoop too long, but Zora would sneak and hide in an effort to hear every story she could. This resulted in frequent punishment, but undaunted, she pushed her willingness to sacrifice for her curiosity as far as she could, devoting much of her life to almighty research. She gathered tales, both formally in interviews and casually in the living rooms of friends, to be written into her novels, essays, and stories. She said, "I had things clawing inside of me that must be said."[6]

In 1973, nine years before the publication of her Pulitzer Prize-winning novel *The Color Purple,* Alice Walker found and marked Zora's grave. Alice and Zora are so linked that we almost can't write about one without bringing up the other. To put it our way, Zora went looking for the Witches she'd been missing, and Alice did the same, discovering Zora's work while doing research on Vodou in the American South for a short story. Author Thadious M. Davis recounted Alice's telling of this discovery in her essay "The Polarities of Space,"[7] stating that Alice had a hard time finding sources that she could trust. Alice felt that the approach of white, racist anthropologists was insulting, rendering their books useless for her pursuits. And then she found Zora, or more specifically, Zora's book *Mules and Men*. She felt soothed by Zora's presence and thus began their posthumous relationship.

Alice wrote extensively on Zora. One of our favorite pieces comes from Alice's "Dedication: On Refusing to Be Humbled by Second Place in a Contest You Did Not Design," which serves as the introduction to a Zora Neale Hurston anthology Alice Walker edited. The anthology's title, *I Love Myself*, came from the response Zora gave upon seeing the results of a portrait photo shoot. She said, "I love Myself when I am Laughing, and Then again When I am Looking Mean and Impressive." Alice covered a lot in her Zoranthology's brief dedication, more eloquently and thoughtfully than we could ever hope to do ourselves, and she did so with a personal love and admiration that could come only from the devoted Zoraphile, Alice herself. She described not only what it's like to read Zora's work, but also how it may have felt to know her.

A friend of mine called one day to tell me that she and another woman had been discussing Zora Neale Hurston and decided they wouldn't have liked her. They wouldn't have liked the way—when her play Color Struck *won second prize in a literary contest in the beginning of her career—Hurston walked into a room full of her competitors, flung her scarf dramatically over her shoulder and yelled, "COLOR . . R . R STRUCK . . K . K!" at the top of her voice.*

Apparently it isn't easy to like a person who is not humbled by second place. ...

We live in a society, as Blacks, women, and artists, whose contests we do not design and with whose insistence on ranking us we are permanently at war. To know that second place, in such a society, has often required more and innate genius than first, a longer, grimmer struggle over greater odds than first—and to be able to fling your scarf about dramatically while you demonstrate that you know. To know that second place is to trust your own self-evaluation in the

face of the Great White Western Commercial of white and male
supremacy, which is virtually everything we see, outside and often
inside our own homes. That Hurston held her own, literally, against
the flood of whiteness and maleness that diluted so much other Black
art of the period in which she worked is a testimony to her genius and
her faith.

As Black women and as artists, we are prepared, I think, to keep
the faith. There are other choices, but they are despicable.

Zora Neale Hurston who went forth into the world with one
dress to her name and was permitted, at other times in her life, only a
single pair of shoes, rescued and re-created a world which she labored
to hand us whole, never underestimating the value of her gift, if at
times doubting the good sense of its recipients. She appreciated us, in
any case, as we fashioned ourselves. That is something. And of all the
people in the world to be, she chose to be herself, and more and more
herself. That, too, is something.[8]

And so with gratitude to Alice, we dedicate this Imbolc, this chapter,
this turn of our Wheel of the Year to the memory of Zora. We dedicate
it to self-evaluation, to the curious and the confident, and to those who
choose—and to those who have to fight—to be themselves.

Zora was born in Alabama in 1891. Some markers have her born in
1901, but it's largely agreed that she had, at some point, lied about her
age in order to qualify to return to high school. Her family moved to
Eatonville, Florida, when Zora was only three years old, so she considered this place her home and set many of her stories there. In 1942's *Dust
Tracks on a Road*, she described an early childhood chasing the horizon
and being chased by the Moon. She took her time learning to walk, she
said, but once she started she didn't stop. "The strangest thing about
it was that once I found the use of my feet, they took to wandering. I
always wanted to go. I would wander off in the woods all alone, following some inside urge to go places. This alarmed my mother a great deal.
She used to say that she believed a woman who was an enemy of hers
had sprinkled 'travel dust' around the doorstep the day I was born. That

was the only explanation she could find."[9] It seems almost prophetic that when she was One Year Old, little Zora's life would already be characterized by this mixture of Magic Powder and the Need to Know and Go.

A lot of her later childhood reads like a fairy tale. Not the pretty princess kind, but the old ones where wicked stepmothers do terrible things to children and idyllic youth is cut short by a cold reality. Zora's mother, Lucy—the woman who had instructed her to "Jump at the Sun"—died. Her father quickly, very quickly, remarried, and little Zora was shipped off to boarding school. She stayed there until her father just . . . stopped . . . paying her tuition.

She started working as a maid at fourteen but, by her own account, never kept a job for very long. That curiosity leading her life again, she said, "No matter how I resolved, I'd get tangled up with their reading matter and lose my job."[10]

"One of the most serious objections to me was that having nothing, I still did not know how to be humble."[11] We can't help but think of our Beloved Witch Ipsita Roy Chakraverti's appreciation of arrogant women or even the time-honored quote, often attributed to Angela Davis, "Well-behaved women seldom make history." Missing Witches maintain that Witchcraft is Activism and Activism is Witchcraft, but WE didn't create the synonymous relationship between Powerful Women, Witchcraft, and Dissidence! Those labels were and are thrust upon us for us to reject, ignore, or embrace. But there's a certain aspect of Witchcraft or being a Witch that almost won't allow us to be sheepish or apologize for not fitting in. Something that claws from within to be released. I spoke to Backxwash, a Canadian rapper Witch who was born in Zambia.[12] She told me about growing up with the echoes of colonialism still ringing in the air. When the colonizers and missionaries came, everything they did not like or understand was labeled Witchcraft. The holy dance was demonized. Her ancestors' ways were nearly erased. So Backxwash wears the label of Witch with pride. It stands for her precolonial traditions and anticolonial perspective, her dissidence and her difference. She named her latest album *Deviancy* because, she told me, as a trans woman, her very existence is seen as a deviant act. In her way of thinking, one of the greatest political actions you can take is to unapologetically love yourself in a society that thinks you shouldn't exist. Part of being a Witch, I think, is allowing yourself to take up space. To exist with freedom and authenticity. And for Zora, there was a steadfast relationship between her curiosity and her confidence. She didn't just have questions, she felt she deserved answers and, empowered to ask her questions, was brave enough to seek those answers at almost any cost.

She worked, for a time, with a traveling theater company, eventually ending up in Baltimore. There she was a manicurist, tried waitressing, got appendicitis, and had to have surgery. She wrote, "When I was taken up to the amphitheater for the operation I went up there placing a bet with God. I did not fear death. Nobody would miss me very much, and I had no treasures to leave behind me, so I would not go out of life looking backwards on that account. But I bet God that if I lived, I would try to find out the vague directions whispered in my ears and find the road it seemed that I must follow. How? When? Why? What? All those answers were hidden from me."[13]

She did live through the surgery and resolved to win that bet with God. "How then did I get back to school?" she wrote. "I just went."[14]

Zora was notoriously charming, witty, driven, ferocious in her dedication, and smart, so I believe this version of the story. She wanted to go so she just went. Delightful and courageous ruffler of the feathers of society, Witch and musician Athena Holmes a.k.a. Big Sissy (they/them), when asked where this bravery comes from, told me, "When I am balanced and cleansed, I can access my bravery." For Athena, and for all of us, bravery isn't something that you have or don't have. You have it. When you are focused on your goals and grounded in your Self, you can access the bravery within you. Athena takes meditative, spiritual baths—just a regular bath, but with the intention of letting go set into the bathwater, allowing the literal and metaphorical dirt of existence wash off of you and down the drain. For Athena, the bath opens up the space for boldness to surface. It's difficult to see your bravery when it's crushed far down into your guts. But it's there, a tiny spark, waiting for you to feed its flame with your acknowledgment.

Zora was gifted with a supremely enviable confidence. She needed no balancing bath. She just went. She worked her way through high school, prep school. She earned an associate's degree at Howard University and studied at Barnard under the legendary Franz Boas, a man who has since been called the "Father of Modern Anthropology." Franz was outspoken in his anti-racism, and his theory of cultural relativism stated that all cultures are equal. No culture or race is better or more correct. Context must inform our judgments. People's cultures inform their values and behaviors. Franz recognized in Zora an unquenchable thirst for stories, so anthropology, the study of human culture and society, made perfect sense. He sent Zora to do field research in Harlem, and it was there that she met and began collaborations with famed poet and essayist Langston Hughes and writer Wallace Thurman.

Zora is perhaps most famously associated with this movement that reveled in its **B**lackness—a Black-fueled, Black-themed explosion of art, music, poetry. A new wave of social Afrocentrism that swept across the New York of the 1920s. The Harlem Renaissance was an incarnation of Black pride whose spirit and influence are still felt throughout American culture. Zora and Langston Hughes and many others would gather at the home of Wallace Thurman—they published a magazine together—and these gatherings soon became the talk of the town. We know that Zora saw the glories of Black culture and was NOT humble, so it's fitting that she became a poster child for what Alain LeRoy Locke, the first African American Rhodes Scholar, hailed as "The New Negro." This term, popularized during the Harlem Renaissance, implied outspoken advocacy of history and dignity and a refusal to submit quietly to Jim Crow. A refusal to hide Black identity, blend in, or be self-effacing. This was a group who rebuked the values of the white bourgeoisie and was not concerned with fitting in. Zora wrote in her essay "How It Feels to Be Colored Me" (and I hope all you Witches will carry this in your hearts), "Sometimes I feel discriminated against, but it does not make me angry. It merely astonishes me. How can anyone deny themselves the pleasure of my company? It's beyond me."[15]

In a way, this statement epitomizes the movement. Soaked in Black history, shining Black excellence, and not humble. Some of her work from this era has been recently anthologized in *Hitting Straight Lick with a Crooked Stick* (2020), but for most of the years that made up the Harlem Renaissance, Zora wasn't in Harlem. Zora was on the road.

Much of what we know about her thoughts and life was gathered from travel letters she wrote to her friends back in New York. Arriving in New Orleans on one of her collecting missions, she wrote to Langston Hughes: I have landed here in the kingdom of Marie Laveau and expect to wear her crown someday. Conjure Queen.[16]

To writer and poet Countee Cullen she wrote, "I have the nerve to walk my own way, however hard, in my search for reality, rather than climb upon the rattling wagon of wishful illusions."

In Haiti she composed her best-known work, the novel *Their Eyes Were Watching God*, while collecting stories for what would become her book *Tell My Horse*. Zora's work was not well received at the time but has gone on to take a rightful place in the canon of literature and in the history of magic. *Their Eyes . . .* and *Tell My Horse* are very different books, but each tells the story of a journey. A search for identity through both history and imagination.

Most modern Witches don't make much of a distinction between magic and science. Rituals are Methods and words cast spells. All is part of natural and cosmic law. One of the mottos of a coven formed by WhiteFeather Hunter in a science lab at Concordia University in Montréal is: Methodology is Ritual. Hypotheses are Prophecies.

In "Graveyard Dirt and Other Poisons," a chapter in *Tell My Horse*, Zora gives us a prime example of the relationship between the real and the mystical, describing the "superstition" of hoodoo men and Witch doctors' use of graveyard dirt. She quoted doctors Domingo Foriero and Louis Pasteur to show that bacteria and illness from a corpse can and do leach into the surrounding soil, impregnating it with deadly power.

We know that graveyard dirt can poison, so we have to wonder what other "silly magic" is, in reality, ancient wisdom as yet "undiscovered" by modern science.

For the Witches' reading list, *Mules and Men* and *Tell My Horse* are essential. They are both packed with folktales and magic, songs and recipes, lovingly and diligently gathered and retold in ways that only Zora could conjure. She talked about the passage of time as "when the moon had dragged a thousand tides."[17] Stories that are vital to the history of American magic are made poetry in her thoughtful and lyrical telling.

She married and divorced twice—her one true love was that formalized curiosity. I want to collect like a new broom.

So, in truest Zora fashion, that's what she did. She just went collecting. Traveling, collecting, writing, publishing. But our brave and bold Zora didn't just document the magic like some scholar outsider. She dug in, got her hands dirty. She was initiated, and fueled by curiosity, opened herself up to all that initiation entails.

> *In New Orleans, I delved into Hoodoo, or sympathetic magic. I studied with the Frizzly Rooster and all of the other noted "doctors."... In order to work with these "two-headed" doctors, I had to go through an initiation with each. The routine varied with each doctor. . . . I began to dream strange exalted dreams . . . that seemed real for weeks. In one, I strode across the heavens with lightning flashing from under my feet, and grumbling thunder following in my wake. In this particular ceremony, my finger was cut and I became blood brother to the rattlesnake. We were to aid each other forever. I was to walk with the storm and hold my power, and get my answers to life and things in storms. The symbol of lightning was painted on my back. This was to be mine forever.[18]*

For Zora, sharing what she had learned was as important as the learning itself. She made her way from Louisiana to the Bahamas and on her return to New York in 1932, she introduced Bahama songs and dances to a New York audience. By 1934 she was establishing a drama school "based on pure Negro expression."

Traveling, collecting, writing, publishing. Traveling, collecting, writing, publishing.

These four words characterized most of Zora's life throughout the '30s and '40s. California, Harlem, Honduras, Florida, Jamaica. Fellowships, patrons, and research grants enabling her ever-growing search for the answer to an impossible mystery. She wrote: Belief in magic is older than writing. So nobody knows how it started.[19]

But she kept looking and listening, driven by curiosity, and everywhere, she found music and magic.

Everywhere, she found music and magic.

Until 1948. There was a scandal. She was falsely accused of sexual impropriety with a young man. I say *falsely* because 100 percent of the evidence spoke to her innocence AND her accuser admitted that he was lying. But despite her clear innocence, a mix of personal vendetta and salacious, profit-driven tabloid reporting ensured the story had already spread. She felt suicidal, betrayed by her community, and eventually left Harlem for good. Another Witch hunted and exiled.

Zora returned to Florida and spent the 1950s working as a writer, librarian, and substitute teacher.

In 1959 she had a stroke. The story goes that in 1960, Zora died in a county welfare home when her heart stopped beating. Her body was buried in an unmarked grave and her personal effects were set to be burned. The fire had been lit. Zora's history was burning. But as luck or the fates or the gods and goddesses would have it, a friend of Zora's, Patrick DuVal, was passing by the place where she had lived. And he stopped and put out the fire, rescuing her papers from being burned as if at the stake. He rescued Zora for Alice Walker to find.

Alice is often credited with breaking Zora into the literary mainstream when *Ms.* magazine published Alice's essay describing her search, "Looking for Zora." Alice and Zora became woven together, with Zora serving as a posthumous mentor for Alice. In her essay "Living by the Word: June Jordan and Alice Walker's Quest for a Redemptive Art and Politics," Cheryl Wall wrote about this Zora/Alice dynamic.[20] "Hurston, who was fond of the Black English word 'bodacious' (bold + audacious), offers Walker a literary legacy as well as a model for living a free life that is marked by unwavering dedication to one's work."[21]

So Alice went bodaciously forward. In *In Search of Our Mothers' Gardens,* she wrote, "We are a people. A people do not throw their geniuses away. And if they are thrown away, it is our duty as artists and as witnesses for the future to collect them again for the sake of our children, and, if necessary, bone by bone."[22] Alice, Zora, Patrick DuVal, and others like them are the unwitting forebearers of the Missing Witches project. We give them love and respect, as we go digging, collecting bones of our own. Ancestors' bones. Witches' bones. Building skeletons bone by bone.

Imbolc is a time to be bold, audacious, bodacious, curious, confident, and NOT humble. It's the time to get real about your accomplishments and your shortcomings. Ask your questions and demand your answers. Gather bones, seek truth, and speak the buried truths that you discover in the boneyard! Be brave, have the nerve to walk your own way. Do your magic, knowing that someday, somewhere, a curious Witch will find it and feel it.

As you make your own dust tracks on a cold and slippery Imbolc road, take with you this page from Zora's autobiography:

The springing of the yellow line of morning out of the misty deep of dawn, is glory enough for me. I know that nothing is destructible; things merely change forms. When the consciousness we know as life ceases, I know that I shall still be part and parcel of the world. I was a part before the sun rolled into shape and burst forth in the glory of change. I was, when the earth was hurled out from its fiery rim. I shall return with the earth to Father Sun, and still exist in substance when the sun has lost its fire, and disintegrated in infinity to perhaps become a part of the whirling rubble in space. Why fear? The stuff of my being is matter, ever changing, ever moving, but never lost; so what need of denominations and creeds to deny myself the comfort of all my fellow men? The wide belt of the universe has no need for finger-rings. I am one with the infinite and need no other assurance.[23]

Changing form is part of Witchcraft. Bits and pieces found and gathered become rituals. Names become spells. So, as Witches, we experiment with words and labels, and play with them in our quest to reach that no-assurance-needed oneness-with-the-infinite that Zora managed to conjure for herself. Before we accept the label "Witch," we have to ask: What *is* a Witch? Do I qualify? (yes, you do). Certainly not all of the "Witches" we've profiled in this book would have called themselves a Witch. Even today, amid the millions of #Witchesofinstagram, calling yourself "Witch" IRL is often met with condescension, a dismissive eye roll, a smug chuckle. This chuckle is, of course, preferable to not just historical but also contemporary Witch hunt reactions of, you know, being killed. . . . All this to say, the stigma is still real—there are myriad reasons a Witch might not want to loudly classify themselves. So sometimes we have to go looking for clues to find the Witches without visible cauldrons, goddess idols, or tarot decks. Sometimes we have to follow the bread crumbs left behind for us to trace.

I discovered Faith Ringgold while doing research on Zora. Now Zora has been known to send messages to her admirers—her biographer Valerie Boyd claims she wrote the book because Zora told her to—so when I saw Faith's absolutely visceral illustrations for Zora's book *The Three Witches,* I knew I had to dig a little deeper. Turns out, one of Faith's most acclaimed works is a series she called *Witch Masks.* One of her most famous stories is about a little girl who can fly. As far as I know, Faith has never publicly called herself a Witch; after all, as her mother reminded her constantly, she is from a good Christian home. But this recurring symbolic equation of freedom with flying through the night sky, these Witch drawings and Witch masks, coupled with Faith's sigil work and alchemy, subverting traditional symbols and forms, reclaiming and politicizing so-called feminine arts. Plus her work as a civil rights and feminist activist, author, educator, and all around magical badass, and I think you'll agree, the Witch is strong in this one. The Tate Modern galleries called her "a rule breaker and a game changer." She said, "*I was absolutely taught by my family as a tradition that nobody tells you what you can't do.*"[24]

Faith is an expert weaver—not just in the textile sense, although she is a masterful textile artist, but also in the way she has managed to stitch together every aspect of her life and self into the expression of her work. Every new skill is carried over to her next medium. Every lesson she's learned, she has woven into her creations, or taken the lemons and made sweet, sweet lemonade. Beyoncé style.

Well now I've brought up Beyoncé, so here's a quick aside for the hive: Check out Faith's quilt, *Dancing at the Louvre,* then go watch the Carters' *Apeshit* video. The connection is obvious at first sight, so I was thrilled to read that the video was inspired, that Queen B herself was inspired by Faith's work.

Amid all of Faith's dualities, there is no infighting. Faith presents seamless. A tapestry both literal and figurative, where every tiny thread disappears so a single image can emerge. In the book *Faith Ringgold: A View from the Studio,* coauthor Curlee Raven Holton wrote,

> *Her work bears testimony to her fight to achieve acceptance and recognition in a world that is both racist and sexist. She is to stuffy boundaries of the art world what a civil rights advocate is to injustice. . . . The Faith I know is subversive in her art making. Her messages can shout or be subliminal at her choosing. She has been called a feminist but she is quick to remind us that the feminist movement did not naturally seek out faces that looked like hers. Rather she, with the force of her presence, pushed the movement and claimed inclusion. She is angry, and yet, she is not consumed by anger.*[25]

This is what I aspire to—as a person and as a Witch. To be not just a human dog pack of dualities and contradictions, snarling and snapping for attention and to be fed. . . . And not the clichéd more than the sum of my parts, but just, like, one complete person. To have emotions but not be consumed by them, and rather, to use those emotions as fuel to pursue a greater good. That's what I want for me and for all you Missing Witches reading this book, out there casting a spell with just your magical being of magical You. Fully you. I was talking to a Witch friend and the subject of balance came up—her desire to balance all aspects of herself and her life. Balance—it's all about balance. And I was researching the beautiful, bold tapestry that is Faith at the time, so I stopped her. "I'm tired of trying to balance; my goal now is total integration," I said. All splashes of color forming one cohesive work of art. I want to stop distributing and redistributing pieces of myself on a scale to be weighed and compared. Like Scrooge's coins or some cuts of meat at a butcher shop. I want to be a shining light of wholeness and authenticity who has left the stress of identity-plate-spinning behind—and my role model for this totally valid Imbolc utopian pipe dream of capital A Awareness and capital B Being will be Faith Ringgold.

Faith was born in our Imbolc destination of Harlem in 1930, surrounded by the icons of the Harlem Renaissance—that staking of artistic and cultural claim to the labels African and American. Both Faith's and Zora's stories overlap a lot not only in time and space but also in the themes these women explored. Faith carried on with Zora's mission in a very real and tangible way, calling her own work a "pursuit of a more affirmative black aesthetic," which is something that Zora could easily have said herself.

Faith says she felt no oppression in childhood because her community shielded her from the harsh reality of race in America. Her mother, delightfully named Willi Posey Jones, was a fashion designer, so their collaborations began early and lasted right up until Willi died in 1981. Faith was also, in a way, shielded by her illness. In the preface to her memoir, *We Flew over the Bridge*, Faith wrote, "My life as an artist began as a child during the many hours I spent bedridden with asthma, picturing my small world and the people in it. By the time I became a teenager I started using my art to tell my story. When images alone were not enough, I added words to my pictures and later quilted them."[26]

But her asthma also kind of changed her life for the better. She couldn't go to school, but she wasn't always sick, so she spent a lot of her days accompanying her mother on errands and adventures. While other children were learning their ABCs, Faith was learning how to live.

With Faith's art, description is difficult. Words are insufficient. Her quilts are colorful; narrative . . . floral granny squares of outgrown Sunday dresses border figures in living rooms and cityscapes, crafted from shapes and strips of textile and texture and paint. The materials are comforting and the subjects are both personal and political. It's almost as if Faith wanted to create a comforter: a visual safe space to lure us into her dissidence, her uncomfortable truths about race, sex, and class. Faith wrote that she made the move to needle and thread when images were not enough. She has also said that she switched from painting to fabric to get away from the association of painting with Western/European traditions. In a world before social media, she made a quilt to call out Picasso's legacy and hung it on a gallery wall. But we'll get to Picasso later.

In 1950 at age twenty, having already been an artist her entire life, Faith applied to art school, City College of New York, but because fine art was often deemed by patriarchal institutions to be an almost exclusively male realm, she was forced to change her application to Education majoring in Art. Faith did so knowing that no one can tell you what you can't do.

She married a jazz musician and drug addict, and because of her courage and determination, she and her two daughters left him before he died of an overdose. Her daughters did not understand why they had been kept away from their father and resented her. She did remarry eventually, but as we've seen with so many of our Missing Witches, her one true soul mate was her Magic. Her Art.

In the early '60s, Faith was painting timid landscapes and tepid still lifes, a trend at the time, likely to fill the new demand for suburban decor. It was a style in line with a gallery she approached about a show. Perplexingly, the gallerist replied: You can't do that.

But leave it to Faith to lemonade those lemons. She said, "You know something? I think what she's saying is—it's the 1960s, all hell is breaking loose all over, and you're painting flowers and leaves. You can't do that. Your job is to tell your story. Your story has to come out of your life, your environment, who you are, where you're from. I realized, I can't tell your story, I can only tell mine. I can't be you. I can only be me."[27]

Faith admitted that that's probably not what the gallerist meant, but that's how Faith took it. In an interview you can watch on YouTube, she said, "I became an artist because I wanted to tell my story as a Black woman in America."[28] So Faith sees telling her story and exercising her freedom to be a tribute paid to her ancestors and to the people who fought the struggle before her. She is relentless.

That gallery moment was a watershed for Faith, and she began the process of becoming the fully formed and developed whole person and artist she is today. Radical, bold, and audacious. Because a gallerist told Faith: You Can't.

Faith turned her art to activism and spent the next few years painting what art critic Andrew Russeth called "some of the most searing depictions ever made of race relations in America."[29] Art history professor Moira Roth was the editor of Faith's memoir. In her foreword she described Faith as a troublemaker, firebrand, distinguished, fiery, independent, savvy, passionate, political, and inventive.

Inventive, subversive, troublemaker. If you ask me, these are the markings of the Witch. In 1967, a year of widespread race riots in the United States, Faith painted a twelve-foot-long visual bombshell called *American People Series #20: Die* in which both Black and white Americans appear, armed with guns and knives, bloodied. At war. But no one looks angry. Everyone looks sad or scared—desperate. Two children, a little white boy and a little black girl, hug each other tightly and tenderly in their shared terror.

In 1968, when the Whitney Museum of American Art organized a show about 1930s American sculpture that did not include a single Black artist, Faith mobilized, organized, and demonstrated against this exclusion of Black artists. Here again we see the weaving that characterizes so much of Faith's life. She was Black, female, artist, activist, teacher—all of these aspects manifesting as one. In one movement, in one moment. Years later, she wrote honestly, if cynically, in her summation: "All the men got something—a show, a sale, a grant for a community project. I got nothing. But that did not surprise me. And today, some 25 years later, nothing much has changed at the Modern except which white man gets the next show."

Of course, when Faith was writing her memoir, back in the '80s, she couldn't have known that she would change the world. That she would have a school named after her, win countless awards, meet the president—a Black president—and be counted among the greatest American artists of the twentieth century. Throughout the '70s, she just went on with her daily business of heroism.

She cofounded the Ad Hoc Women Artists' Committee, Women Students and Artists for Black Art Liberation, the National Black Feminist Organization, and "Where We At" Black Women Artists. She painted a mural *For the Women's House* as a permanent installation at the Women's House of Detention on Rikers Island. As a result, Art Without Walls, an organization that brings art to prison populations, was founded.

And that's honestly just a sample of Faith's initiatives of the '70s.

As Witches, we encounter a lot of iconography. We know that symbols have power. Some we use to concentrate our own intentions, but we also know that other symbols must be deconstructed, must have their power examined, and, if necessary, subverted. Faith is no exception—some of her most acidic work is based on those fifty pentagrams and thirteen wands—old Stars and Stripes, the American flag. It is a symbol of both freedom, on one hand, and oppression, on the other.

In 1970 she helped organize the *People's Flag Show* in Manhattan, an exhibition that was a protest against laws restricting the use and display of the American flag. Faith and two other artists, Jon Hendricks and Jean Toche, were arrested and charged with desecration of the flag, and the exhibition was shut down. The American Civil Liberties Union came to their defense and all of the charges were dropped.

In a 2018 lecture at the Humboldt University of Berlin, Faith said, "The '60s was rough. . . . Most artists were not paying attention. . . . They were painting beautiful paintings abstractly . . . but they were not telling the story of what was going on in America, and I thought I wanted to be that person. For that, I paid a terrific price. It was hard. They put me out and tried to keep me out, but I persisted."[30]

Faith's work with the American flag is shocking and incendiary, even by today's standards. She hides provocative messages in common imagery that require only a slight tilt of the head to see. Like America itself, these paintings show themselves to be one thing, but on closer inspection reveal themselves to be something else, something more sinister. At Imbolc, look at your life the way we look at Faith's artwork. Inspect it from different angles. What does it seem to be saying? What is the darker truth? What can be revealed with the tilting of your head? Who are you and what is your vision?

In an interview with *Oxford Art Online*, Faith said, "I found my artistic identity and my personal vision in the '60s by looking at African masks; and my art form through the serial paintings of Jacob Lawrence. The powerful geometry of African masks and sculpture that informed modern art is what I like best about Picasso, Matisse, and the other modern European masters I was taught to copy. It is their exquisite compositions of shape, form, color, and texture that make Picasso, Matisse, and Jacob Lawrence's work so wonderful."[31]

You've probably seen and can picture that Picasso face, hard lined, deep set, beautiful, and grotesque. But unless you've studied art history, you might not be aware that cubism was directly inspired by African mask art. But now that I've said it, it seems so obvious, right? Picture a Picasso face, now picture an African mask. The similarity is so clear once it's been pointed out, but whitewashing is brainwashing. That's what colonialism does. It takes the sacred and rebrands it until we all forget where it came from. Mass produces and mass markets until all power and meaning are scrubbed out. The mighty divine that is a portal of transformation and connection to the spirit world is rendered object. Kitsch. Hung on a wall and stripped of its rightful place in the holy dance. Faith said, "I researched African—my own art, the classical art form of Black people—on my own. I really taught myself because there were no courses being taught on African art and artists. . . . I had to get my education [and] then I had to get my reeducation which was what I gave myself."[32]

Picasso denied the influence of African art on his own paintings despite the fact that he previously said he experienced a revelation while viewing African art at the Ethnographic Museum of the Trocadéro in Paris. The expansion of the French empire into sub-Saharan Africa meant that African artworks were being brought back to Paris museums for exotic displays. Media buzzed with stories of cannibalism and other gossipy tales of the African kingdom, the *dark* continent. In 1991 Faith made a fucking masterpiece quilt *Picasso's Studio*. Where a beautiful

Black woman poses proudly, natural, powerful, at the center of the space, surrounded by white women, faces abstracted in the style of cubism. The figure of Picasso himself is pushed off to the left. To the past. He is Blue. Old. His canvas blank and empty. It's like Faith called out the entire art world, and all of Western culture with a single quilt. It's phenomenal and it shows that Faith can do it all, all at once, all the time.

Conjure in your mind a Picasso painting; now picture an African mask. Think about how many times something ancient and sacred has been stolen and put on display. Or whitewashed, repackaged, sold, and had its roots denied. bell hooks wrote, "Such appropriation happens again and again. It takes the form of constructing African-American culture as though it exists solely to suggest new aesthetic and political directions white folks might move in."[33] So, Witches, let's give back some stolen time and energy to the magic of African masks.

Mask making is one of the oldest art forms in the world. There are so many mask designs among African cultures. And so many materials used—wood, leather, bone, bronze, ceramics, ivory, straw. Each mask is one of a kind. Traditional masks used in ceremony are owned and passed on by families and clans who, from generation to generation, enlist the spirits to help and protect them, honoring the spirits and asking for their blessings.

The designs are infinite, but the most common are animal representation and ancestor representation. Animal and ancestor masks connect people with the spirit world that traditional African beliefs say inhabits the land. Wearing masks, they are transformed, possessed—at other times, masks make the spirits visible to enable communication. Masks were part of most if not all rituals. Funeral ceremonies, initiation rites, to ward off destruction, to bless soil. The Nuna of Burkina Faso seek the help of powerful spirits who live in the wild forests, bush country, and rivers surrounding their villages. They create animal spirit masks depicting nature spirits of hawk, buffalo, and crocodile, which live near the village. For the Dogon of Mali, who are expert agriculturists, the antelope is the symbol of the hardworking farmer. Dancers wearing the masks hit the ground with sticks to represent the pawing of an antelope, and the hoeing motion of the Dogon farmers. A signature piece of Angolan mask art is the female mask *mwana pwo* worn by male dancers in their puberty rituals. This female ancestor mask is worn by boys turning into men as a symbol of power and fertility.

There are masks to represent tranquility, used to portray the virtues of self-control and patience. Bulging foreheads carved with designs symbolize wisdom. Scowling, teeth-baring for war masks. Myths, histories, morals, and lessons are all bound up in these sacred objects, essential to preserving oral tradition.

Faith began her *Witch Mask* series in 1973 using a combination of raffia, macramé, appliquéd fabrics, and beads of yellow, gold, red, and green. Some masks had glass beads, hung from their eyes as teardrops. All the masks included costumes and were hooded so that they could be worn. Faith said, "It made the masks a complete spiritual and sculptural identity, and stressed the fact that masks are not objects to be hung on a wall but are to be worn."[34]

Women's Liberation Talking Mask: Witch Series #1, for example, has a nose shaped like an arrow, pointing down toward the mouth. Art historian Lisa Farrington wrote, "For Ringgold . . . these stylistic devices manifest her concerns with issues of voice—particularly the chronically silenced voices of African American women."[35]

Back to bell hooks, who I was delighted to discover was herself inspired by Faith! If you haven't heard of activist and philosopher bell hooks, google her. You won't regret it. From bell's book *Belonging: A Culture of Place* in a chapter "Aesthetic Inheritances: History Worked by Hand," she wrote:

> *This writing was inspired by Faith, who has always cherished and celebrated artistic work of unknown and unheralded black women. Evoking this legacy in her work, she calls us to remember, to celebrate, to give praise.*
>
> *Even though I have always longed to write about my grandmother's quilt making, I never found the words, the necessary language. At one time I dreamed of filming her quilting. She died.*

71

Nothing had been done to document the power and beauty of her work. Seeing Faith Ringgold's elaborate story quilts, which insist on naming, on documentation, on black women telling our story, I found words. . . . To [my grandmother], quilt making was a spirit process where one learned to surrender. It was a form of meditation where the self was let go. This was the way she had learned to approach quilt making from her mother. To her it was an art of stillness and concentration, a work which renewed the spirit.[36]

There is a long and heartwarming history of women forming covens, although they called them Quilting Bees or Sewing Circles, to renew their spirits and tell their stories to each other and to the world through their quilts. Faith also conjured a history of resistance in what has come to be called Freedom Quilts. During the time of the Underground Railroad, directions and instructions were coded into patterns, quilted into blankets, then hung on porches and clotheslines, acting as guideposts, hiding in plain sight. Patterns like *Flying Geese* and *North Star* instructed escaped enslaved people to head North. A *Log Cabin* design was code for a safe house, and a *Bear Paw* suggested that the freedom seeker should follow nearby animal trails to source water or food.

Faith continued to stitch together her art, resistance, politics, and experience and in 1991 wrote her children's book *Tar Beach*, which weaves fantasy and reality with themes of race and class and does so with whimsy and hopefulness. Based on a quilt she made in the mid-'80s, *Tar Beach* is about a little girl who can fly and takes ownership of all she surveys, including the Washington Bridge, an ice cream factory, and the union building where her father is not allowed to be a member. Of course it's never explicitly mentioned that the main character, eight-year-old Cassie, is a Witch, but in my reading, it's implied. The book itself is a tapestry of human experience, and Faith's illustrations illuminate her manuscript with an energy you can feel. The story begins like this: I will always remember when the stars fell down around me and lifted me up above the George Washington Bridge. And ends like this: It's very easy. Anyone can fly. All you need is somewhere to go that you can't get to any other way. The next thing you know, you're flying among the stars.[37] Faith, the radical provocative incendiary political artist, has written sixteen more children's books since *Tar Beach*. The Guggenheim Museum purchased the *Tar Beach* quilt in 1988, but as far as I know, it's locked in a vault, never yet placed for public viewing.

Healers and scientists can harness the power of natural poisons and turn them into medicines. It's a very Witchy thing to do. We make medicine from poison and Art out of grief, grab calm from inside a storm . . . And this lemonading is, again, I think, a large part of Faith's magic. She wrote: "I borrowed the story of our ancestors when they were down and out and singing the blues. A beautiful artform came out from all of that misery and suffering. So I said, let me turn this into something beautiful. This doesn't have to be something ugly. This can be something beautiful. I can beautify this. I will beautify this."[38]

But Faith reminds us, in her work, in her life, that obtaining freedom is not the same as maintaining freedom. We can make all the progressive laws we want, but the laws of man are not the laws of physics. They can change. Be revoked. Backslide. Be unjust from the jump. In the States you have your bill of rights, in Canada we have our Charter, and it certainly is magical thinking to believe that so it is written, so it shall be done. . . . But how we treat people is an entirely individual affair. Passing laws helps, but we can't mandate shifts in consciousness. Plus certainly, passing a law is one thing. Enforcement is another. And what do we do when even ethical laws are used as ammunition for systemic racism? We know that Laws are one thing. But Justice is quite another. We cannot count on Laws to be Just. Freedom is a delicate flower that requires daily nurturing and constant questioning. As she ages, Faith continues to exercise her freedom at every turn. She got a new house and wanted to add a studio onto the back. Her racist neighbors complained when she applied for the permits, saying they didn't want "those types of people" coming and going. Faith could easily have moved to a more welcoming neighborhood, but she stayed and fought, and built her studio. Curlee Raven Holton wrote, "As Faith told me her story I asked her, 'When you look out your studio window, what do you see?' 'I see my determination to be free in America. And I'd like to pass that on, because I know that a lot of people have had the problems I've had. And a lot of people had to give up because they couldn't afford to persevere. You see, they couldn't afford to win! And freedom is not free. You've got to pay for that dream.'"[39]

To me, Faith's work is and has always been spell-casting—an alchemy, changing forms, transforming spaces, minds, matter, and emotion. She doesn't call this spell-casting, but I'll let you decide if these are the words of a Witch making magic: To make up for some of the closeness I missed with my daughters, I made a number of works of art. Through Art I tried to create the peace we could not achieve in real life.[40]

When her daughters began to fall in love, Faith made wedding installations in gallery spaces to contend with those motherly feelings of both profound joy and profound loss. When her own mother died, she made a quilt. In just two days.

In her home she keeps an altar, though she calls it a shelf, with pictures of ancestors and a painting she did when she was eighteen years old to remind her of her growth.

With a multidisciplinary joie de vivre, Faith resolves the unresolvable—self, other, future, past, love, death, history, equality, fantasy, reality, root, and bloom—this, again, I think, is her magic. And maybe even THE truest magic. Total Oneness in Total Freedom. Honesty. Authenticity. The You-est possible You. The Faith-est possible Faith. But if you're still not convinced that she, the illustrator of Witches and creator of Witch Masks, transmogrifier of materials AND minds is not herself a Witch at heart, I'll end this story with a song Faith wrote, Witchily titled, "Anyone Can Fly." So Grab your broomsticks, my Witches! You Can Beautify this, Be wholly yourself, Gather, Remember, and Fly:

> Anyone can fly
> If one can
> Anyone can
> All you got to do is try
> Spread your arms to reach the sky
> And you'll know the reason why
> Anyone Can fly

You must use the power of the flight command
You must learn the magic of the helping hand
Love yourself and others too
Believe in them
And believe in you
And try hard
At everything you do
Anyone can fly
If one can
Anyone can
All you got to do is try
Spread your arms to reach the sky
And you'll know the reason why
Anyone Can fly[41]

Both Zora and Faith are Witches who changed the world. But to do so they had to ask hard questions about themselves, about their lives, and about the Universe they inhabit. We can't fill the gaps like Zora, or stitch social justice together like Faith, or make a needed contribution to our community if we don't first ask: what's missing? So at Imbolc, go looking for the Witches you've been missing, but start with Witch No. 1. You. Remember this: You are the only person whom you're stuck with forever. That's why we Witches need to check in and make sure every year that we ask hard questions and make choices that aren't based on society's rules or our parents' expectations or our friends' priorities, comfort, and fear. You are the only person who will look back from that mirror for the rest of your life. Who are you and what are your goals? What is your vision? What are your limits? Zora and Faith teach us that we cannot make positive changes if we refuse to acknowledge what is wrong. We won't go looking unless we understand that something is missing.

At Imbolc, we encourage you to acknowledge your victories and second- (third-, fifth-, ninth-) place ribbons (COLORRRSSSSTRRR-RRUCK!!!!) as well as your missteps. Acknowledge your effort and what you took for granted. Acknowledge that your existence has untapped potential! Ask yourself what you need to tap into that potential. The Wheel of the Year will continue to turn, but at Imbolc we make a choice: will we repeat our uniform patterns or make a bodacious new quilt from the scraps of last year? Will we sit in the dark and curse the inky gloom or will we craft a candle and light it? Will we cling to last year's crop as it rots, or prepare to plant new seeds in our own lives and for the future? Will we recognize the subtle difference between being unable and being afraid? Witchcraft is about being aware and making a choice. As the Groundhog knows, if you truly need six more weeks of winter sleep, that's OK. You are not obligated to be perfect or epic or sensational. As a Witch, your existence is a political act, and loving yourself may be all the resistance work you need to do. You are allowed to stop asking how to be a better person and start asking how to just be good to yourself. You may find that this too can change the world. You are one with the infinite, and anyone can fly.

Ritual

You'll need a pen and paper. Ideally you'll use a red pen for courage and a blue pen for patience, but any writing tool will do.

Go to the space in your home where you spend the most time. Get comfortable. Close your eyes and take a deep breath. And another. When you are ready, open your eyes and look around. Take an honest assessment of your physical surroundings (your apartment, your bedroom). What do you see? Take as long as you need to really analyze your space in this moment. What do you have too much of? What are you missing? How much of your identity is reflected in your space?

Now you're going to make two To Do lists. The first (in red pen for courage) isn't so much a list because you're just going to write down ONE THING you can accomplish TODAY that involves taking stock and cleaning and/or organizing. Be realistic.

Choose one closet or pantry shelf or a single drawer if that's all you can handle today—your email inbox, even (my inbox shows 2,976 unread messages, so I should probably spend my own Imbolc in there this year). If you're super on the ball and organized already, then look inward instead. What is your life missing? What does your heart hold that you don't need? This is both a practical and a symbolic act, so get creative if your intention is a little less tangible. Choose something that resonates with your vision. For example, if you'd like to eat healthier, clean out and organize your fridge. If you want to be better with money, organize your purse or wallet. If you want to be a better communicator, sanitize your phone and keyboard. If you want to be more grounded, scrub the floor. Whatever task you're drawn to, do it with this new awareness. If you honestly can't find a single thing in your home or life that needs your attention, then congratulations! Your task is to go help someone else.

Once you've decided on your real and symbolic act of assessment and organization, be sure to write it down on your To Do list.

When you've finished your task for the day, swelled by your sense of capability and accomplishment, grab your blue pen (patience), cross out your finished task (so satisfying!), and start another list. This time, it'll be a single bigger goal, or two or three small goals that you can achieve in six weeks, or by the next Sabbat, Ostara. Again, use what you perceived in your earlier assessment and be realistic.

Fold your list and draw a Sun on the folded paper. Now place it somewhere in your newly organized space and speak the following invocation. Stay focused on the goal(s) you wrote down and by the first day of spring, you'll be fully aware and ready to open yourself to the new world.

INCANTATION

I am bold and audacious.
No one can tell me what I can't do.
I have the nerve to walk my own way.
I can beautify this.
I will beautify this.
I am one with the infinite
and need no other assurance

3

Ostara

This circle is led by Risa

IT IS OSTARA, EOSTAR. It is the spring equinox. Dark and light reach another point of balance on the spinning wheel. Light is increasing quickly, and the darkness will recede; but for this moment they breathe together. This is the ancient goddess holiday that gives us bunnies and baby chicks; this is the pagan story overwritten by the peace-loving anarchist hippie Jesus's execution, descent, and return. In honor of the beginning of spring, we can ritualize an opening for new ideas and new ways of thinking. On the spring equinox, day and night are equal, our shadows—personal and collective—look us in the eye . . . and they can heal and guide us.

This chapter tells two versions of the story of how colonization has used Witches. And how Witches have survived and planted themselves like seeds to change the future.

We trace the history of a woman, born a slave, who was beloved and feared as a healer and a dealer in love medicine in seventeenth-century colonial Colombia. A woman named Paula de Eguiluz, who was tried three times for Witchcraft and survived, still imprisoned, while the bishop himself paid for her services.

We also tell the story of mind-changer, *curandera,* and poet María Sabina. How she gave the world the healing and insight of psilocybin, or magic mushrooms, as well as her tremendous visionary poetry, and the ways she continues to shape the opening world today.

We anchor our gratitude for and our fury at the injustices of the present with these deep roots. We honor the shadows in our histories.

For Ostara we remind ourselves that things can change.

Eostar is the promise of change and revelation. The promise that the world will turn. That light will come out of the dark; and the gentle dark will follow the blinding. We will use the stones that have been thrown against us to build new homes. If you have been hunted or slandered for your healing and your magic and your knowledge, then you are a part of the history that the world has been missing.

Paula's story deserves more telling. María's connection to the Earth needs more study, and the power of her poetry merits being included in the big tent of postcolonial literature, feminist history, and Witchcraft.

For all those who have been persecuted under the rubric "Witch," or dismissed and fetishized with "Witch doctor," we want to own those names. Burnish these names by the light of our own fires and claim their power.

Paula went by the nickname Aleluya, and she was both dangerous and divine.

She can be an icon for us of surviving, and for giving ourselves new names as we become our own songs of joy and of redemption, even in the darkest circumstances. An icon of resilience though the odds are stacked against you again and again, season after season. Patron Saint Aleluya of learning the game and playing it better than them, and escaping with your life while the people who hunted you pay you for your services, thank you very much. And Aleluya.

Aleluya was born without freedom, born into slavery and sold away from her mother whose name was Guiomar. She was moved from Santo Domingo to Havana, and then was sold again, this time to Juan de Eguiluz. She began to practice as a healer in the fervent colonial port city of Cartagena de Indias. They married, and he granted her freedom.

Cartagena de Indias began to thrive as a colonial port city when Spanish settlers discovered treasures in the tombs of the Sinus Amerindian tribe, who buried their dead with all their riches. Less than one hundred years later, picture a city being built of stone, still haunted by its origins in a pillaged graveyard. Cartagena was the largest port in the Americas and a hub for the international slave trade.

Over 1.1 million captive Africans entered the docks at Cartagena de las Indias . . . The Spanish Crown had the system of trafficking African souls down to a grizzly science, and made it their most profitable business, according to the governor of Cartagena Province during the 16th century . . . We will never know even close to, much less exactly, how many ancestors passed through Cartagena . . . Some of the more wicked slaving ships during the inspection process at Cartagena would declare just over 40 souls on board, when in reality there would be over five times that number, chained to the walls below in the hold . . . Among the more egregious cases of contrabanding . . . slightly more than 40 souls were declared at customs, when in reality an inconceivable 600-plus captives were on board, never to be officially recorded.[1]

Picture this place, and a teenage girl alone here, far from family. Who by some combination of personal power, cunning, luck, education, and magic finds a way to freedom.

Picture this person. She had a real life of her own, at least for a while. A freed woman. A sought-after healer in Cartagena, who was known for having spells for the kind of good love that might protect a woman and offer her a little freedom of her own. With damask skirts of blue, and purple and golden braid.

Her neighbors first accused her of being a Witch in 1623. She was accused, tried, and punished three times from 1623 to 1636.

Eostar is a day to gather your strength, because the fight will come like waves in different shapes over and over again.

The first time Aleluya's Cuban neighbors accused her, it was of killing a newborn by sucking on its navel; jumping out a window to avoid a blow from her master but suffering no injuries; practicing erotic magic; and making a pact with the devil.

By the time of her second arrest, she had lived in Cartagena for eight years, first as a prisoner in the Tribunal secret prison, and then a menial servant at the Hospital of the San Juan de Dios friars. . . . They did not immediately reveal the charges against her, but Paula quickly assessed her vulnerable position. At this time, she described her position as a curandera; she was a popular healer in the city of Cartagena and its surrounding regions. She worked and socialized with a number of other Afro-Caribbean women who sold love potions and taught incantations and conjurations to a large clientele of women, rich and poor, white and black.[2]

We don't know where Aleluya learned her magic, but this was the community, culture, and world she moved in. "She definitely took part in 'cures' that had nothing to do with the official European understanding of physical disease. Even when dealing with physical ailments, she undoubtedly used herbs and methods contrary to those . . . in a Spanish hospital. Paula may have learned curing from her mother or other Africans, working within a broadly Atlantic school that drew on African, Indigenous American, and traditional Iberian healing techniques."[3]

Colonial Cartagena de Indias was rich in interwoven spirit knowledge, and it could be a very dangerous place for a woman to be noticed for her power.

In a colonial context—and we still live in one—there will be a market starving for anything that might offer a step upward. But there will also be a deadly fetishization of the colonized body that will in one moment turn to you for secrets, and in the next moment hunt you for selling them.

Be careful out there.

And work hard to be better: white women who have focused on positivity culture, burning sage, and going to yoga retreats but not displacing their egos to listen to and be unsettled and changed by Black and Indigenous voices (or voting for Trump or not voting at all) need a "come to Jesus" moment about the violence they participate in.

Or better yet, why don't we come to Aleluya? Not to idolize or deify her or to erase her again with a sanitized history, but to attempt to hear and tell the honest truth. One with room for her healing, for her bravery, for her community of praxis, and for the vast sanctioned cruelty that strangled her life and cornered her into her own kinds of violence to survive. Let's be honest about that, too, about what a culture of enslavement and inquisition, fear and torture does to our values and our potential and our magic.

According to Nicole von Germeten in *Violent Delights, Violent Ends: Sex, Race, and Honor in Colonial Cartagena de Indias*, in order to survive the Inquisition, Paula accused other women of sorcery. She used strategic accusations to deflect and manage the violent attention of the inquisitors. Based on the transcripts from the Inquisition—and my access to these is limited to Nicole von Germeten's interpretations—Paula would also influence other imprisoned women's confessions by communicating with them in the secret prisons of the Holy Office.

She was able to carefully negotiate the violent tangle of the Cartagena Inquisition by sending messages, extricating herself from the violence of torture, drawing others into the trap but also helping to direct their forced confessions based on her knowledge of the needs of the inquisitors. She survived in this precarious way until she accused someone who made it his mission to destroy her.

The fly in the ointment of Paula's maneuvers was the free mulatto surgeon Diego López, born to an enslaved mother in 1593 in Cartagena. Paula had mentioned López in passing in one of her numerous confessions, leading to the surgeon's arrest and interrogation . . . López formulated his entire defense around the notion that "Paula was the dogmatizer and master of all . . . the maleficio that led to crimes and irreparable damages notorious all over this city harming important people of this republic," thus directly contradicting Paula's defense tactics and carefully worded confessions. . . . he passed on several rumours that Paula has poisoned people with powders . . . López was an untrustworthy witness, but he sensed what the inquisitors wanted to hear and whom they would target next.[4]

López attacked the free, prosperous women of Paula's circle. He worked to distance himself from their craft and healing, to draw a line between himself and the women who healed. He saw the Inquisitor's sublimated desires to violently dominate powerful women and he whipped them into a frenzy aimed particularly at Paula.

Recognize this pattern from the European Witch hunts: "More than a persecution of magic broadly put, the Witch hunts were a gendered class war wherein elite males forcibly took over both the conceptual and practical realm of healing from peasant women; as the fifteenth-century *Malleus Maleficarum* explains 'if a woman dare to cure without having studied she is a Witch and must die.'"[5]

Diego López also saw the potential to turn racist violence away from himself—a mixed-race man selling healing to colonizers—toward Jewish immigrants, and he "started an anti-Jewish frenzy in Cartagena through his lurid and extensive accounts of local Portuguese including a fellow surgeon."[6] Anti-Semitism, misogyny, anti-Black, anti-Indigenous, and anti-queer violence ricochet across time and across bodies, tools of oppression. Turning us against each other in our desperation, where instead our experiences of injustice could call us into each other's circles.

We can reclaim spaces for that anchoring. Sharing knowledge, stories, and rituals can tie us to each other. Common ground—both metaphorical and literal—can root us in the fact of a shared Earth.

> *From a feminist viewpoint, one of the attractions exercised by the idea of the commons is the possibility of overcoming the isolation in which reproductive activities are performed and the separation between the private and the public spheres that has contributed so much to hiding and rationalizing women's exploitation. . . . Reproduction does not only concern our material needs—such as housing, food preparation, the organization of space, childrearing, sex and procreation. An important aspect of it is the reproduction of our collective memory and the cultural symbols that give meaning to our life and nourish our struggles.*[7]

To ritualize the reproduction of our common memory we put true stories on our altars. We share symbols and songs that give our lives meaning and nourish our struggle. We make sacred the many ways of reproduction in order to stitch ourselves with all our craft into a dedicated alliance. This common ground gives us strength so that under the pressure of violence, the grind of poverty, the almost invisible choking net of systemic injustice, we can answer together the essential healing question: how do we stop the cascading failure of exploitation?

As far as Nicole von Germeten was able to discover in the records from the Cartagena Inquisition, in her later life de Paula "remained in prison but allegedly enjoyed furlough to travel in a sedan chair, luxuriously dressed and well paid, to advise bishops and inquisitors on their medical care."[8] She was incarcerated while Diego López was allowed to regain his medical practice in Cartagena. Both were violently tortured but in the end, Diego López was allowed a public redemption denied to the famous Witch, and she was kept much closer to the heart of power. Buried in the injustice there is that kernel of rhizomatic, undeniable truth of the dominated: In the dark of inquisitorial prison, in the unwritten history that sprawls beyond the official documents, she flourishes. Powerful men pay her well and rely upon her wisdom. They can imagine they control her, while her roots and tendrils change the flow of the mainstream quietly and unseen.

This is a piece of the story of how *curanderas* were contained and used in colonial Latin America, and this story suggests a shadow history of how they carried their knowledge forward, buried their seeds in the dark, and survived.

In the 1960s commercial culture "discovered" another Indigenous ancestry of visionary healing, and sought to commodify it and struggled to understand it yet again. But this inheritance exceeds containment.

I take Little-One-Who-Springs-Forth and I see God. I see him sprout from the earth. He grows and grows, big as a tree, as a mountain. His face is placid, beautiful, serene as in the temples. At other times, God is not like a man: he is the Book. A Book that is born from the earth, a sacred Book whose birth makes the world shake. It is the Book of God that speaks to me in order for me to speak. It counsels me, it teaches me, it tells me what I have to say to men, to the sick, to life. The Book appears and I learn new words.[9]

María Sabina is the most famous *curandera* to allow outsiders to participate in the healing vigil known as the *velada*. Mexican poet Homero Aridjis called her "the greatest visionary poet in twentieth-century Latin America."[10] Purified and late at night, high in the mountains in Oaxaca province, surrounded by her daughters and uplifted by their voices, she would become one with God and heal with words. María had her story told on the cover of *Life* magazine, and saw her tiny, isolated community transformed into a transcendental hippie mecca and madhouse that shaped the world.

María's image is printed on T-shirts and sold at head shops. She gave the world magic mushrooms and so hundreds of thousands of tech bros microdosing in glass towers in Manhattan; steampunk music lovers in the desert; middle-aging parents on vacations in the woods; artists looking for other vision; and overprescribed depressives looking for a better way all have her to thank, though they may not know her name. They may not know or remember that a 1960s subculture beat a path of hippie seekers to her door once the news broke about a magic that opened minds and brought you face to face with God.

María was a Mazatec Indigenous woman born in 1894. The Mazatec trace their origins back thousands of years, and by the 1300s were a free and independent people with two empires, one in the highlands and another in the lowlands.

These kingdoms were first invaded by the Mexica and the Aztec Empire, and then the first Spanish colonizers arrived in Mazatec territory in 1520. The colonizers tried to eliminate the Indigenous rituals and religion. They built churches, worked on conversion, and played out a violent repetition of the European Witch hunt and Inquisition in their territories. But they also documented the use of ritual hallucinogens, and, a couple hundred years later, this is how the wider world finds María.

In the 1950s hydroelectric dams were built and large tracts of the jungle were mown down; private banks supported the monoculture of sugarcane and the annihilation of complex ecosystems required for industrial cattle farming. The lowland Mazatec lost the equivalent of 50 percent of their usable land. About 22,000 Mazatec who had territorial rights to the basin dating back hundreds of generations were relocated some two hundred fifty kilometers away from their traditional lands.

The isolation of the mountain Mazatec communities gave them a reprieve from this onslaught until two independent researchers, fascinated by mushrooms, made their way to María Sabina's door: Gordon Wasson and Valentina Pavlovna Guercken.

Gordon repeated an origin story several times in his books and articles of how his lifelong fascination with mushrooms began by following his Russian bride, Valentina. One day he was out walking in the woods in New York with Valentina when she exclaimed with glee and headed off to gather some mushrooms she spotted growing in the woods. He thought this was a macabre idea, a dangerous dealing with death and rot that would probably make them all sick. Instead the mushrooms were delicious, and he started to pay attention as she explained that cultures outside of North America have loved and valued the mushroom.

Over time, the Wassons traced their opposing reactions and suggested that these extremes might stem from the same lost history. They dedicated their life work to exploring the idea that the mushroom in ancient history had been deeply sacred. They argued that the mushroom is, in fact, the revelatory component at the heart of many world religions and ancient mysteries, as well as exceptional advances in prehistoric cultures; and that this heritage produces extreme and opposing reactions today.

This idea, that a splitting into binary suggests a potent sacred *something* beyond the binary, before the split (and in between), is at the core of Witch knowledge.

White culture loves to worship and commodify Indigenous knowledge, casting itself as saviors in the process. But when this is not convenient, Indigenous people are caricatured as violent, drunk, a threat. Both obfuscate the real truth of a living, thriving people who have knowledge that the dominant culture lacks and longs for and endlessly seeks to destroy.

A similar pattern plays out with women, and the power of girls and womxn. Call her Whore on the one hand to justify your violence, or place her carefully on a fragile Virgin pedestal; either way, you are making a small container for something vast.

Noticing the container that is binary is a step toward seeing the infinite around it.

On Ostara let's instead listen to our dreams. Let's fill our altars with people, stories, and symbols that resist simplification. Let's listen for the things that sing with this in-between tension of both life and death, maiden and crone, darkness and light, victim and perpetrator, man and woman, and whisper of a wholeness beyond the divides.

Gordon and Valentina traced scattered references to sacred mushrooms all over the world, and eventually, following the colonizers' documentation of the Mazatec ancient holy relationship with the fungus they called God's Children, they found María.

She was not the first to let them join a ritual, but she made the greatest impact, and Gordon's experience with her is the one he ended up writing about for *Life* magazine.

The Wassons went to Huautla de Jiménez, Mexico, on a small grant that appeared to be a regular research grant. We now know, since the publication of the Project Artichoke/MKULTRA documents, that these funds were made available as part of the Central Intelligence Agency's widespread investigation, which began in 1953, into the possibilities of mind control. The secret CIA program MKULTRA involved torture, including performing electrical and chemical experiments on veterans, the mentally ill, and the homeless.

Were the Wassons willing players in this vast program of theft and abuse? They wrote several beautiful books, and they coined the term "entheogen": a class of psychoactive substances that induce spiritual experience. They wrote about entheogens as the origin of human religion. This is a lot of loving effort to go to if your real goal is to disguise mind-control research. But Gordon's day job was vice president of public relations for corporate industrial giant JP Morgan. He worked at the highest level to make a positive brand for multinational industry and banking. The Wassons promised María not to reveal her identity or location, but somehow both promises were broken and not long after, the essay appeared in *Life* magazine—with Gordon on the cover. Capitalism had "discovered" magic once again.

There are stories of young hippies taking seventeen hours on the bus through the mountains to arrive in Huautla, only to find the Beatles' private plane parked in the town square. Others claim that when swimming by a waterfall after taking a mushroom trip, they found Walt Disney's signature carved on a rock face. The Rolling Stones slipped out of the public eye for a bit and reappeared with a hallucinogenic art film, *Performance*, which a 1970 *Rolling Stone* review called a heavy trip, "stunning in the sense of a body blow, and if Woodstock presented one sort of reality, *Performance* presents another sort, a dark yin to Woodstock's yang . . . a slow love/death dance, liberally spiced with magic mushrooms."[11] Pete Townshend of the Who, Bob Dylan, John Lennon—according to the stories all were there, and they brought legions of hippies behind them.

With so many tourists arriving, it became clear there was money to be made, and various residents started selling white people a ride on the sacred psilocybin. A ritual that required a gifted guide, poet, and seer—a blessed representative of God's Children—was ripped from its context. People struggling to make a living sold it for a profit, and the kids just used it to get high.

María saw it all coming. The mushrooms, which she referred to as the Holy Children, showed her the white men and then the waves that would follow if she shared the mushrooms' power. She saw that the Holy Children's power would diminish from this dilution, but the Children showed her she must do it anyway. Maybe there are reasons beyond reasons, roots of the roots. Maybe she saw an even further future.

There is a lot of heartbreak in this story. María married twice, both times to abusive men who cheated on her. But there's ferocious strength as well, a constant force of will and burning light of revelation. And a deep resilience and the strength of mountains. Trauma cannot give you strength, and you don't owe it gratitude, but it can reveal the strength you always possessed.

She saw her son's murder coming before it came, and she had to live and relive it. She saw the future coming for her, and she waited to be hit by the wave. The strength required to endure this unbearable mix of power and powerlessness is a message from healer to healer and woman to woman throughout centuries of surviving patriarchy.

María is often described as "humble" and then "tragic." This is another subtle slippage, another spell settler discourse casts to erase Indigenous people, especially women. Seeing this powerful healer and poet as a victim doesn't do justice to the complexity, intentionality, knowledge, and power of her experience.

And María had deep knowledge.

She spent decades of nights on her mountaintop using the power of her language to commune with "the book": the entire tradition of Mazatec language, "time was her page."[12] Gordon and others described multiple occasions where in the course of a *veleda*,[13] María—riding the lines of sight provided by her communion with the Holy Children—provided information about future developments in distant places that over time would all prove true.

When I try to understand what those years of María's life were like, I imagine the vast spores of a species we are only beginning to understand, and how a poet and healer could have found a way, through songs and rituals, learned and crafted, to travel with them, connecting her to the greatest web. Ninety percent of the estimated 3.8 million fungi in the world are unknown to science. She was a word Witch whose scope was the great mushroom of language itself. She spoke of the god who emerges from the Earth. She had a vision beyond common comprehension. "Words for her are a therapeutic instrument and a way to depict visions, but also a self-conscious flesh that remakes and investigates prior texts."[14]

She is the woman who shepherds the immense.

She first glimpsed this immensity as a kid, just hungry, eating the sacred mushrooms and seeing what they showed her about her life in the years to come. Her life as *curandera* began after her husband's death. Her daughters stayed with her, braided her hair, and lifted up her songs at night when she grew tired.

Celibate as the Holy Children require, she listened to the messages they sent her from across the planet, through the Earth and air. She was awed and lit up by the poetry that came to her. She was generous with her gift, her community relied on her, she was the gifted guide. If she agreed to help you, she and her daughters would sing all night long, and they would surround you with their voices until you saw a way for healing, a path for you to follow, through darkness or light.

When outsiders came she welcomed them as well.

But the tide of public opinion turned against her. Not all seekers are scrupulous or respectful; and as more and more came they drew too much attention, and attention of the wrong kind, to beautiful, isolated Huautla de Jiménez. The Mexican Army can't ignore the drug trade happening in the mountains. They harass, lurk, trouble the community. At a breaking point, about a thousand hippies were rounded up and arrested. María's small adobe home was burned to the ground. Most accounts suggest this was the act of frustrated villagers, but it could have been the Mexican Army trying to shut off the source, or even imaginably a frustrated MKULTRA.

Frustrated—because their investigation into mushrooms for social control didn't work out so well, did it? Though the hordes of hippies were messy and troublesome you could at least say, on some level, their minds were opening. Once the idea was lit in the young, frustrated imagination that there could be more to life than the two-car garage, simple patriotism, consumption, and happy obedience, there was no putting that particular Pandora back in her box.

The story goes that María mourned Wassons' publicizing of the "saint children." "Before Wasson, nobody took 'the children' simply to find God. They were always taken to cure the sick. . . . From the moment foreigners arrived, the 'holy children' lost their purity. They lost their force, they ruined them. Henceforth they will no longer work. There is no remedy for it."[15]

In *Women and Knowledge in Mesoamerica*, Paloma Martinez-Cruz put a twist on this popular, heartbreaking end to the story of María, the great poet, the great healer of the Mazatec people. Paloma Martinez-Cruz suggested that María's language always contains multiple realities, she is a multiplier of possibilities, a trickster. And if she told you the magic was gone, maybe that was because she wanted you to believe it.

Heriberto Yépez is a poet who takes María seriously as a poet. I spent a long time looking for a historian or theorist of María whom I could really love. One who could explain and explode all the heavy, layered histories around her and obscuring her. It seems appropriate that when I finally found who I'd been looking for, he is a poet, a boundary-slipping theorist from the Mexican border town of Tijuana who has cast light on gay Mexican voices and conjured a true poet-shaman understanding for María Sabina.

Heriberto Yépez wrote, "Sabina was a wise-one not because she ate mushrooms and got into trips, but because she dominated a dynamic dictionary of meanings. She reproduced those meanings in the ceremonies; she rewrote that dynamic dictionary throughout her life. She was trying to revolutionize the praxis. That's why she even allowed foreigners to participate. She was trying to go beyond. She wanted to open the book."[16]

Rather than casting her as the Wassons' victim, Heriberto Yépez called out her choice, the incredible power inherent in the choice she made and the way she made it. She went beyond. She opened the book.

This poet saw her in an iconic line with La Malinche:

The historic Malinche was given to Cortés as tribute by the Indian leaders in Tabasco, along with 20 other women, gold and poultry. She later served him as mistress and translator during the Conquest . . . The great shadow that Malinche has cast on the Mexican psyche secretly reappeared when María Sabina was "discovered" by Life and Gordon Wasson . . . Like Malinche, Sabina, in an act of cultural infidelity, had betrayed the secret knowledge of Mexican culture to foreigners . . . both were Tongue-Women, interpreters of Language, women who with their power over words guided men on their crucial journeys—one to the Conquest of Mexico, the other to the Conquest of Self. Both were Translator Women of the Book of Language. Both Sabina and Malinche were women-poets, women with power over language.[17]

In a world of powerful machines, it can be easy to forget that language itself is a world-making power. Your spells and your poems actively order reality. Language can produce and reproduce power structures, tell us who we are, limit what we imagine we can be, or it can make us all see new things. It can move us from isolation to communion and stitch us into possibilities.

Think about what belief in a right to care communicates. Believing in each other, in our right to care, and to be cared for, changes us. It opens new possible paths for our future. It goes beyond what is possible.

Canada has its own nightmare history of colonialism, and perpetuates systems of ongoing racism and health disparity today; it has a long way to go in expanding the power of this magical idea. But the kernel of thought that believes health care is a right has expanded rapidly here. Within ten years of Tommy Douglas, "the greatest Canadian," fighting for free health care in his province of Saskatchewan against what seemed to be insurmountable odds, it had spread across the country. Doctors demonstrated against Medicare, politicians howled, but now we live in a world where when our daughter goes into anaphylactic shock as she did that summer, a small life flickering out in our arms, we call for help without the added terror of how much this will cost, and will it break us.

How can the lifting of fear liberate us?[18]

On Eostar, why not begin to trace a map of the freedoms your people have fought for?

Add a freedom fighter of some kind that matters to you to your altar. Choose one place of darkness where you will recommit to bringing light. With María Sabina lighting up our hearts, let us recommit to her sacred work of healing. Of health. Of care.

> *She is declared the Last Shaman, the one who brought the whole tradition of revelation down by revealing its secrets . . . Why was María Sabina so painfully punished? . . . She stood in contrast to the process of modernization that preoccupied the nation. Still more dangerous, she led an extraordinary life but had a very common death. . . . Book Woman, Jesus Woman, Light Woman died as Malnutrition Woman, Anemia Woman, Bleeding Woman, her social misery was public evidence of the failure of the Mexican state to maintain even the most basic conditions for the preservation of physical and spiritual life. At the end of the 20th Century, according to the Mexican government's estimates, 74% of Mexico's 100 million people lived in "moderate" or "extreme poverty."[19]*

We need to seek and uphold stories of lives that show the cracks in our systems, as well as the wisdom of the lives pushing through there. We can emerge from the sad trough of victimizing her and blaming her in order to craft a new story, one in which we meet the Immense she has been shepherding toward us all.

It is a flower of fresh water
A flower of clear water
Fresh flower
Translucent flower
Because there are clean flowers where I am going
Because there is clean water where I am going
Clean flower, clean water
Fresh flower
Growing flower
Mine that is increasing
Green mine
Budding mine
There is no wind, there is no spit, there is no garbage, there is no dust
There is no whirlwind, there is no weakness in the air
That is the work of my santos, that is the work of my santas[20]

Heriberto Yépez and María are both together poet champions and shepherds of true stories. Healers who use the magic of their craft to "re-enchant the world":

Sabina was without a doubt a poet. She was not only a poet, but more importantly poetry's wholeness. Her activity's goal was totality. She reached for the impossible. Searching for a book-beyond-the-book. Having a new poetic body. Breaking the differences between writing, reading, chanting, talking, dancing, and silence. Removing pain from others. Fighting for the survival of a great culture. Investigating sounds, meanings and languages. Increasing wisdom. Teaching. Being radically self-critical, recognizing when one fails, when one is dying.[21]

Contemporary research into the power of psilocybin—the active ingredient in magic mushrooms—has focused in part on its ability, when coupled with careful therapy, to teach us about death.

Like the therapeutic potential in ritual and tarot (and the world-shaping power of poetry), these ancient fungi have a long history of getting pushed back under the rug.

> *Stanislav Grof, a Czech-born psychiatrist who used LSD exten-*
> *sively in his practice in the nineteen-sixties, believes that psyche-*
> *delics "loosed the Dionysian element" on America, posing a threat*
> *to the country's Puritan values that was bound to be repulsed . . .*
> *Roland Griffiths, a psychopharmacologist at Johns Hopkins Univer-*
> *sity School of Medicine, points out that ours is not the first culture*
> *to feel threatened by psychedelics: the reason Gordon Wasson had to*
> *rediscover magic mushrooms in Mexico was that the Spanish had*
> *suppressed them so thoroughly, deeming them dangerous instruments*
> *of paganism . . . There is such a sense of authority that comes out of*
> *the primary mystical experience that it can be threatening to exist-*
> *ing hierarchical structures.*[22]

María shepherded these dangerous, Dionysian instruments that threatened hierarchy directly into the minds of multitudes of seekers.

But what is it that the mushrooms actually do? Is it the same thing that Heriberto Yépez thinks poetry can do—breaking boundaries and healing? Freeing us from the narrow constraints of binary? How can a temporary shift in brain function threaten hierarchies in society? And is this what a Witch does?

> *Neuroscientists assumed that the drugs somehow excited brain*
> *activity . . . But when Carhart-Harris looked at the results of the*
> *first set of fMRI scans . . . he discovered that the drug appeared to*
> *substantially reduce brain activity in one particular region: the*
> *"default-mode network." . . . Carhart-Harris describes the default-*
> *mode network variously as the brain's "orchestra conductor" or*
> *"corporate executive" or "capital city," charged with managing and*

"holding the entire system together." It is thought to be the physical counterpart of the autobiographical self, or ego . . . with the ego temporarily out of commission, the boundaries between self and world, subject and object, all dissolve.[23]

Our brains have an ego executive in a corner office making sense of the world, giving it order, and barking out orders. When in overdrive, the default-mode network becomes a tiny tyrant tied to depression and anxiety. Certain experiences can calm it, allowing us to experience the world from other places in ourselves: move us from default mode into our beating hearts, taste buds, lungs, and toes and out along the waves of love and lights of every color that permeate us and have their own logic about life and death and time.

Not that I really know what a mushroom trip feels like. The extent of it for me was one glorious, brilliantly cold day at the lake house with a beautiful Witch artist friend who had recently weaned herself off anti-depressants and was microdosing mushrooms instead, so we joined her. Not enough to trip, just enough to paint and play music and laugh all day like kids. The closest I came to feeling anything like what I've read described was after a crazy-carpet run, heart beating hard in the white, cold, diamond Sun, wind brilliant in the trees, and the world feeling like it was inside of me.

I was medicated from chronic pain during the decade when my social circles were adventuring with mushrooms and LSD. And maybe those things could have helped me. My pain grew as I clenched with fear around an injury; I turned some parts of my spine to stone and I can imagine now how soothing my default mode could have saved me some tears and some time. But those drugs were for other people, they were on the long list of things that terrified me. To be fair, some of my fear was reasonable. I knew people who got lost on unguided trips, young men for whom drugs pulled a schizophrenic trigger and caught them in a trap that was never unsprung. There are dangers to messing with this stuff unguided.

María would ask you to be as honest as you could about what needed healing, and then she would stay with you and sing and dance and treat you with her identity-changing poetry all night until the effects of the Holy Children passed.

In current clinical trials, a therapist is with you through the entire experience, helping you find your way through what are often described as visions of birth and death, the patients emerging with a new belief that death is not an end.

Amy's experience was different.

LSD was the first drug I ever took. I'd love to say this was some grand plan spiritual quest, but the fact is, I just took whatever someone handed me first. I discovered psychedelia before I discovered psychedelics, and was enthralled by the music, art, and fashion of the mid/late 1960s to the point of obsession. I knew by age ten that I wanted to "open the doors of perception," whatever that might mean! "Expand your mind"?!?! Sign me up! So lemme tell you. On one hit of acid, you might feel strange, giggle, your reality may start to shift, but on four hits, you might discover the secret of the universe. At fifteen years old, all pupils and grins, a girlfriend and I discovered that the secret of the universe is as follows: Everything is a Circle. Now this is vague and probably not super helpful, but I stand by it even today. And now, as we wax philosophical on the Wheel of the Year and the turning dance of the Earth and galaxy, it seems especially apt. Everything is a circle.

There is something very profound about a controlled hallucination (and by that I mean one that you've intentionally brought upon yourself rather than one caused without knowledge or consent by mental illness). From having taken LSD, I know that my brain is capable of seeing things that are not there. Of producing strikingly realistic visuals that are only available in my perception of my surroundings. Once I experienced this, I understood that this is true at all times. Even without the benefit of chemical drugs, the entire universe is filtered through your perception. How you see the world will not be the same way others see it. There is beauty in that. And relief. No one needs to "get" you but you.

I don't recall the first time I ate mushrooms. This is probably because where I come from, psilocybin wasn't a sacred magical tool for healing. It was a party drug, eaten by the fistful in an attempt to, for lack of a better term, trip balls. That said, I was always kind of the mystic of the group, and on these nights where the Holy Children were consumed, I could most often be found dancing alone in a dark bathroom or wandering off in search of nature, adventure, train tracks, or a moment of stillness. I didn't know it then, but I was listening for their instructions, directions, and poetry.

Lucky for me, it was my same reverence for '60s culture and music in particular that kept me from going too far into my experimentation with drugs. I knew that speed, heroin, and heavy drug use had killed many of my idols, my favorites. Nick Drake, Gram Parsons, Janis Joplin, Jimi Hendrix, Alan Christie Wilson from Canned Heat, and so very many more. I knew for certain that certain things were deadly. And as I've gone through this life, I've lost friends too. Someone I loved died the first time he tried heroin. One of my oldest friends moved to the UK and thought it would be fun to try heroin on her birthday. Through her years of addiction and homelessness, living in squats, she'd find a way to contact me every few years or so. A comment on a blog post I'd written about Daft Punk that she'd found by googling me was probably the most random. She told me once, "Amy, heroin is the best thing ever. Don't ever try it." Years later I was at her funeral, hugging her mother. So I'll give you that same advice that she gave me. It might sound like a no-brainer, Witches, but if a drug can kill you from trying it once, don't ever try it. Don't ever try it.

As Risa and I were learning about María Sabina, I realized that it had been a long time since I had taken magic mushrooms, and wondered if it was time to reacquaint. I got some from a friend, and we ate them in the sunshine and frolicked in the creek in the woods behind my house. The overwhelming message whispered to me by the Holy Children on that day was: You don't need us. And I understood.

We spoke to a mixed-Indigenous medicine woman named Annie Lamoreaux who has been traveling the world, studying the shamanic journey. On one trip to Mexico, she decided it was time to try the drug that locals used for their journeys of the mind. On the way there, they got into a car accident, and Annie took this as a sign that drugs were not meant to be her way of connecting with the Great Spirit. Instead she uses her drum to enter this trance state and receive messages from beyond.

I honestly don't advise that you use drugs. There are many, many ways to connect. Just take it from me and the lessons I've learned on my long strange trips. Everything you sense is filtered through your perception. And you can change your perspective without drugs, just by shifting focus. But when you change your mind, you change your reality. THAT's Witchcraft. THAT is sacred. As María Sabina said and Risa and I agree: "the drugs will only take you so far."

To really open the doors of perception we can take insight from the psilocybin and turn down our default mode, decenter our ego, and listen. To escape the violence we're doing to the world and to each other, we need a language that enshrines our collective right to health. To re-enchant the world, we need a common ground of both soil and stories that makes safe space for binaries to ease and twist into new life, and into each other. We need a spirituality that understands love on a scale so big it roots us throughout space and time.

For this great big view let's take María, her bravery and vision and poetry, as a patron saint and guide.

Because I can swim in the immense
Because I can swim in all forms
Because I am the launch woman
Because I am the sacred opossum
Because I am the Lord opossum

I am the woman Book that is beneath the water, says
I am the woman of the populous town, says
I am the shepherdess who is beneath the water, says
I am the woman who shepherds the immense, says
I am a shepherdess and I come with my shepherd, says

Because everything has its origin
And I come going from place to place from the origin.[24]

Long before María Sabina sang these words into the world, a girl who went by Aleluya learned healing from a mother named Guiomar, who traveled in a death ship and was sold, and who survived.

Aleluya learned how to craft the spells for good love that in those days—and in ours—conjure the possibility of homecoming, and the kinds of opening only possible when we are safe.

Aleluya talked to the stars.

Under torture and threat of death she started a craze of Witch hunts and lost control, and people got hurt. But she survived and even held in darkness, she retained a power.

Let's call out to them as well, mother and daughter.

María Sabina and your daughters, Aleluya and your mother, please bless the fight to free every single human used against their will. Please offer your rage and light and power to the estimated thirty million people enslaved today.

Please be with the families and refugees fleeing climate crisis and collapsed governments following decades of capitalism's rape of the global south.

Please help us mourn the sickness of our present moment, and then bless our rising power.

Witches alive, and those who have returned to the fabric of it all, on Ostara raise your knowledge of the darkness like a cup, and gather your powers.

We are here to shepherd the immense. We are here to open the book.

Ritual

A few years ago, in an effort to get to know my own subconscious, I committed to writing about my dreams every day. I'd make notes from bed the moment I woke and then process them in more detail later in the day.

The note from my dreams last night reads "an altar to loneliness" and I don't remember this dream, but I can relate to this feeling. If I'm being honest, I am jealous and totally enamored with every pregnant person and every expectant partner. I am 37 and not there yet, so maybe it's too late. If I'm being dramatic then: My Womb Is an Altar to Loneliness.

My therapist once asked me if I had an altar. She suggested making an area in my home clean and beautiful and full of personal symbols of my own health, Self and triumphs.

I was great at altars when I was a teenager. I had a table covered in candles dripping dramatically in my mom's basement, images in heavy metal frames, icons, incense, selected rocks, a small jeweled frog. I liked to lie on the floor near it with the lights out listening to Billie Holiday's "Lady in Satin."

"If I'm going to sing like someone else, then I don't need to sing at all."—Billie Holiday

I have gotten good at altars again, following the advice of a thoroughly respectable therapist. There is something to the idea of making spaces in my house that look like the inside of my heart or my unconscious or my hopes. There is something empowering in making up my own symbols: pine trees, rose petals, select rocks, a sculpture of an ear, a small wooden doll.

And admittedly, there is something to the idea of an Altar to Loneliness.

An altar puts the loneliness on the outside where I can sit with it, companionably.

I look at it and it looks back into me. Together we make something that wasn't there before.

I try to write about my dreams every day. It's a different kind of fertility, and for now it's enough.

Or at least, it's what I'm doing.

To celebrate and ritualize the coming fertility of spring, this turning in the air and in your life, let us spend some time with our altars.

Start from the mundane. Think about Spring Cleaning and focus that bright, windows-open energy, on your altars. If you don't have a space you think of as an altar, now is a beautiful time to begin. If some part of you resists the religious and authoritative history tangled up in the word "altar," take inspiration from artist, activist, icon Amalia Mesa-Bains.

Mesa-Bains . . . creates large installation works comprising dozens, at times hundreds, of objects: photographs of friends and family, strings of beads, scientific instruments, perfume bottles, her personal medical equipment, holy cards, her wedding veil, Mexican flags, her father's glasses and mother's necklace, statuettes, fabric and clothing, sugar skulls, crucifixes, calendars, stamps, candles, shards of glass, dirt, scattered woodchips, plants. At the beginning of her career, she took inspiration from home altars and Day of the Dead ofrendas, adapting them for her own artistic aims. Her installations are sacred spaces imbued with memory: of the dead, of history and all its atrocities, of innocence lost, of the mystical and mythological.[25]

An altar in your home can be as simple as a candle and plate where you burn a cinnamon stick next to your favorite plant, or it can be a glorious assemblage that looks like your soul and family history looking back at you. Either way, it is a choice and a declaration and a space for yourself that makes a container for your power.

Choose a space to be an altar. I like windowsills, the space along the back of my desk where I sit facing the window writing, the tops of shelves, inside drawers, even inside a nice mug. An altar can be very small, and it is by nature very personal.

Polish and clean and offer yourself this space like a gift. First empty the space, and clean it lovingly. Use a little lemon juice or some of your own nice soap.

Visit your altar before you go to sleep, clean and fresh and waiting. Let that clean and waiting energy enter your dreams, where your subconscious can work on how to flourish and fill.

For Ostara, add ancestors to your altar. Choose an ancestor who speaks to your heart about resistance and survival. Someone who has represented loss and hardship and then change and new growth. Find an image of them and light them a candle.

Bring them an offering you think they will like: a song, a story, a glass of beer, a cookie. Clean this away at the end of the day.

Over the coming days, take notes from your dreams, and watch for items passing through your day to day that carry the strange lovely light of dream worlds. Some things will just seem like they belong on this altar. They make a kind of sense to you. They resonate with the same frequency, or they expand the idea for you of what the altar can be.

Years after making my altar to loneliness, and after the subsequent strange magic of getting pregnant, I noticed something that had been sitting on that altar unseen and unremembered by me. In a small porcelain cup I had put a tiny silver spoon and forgot it there as the years intervened. I chose my daughter's name without noticing that it had my daughter's first name inscribed on it above an image of the flower that is her second name; May Marigold was sitting on the Altar to Loneliness the whole time.

Full of overwhelming love and gratitude, I made a new altar of gratitude and protection. This time, I surrounded baby May with stories and symbols of the women who gave her her name.

You will know the pieces of your altar when you see them. The time you spend curating this space of love will honor the people who have fought for your future. And it will give you strength and weave you— and all that you will give birth to—into that fight.

INCANTATION

I open the book
I talk to the stars
I am dangerous and divine

I am gratitude and fury
I am rooted in the common ground
I shepherd the immense

Because everything has its origin
And I come going from the origin

Everything is a circle
Everything is a circle
Everything is a circle

4

Beltane

This circle is led by Amy

BELTANE, USUALLY MAY 1, MARKS THE HALFWAY POINT BETWEEN THE SPRING EQUINOX AND THE SUMMER SOLSTICE. These halfway points might not have as much solar pizzazz as the solstices and equinoxes, but there is so much power in the very middle of things. Halfway is a marker of achievement. It's also the place where one decides, once and for all, if they will turn back or keep going. Except with our Wheel of the Year, there is no turning back. When we reach our halfway points in this Wheel of the Year, we must continue. We just have to keep going. Just. Keep. Dancing.

Here are the roots of the root of the root.

You have power. You can change your life. You can change other people's lives.

You are connected to Nature in ways that we will likely never fully understand.

But there are clues. There is music if you listen, a dance if you watch for the steps, a rhythm inside and outside of your body. We dance in a circle with the Wheel of the Year.

One of my favorite sayings is a quote commonly attributed to Robert Ersolt: *"[An] optimist [is] someone who figures that taking a step backward after taking a step forward is not a disaster, it is a Cha-Cha."*

Life is a dance. Witches hear the music and learn the choreography. Our movements and our progress are not always linear. We dance in circles, we sway back and forth, we flail and fall in wild, eternal figure eights, gesticulating as we attempt to free our bodies from the repetitive motions of daily life or the stillness of sleep.

A Beltane mainstay, the Maypole, is a tall wooden pole with long colored ribbons attached to the top. Each dancer takes a ribbon and they are off, twirling in a circle around the pole, jumping and ducking as they go over and under each other, around and around and around to weave a complex braid around the pole. Risa and I made a makeshift Maypole in my living room to celebrate Beltane many years ago, and it was a fabulous disaster. Cobbled together from leftover birthday streamers, a broomstick, a plunger, and some duct tape, our Maypole was neither beautiful nor stable, but it provided a centerpiece for our laughter as we stumbled through the dance and stumbled through our lives.

Maya Angelou said, "Everything in the universe has a rhythm, everything dances."[1] Everything dances. Cells in a petri dish dance as they draw together. Magical beanstalks spin around the Maypole as they grow. The Moon does a little shimmy as it passes through the sky. Each planet has its own specific twirl as it rotates around the Sun, creating looping spirographs as pathways. Dance connects us to Nature from a celestial to a molecular level. Like tarot cards and candles, Dance can be an instrument for your magical practice. If your index finger is a magic wand (which it is), your body in dance is a whole tool kit for ritual magic and self-expression.

At Beltane, the last of the snow has turned to water and sunken back into the soil. Things are heating up. It's no wonder then that the most major symbol of Beltane is the bonfire, an effigy of the Sun, around and around which we dance. Ceremonial dance shows up in every culture throughout time, and indeed our dances reflect our culture—from the Charleston to the twist, from the moonwalk to the whip and Nae Nae, the way we move our bodies is a reflection of our times. Elvis Presley shook his hips and scandalized the nation, giving birth not only to a dance craze, but also to a whole new target audience: teenagers.

If you've ever danced in a group in pretty much any situation: wedding, bar mitzvah, nightclub, then maybe you can conjure that feeling. Where the beat guides all of you, and the crowd becomes one. We become strings vibrating on the same guitar, making chords. The beat drives and we are in sync, a living, breathing, dancing entity of untamed joy and connectedness. When dance becomes ceremony, when dance is a ritual, this connection goes beyond the dancers and connects us with Nature as a whole, and some believe, to the gods. The beating of the drums becomes the beating of the heart, hearts become one, participants may even fall into a trance. For some, this trance is the Shamanic Journey, for others, it's simply Letting Go. Indigenous shamans of North America use the beat of the drum to induce a trance that connects them to the Great Spirit. In this trance they receive messages and instructions. And the practice is similar for a Haitian priest or priestess of Vodou. The dance begets the trance, the trance allows the dancer to be possessed, the possession allows for communication with ancestors and deities.

Anna Halprin is a choreographer and pioneer of postmodern dance who believes in the very real and tangible healing power of dance. In her book *Returning to Health: with Dance, Movement and Imagery*, she wrote, "We are all connected to each other and to the natural world in which we live. The power of dance to heal reaches its fullest potential when we are able to tap into this sense of wholeness, and to feel this connection to all that is around us."[2]

Dance is the bridge between Thinking, Feeling, and Doing/Moving, so it connects us, not only to Nature and that which surrounds us, but dance provides a greater connection also to the self. A resolution to the mind/body dilemma. There is no dilemma. There is no separation. We are one.

With this in mind, as we conjure a Beltane bonfire in our hearts, bodies, and minds, we take a spiraling dance through land, sea, and time to trace the history of Haitian vodou through dreams and under water. As the flames of our imagination bonfire lick up toward the sky, we are assured that anything is possible when we allow ourselves access to our power—the power that lives within us at all times. The power to help, to heal, and to change.

For Beltane we are guided by Marie Thérèse Alourdes Macena Champagne Lovinski—born in Haiti, pregnant at 14, a former singer, dancer, sex worker, and tobacco inspector, a woman whose own face did not appear on the first edition of her biography. She would go on to become the most famous Vodou priestess living in the United States, only when she turned herself over to her Spirit and to her own power. This is a woman who was given her last rites TWICE and lived to tell the tale. If you know her, you likely know her as Mama Lola.

In *Mama Lola: A Vodou Priestess in Brooklyn*, Mama Lola's biographer turned lifelong friend Karen McCarthy Brown described her as "a strong woman who provides the main financial and emotional support for a hard-pressed family. She is also a fighter, a survivor who has had a hard life but nevertheless shows little trace of bitterness from her suffering. She is a presence to be reckoned with, someone who commands the respect of others. But Lola is also a giver, a caring and empathetic person who takes pleasure in helping others. By necessity, she has become adept at balancing this desire to help others with the need to care for herself."[3]

If you are a woman, a parent, an empath, or especially if you are a Witch, heck, if you are a decent human, you know that this balance of Care is not easily attained. Some go their whole lives without ever coming close to the kind of compassion and fierceness and awareness and, yes, arrogance in the style of Zora or Ipsita Roy Chakraverti that is required to balance Self and Other. Worse, some never consider that maybe the two (Self and Other) are one, going their whole lives without ever knowing what it means to truly Care. Different dances bring different ends. When we dance alone, we are free, frenetic; when we dance with a partner, we are in intimate sync; when we dance with a group, we are electric, a charge that fills the room. Each dance has something to offer—a connection to ourselves, to the gods, to Nature, or to other people. We balance this need to dance alone with the desire to teach our dance and learn the dance of others; to reach with an outstretched hand and pull our loved ones spinning into an embrace.

Mama Lola was born in 1936 in Port-au-Prince, the capital of Haiti. Conceived at a (not altogether unfinished) time when Haiti was going back and forth, fighting for the power to define its national identity—legalizing and criminalizing and legalizing what were called in the law "superstitious practices." There had been a longstanding prohibition of Vodou ceremonies as a result of colonization, the Catholic Church, and the near twenty-year US military occupation of Haiti that ended just two years before Mama Lola's birth.

Sténio Vincent, Haiti's president at that time, maintained a ban on some public rituals, but in 1935, affirmed the right to "popular dances," though it's been claimed that Sténio did so only to allow for Haiti's tourism to better engage tourists' curiosity. Nonetheless, on the heels of this announcement, as if to heed the call of the dance, Mama Lola was born. Into the great and eternal dance, Mama Lola was born.

Her mother, Philomise Macena, known as Philo, was also a reluctant Manbo. Manbo—sometimes Mambo—is a term for a High Priestess in the Vodou religion. They are physical and spiritual healers. They give blessings, songs, prayers, and advice, clear hexes, lead and perform rituals and ceremonies. . . . One can study, train, and go through a complex set of protocols to reach the status of a Manbo, or one can *become* a Manbo, *chosen* via a dream dragged under water . . . a calling to serve the spirits that cannot be ignored.

Any person who is called or calls themselves Manbo or *curandera* or *yogini* or Ayurvedic practitioner or bruja or *sangoma* or WITCH is sure to have a spiraling story to tell. Mama Lola is no different. In order to understand her story, we must learn about Vodou. Not the racist, outdated, Western portrayals of Voodou as a dark and evil conjuring of bad spirits and sacrifice to the devil. Zombies. Bloodlust. Black . . . magic. But the real, spiritual faith that guides our Manbo.

Vodou is a belief system of uncountable age, but the word is derived from the Dahomean word *vudu*, which means, simply, "spirit."

Milo Rigaud wrote in *Secrets of Voodoo:* "To the uninitiated, Voodoo has long been thought of as a primitive form of magic and belief in ghosts. Most of what the average layman knows of Voodoo comes only from misleading use of it in Hollywood horror movies and paperback thrillers that emphasize 'Witch doctors' or the sticking of pins in 'Voodoo Dolls.'"[4]

Beyond Hollywood, these images, based on racism and control, demonizing the ancient ways and painting them as bloodthirsty, sick, and savage, have infiltrated Western culture with violent results. In 2010, more than forty Vodou priests in Haiti were attacked and killed by a lynch mob who blamed them for the spread of cholera.[5] After the devastating earthquake, American televangelist Pat Robertson told his many followers that the founders of Haiti had made a "pact to the devil," blaming Vodou for the natural disaster.[6] When a patient in the medical office, where Mama Lola's daughter Maggie worked, learned Maggie was Haitian, she refused to allow Maggie to touch her. The reasons the woman gave were: Vodou and AIDS.[7] Reasons that are still used against Haitians today. But when you brush away the dirt and cobwebs of religious, racist propaganda, the passion, wisdom, and oneness of the universe of Vodou are revealed.

Rigaud also wrote,

The fact is that Voodoo encompasses an exceedingly complex religion and magic with complicated rituals and symbols that have developed for thousands of years—perhaps longer than any other of today's established faiths. The believer in Voodoo . . . centres his hopes and fears as strongly on it as does a follower of Christianity, Judaism, Buddhism, or Islam. Indeed, the Haitian atmosphere seems ever impregnated with it, as if with a rich, mystical aroma of Africa—to the extent that individuals as well as families are conscious of Voodoo's effect upon their lives with a curious mixture of glory and dread.[8]

I'm writing this chapter with the same "curious mixture of glory and dread." In learning and telling Mama Lola's story, we have to explore the story of Vodou itself, Ifa . . . Yoruba . . . The roots of the roots. It's extremely vast and beautiful but intimidating territory since I have no birthright, no ancestral claim to Vodou. None of my ancestors died to protect it, it does not run in my blood in the same way it does for those of African descent whose ancestors practiced for generations. But I do have a tangible connection to Cuban Santeria which is, like Vodou, another child of Yoruba Ifa. I didn't plan my experience and I certainly didn't expect it. All I can say is, it happened to me, and it changed my life.

When I was in my early twenties I had a trauma that I'll characterize as a violent betrayal. And after it happened, all I knew was that I had to go away, I had to go far, and I had to go by myself. I needed a break from everything and everyone I knew. I needed a break from the life I had somehow created, so I looked for a destination that was the farthest away I could get on my meager savings. I was working at a gas station at the time so I wasn't exactly flush, but after a few months of penny-pinching austerity, I was on a plane to Cuba. My plane landed, I went to my hotel and slept for fourteen hours.

I woke up in Havana with no real plans. I had arranged to spend a couple days there before taking a bus to the beach for the rest of my stay.

I'm not a resort person by nature, but I was in recovery from my life's recent and total upheaval. I needed to stare at the ocean for a few days.

So I set off along the Malecón, walking the streets, stopping for coffee, taking in the sun, art, and culture of Havana. Eventually I was approached by a Cuban guy about my age. He spoke English and an unspoken deal was struck. I'd buy the drinks, and he and his friends would show me around town. This is not unusual. The people of Cuba are largely poor, and the sight of a tourist alone is an opportunity to take care and be taken care of. They took me to places that tourists don't go. We talked about music and politics, communism, the Cuban government. We laughed and sang and made connections beyond your typical tourist shakedown. At a certain point in the night I completely ran out of money. This was way back in 2001 so I didn't have a cell phone and online banking wasn't a thing. So I told my new friend that I was officially broke. I was out of money, and I understood that this might be the end of our arrangement. He smiled, and changing his plans, asked: do you want to go to a party?

We arrived at a small row house with concrete walls and a dirt floor. A bare light bulb hanging from the ceiling. A buffet was set up, but no one was touching it. The food sat, laid out in perfect arrangement. The table's centerpiece was a tall, plastic, female saint—the kind you'd see on someone's front lawn at Christmas. MIDI Christmas carols beeped and chirped on a loop from a tiny speaker attached to a strand of twinkling lights. I sat on a hard, wooden bench against the wall, laughing with the children as the room began to fill. The sound of drums—metal and hide—grew in volume and intensity. Ecstatic banging and clanging filled my ears, and the crowd parted as a man and a woman, dressed all in flowing red robes and loosely wrapped turbans, entered the space. It was like a dream. A beautiful, hazy dream.

I remember being in front of the priestess. She squirted some kind of scented oil from a plastic squeeze bottle into my outstretched hands, then she rubbed her hands together, instructing me by pantomime to do the same. She grabbed me by the shoulders, somehow both tenderly and aggressively, with authority, and spun me in a circle until I was dizzy, her last spin flinging me out onto the crowded dance floor. Some time passed, drums beating, limbs flailing, sweat pouring from our bodies, and the Santera reappeared with the priest/Santero and a live, flapping, clucking chicken. In all honesty, my first thought was, "Holy shit, they're gonna sacrifice a chicken."

There was a sacred and powerful energy in the room. The Santera held the chicken high above her head, pulling feathers from its body and tossing the blood-speckled plumage into the air. As the feathers rained down on all of us, I wasn't scared. I felt honored to be there. And still dizzy.

Swiftly, with a long, sharp knife, the chicken's head was removed from its body in one clean swish of the blade, and the priestess was swept up by her people, disappearing again into the crowd.

At this point I was thinking that's the most intense thing I've ever seen or will ever see. And then they brought out the goat.

And it was praised, petted, and paraded around and outside the house with chants and cheers. And it was close to me and I saw its eyes. We looked into each other's eyes, and then, almost immediately, I saw the inside of its neck, the smooth edge of a sliced throat and spine, and the blood dripping into the ceremonial bowl. I wasn't afraid. I was humbled and ecstatic. I had come to Cuba to reassess my life and had found myself, by luck or fate, taking part in an ancient ritual sacrifice. I was reborn.

The party continued and, I was told, would continue for three days. I stayed until I couldn't keep my eyes open and was lovingly helped into a taxi by my new friends.

The next morning I got on the bus across Cuba to my shabby but luckily all-inclusive hotel and stared into the ocean for three days.

On my last morning in Cuba I awoke and knew what I had to do. I had to move from Ontario to Montréal, Québec. I had to study at Concordia University and complete a degree in literature. I woke up and the instructions were there, waiting inside my head and heart. It was so clear. So that's what I did. I changed my life completely.

The anger I had for those *friends* who had betrayed me with violence and lies turned to gratitude. If they had never come to my apartment, throwing vitriol and punches, I may never have left my little hometown. May never have earned my degree, or met my husband, or written this book. My experience with Vodou allowed me to reclassify the violent mob from villains to neutral agents of change.

Over the years since, I've studied a bit and learned what I could to honor my experience. I was in Cuba in early December, so I figured out that the plastic saint was Saint Barbara, a stand-in for the Orisha Chango, whose feast day in Cuba is December 4. Chango also appears as Saint Jerome, which is a big town about halfway between my home and Risa's home these days, out here in the mountains north of Montréal. It feels like destiny, so I give it up to Chango on the daily for calling me to Cuba to be cleansed and blessed, freed and guided.

I'm still trying to understand my experience—what it means and what I owe. I never ask Chango for anything, other than to accept my gratitude into his great universe. He has already given more than I have earned.

As an act of simple thanks, acknowledgment, and appreciation, I keep a statuette of Chango on my altar, in my pantheon, with his lightning bolt, axe, and red and white beads. Manbo Mireille Ain, a Vodou priestess in Jacmel, in Haiti, said, "Vodou never excludes anyone. We are a religion of transformation. We assume it is not us who decide the value of someone. It's the Lwa [spirits]."[9]

I hope my experience means that the spirits deem me worthy to share these stories. I pray that Chango is glad he led me to this moment. Keeping in mind the colonial history of appropriation and begging permission from Elegba, here is my small offering, the doorway I have found to this most sacred knowledge: the roots of the roots of Haitian Vodou. Mama Lola said that one of her goals was to "open doors for others,"[10] and I hope that's what I'm doing here.

Karen McCarthy Brown wrote, "Alourdes moves in a spiral fashion over and over the same ground when telling an important ancestral story. Each pass over familiar turf creates redundancy, but it also brings out some additional nuance or detail. To listen, it is necessary to relax with the rhythm and to trust that it will eventually bring her around to fill in the gaps."[11]

This is how these stories must be told, as we wind our ways in and through. Not marching in a straight line, but dancing—over, under, and around. Mama Lola once said, "I GOT PLENTY CONFIDENCE IN MYSELF. YOU WANT SOME TOO?"[12] So with a "yes, please, and thank you Mama Lola," let's humbly open the gateway and spiral back to the beginning. The source of Vodou and its many siblings: Ifa.

There has been an eternity of discussion about the birthplace of this great and sacred collection of knowledge. Perhaps the Yoruba of Nigeria are descended from a people who were living on the banks of the Nile in Egypt. Others claim the ancestors had traveled west from Ethiopia. There is no singular authority on the subject, partly because Ifa was an almost entirely oral tradition, and partly because colonialism has done its racist best to erase what we might have known.

But many authors of African descent are decolonizing their belief systems, learning and relearning the ancient ways.

Nigerian *Babalawo*—High Priest in Ifa—Osunniyi Olajide Ifatunmo said, "People often ask me if there is a 'complete' written copy of the Odu Ifa. However, within the Odu Ifa it explains that there is no *babalawo* who knows all of the Odu Ifa because the pages in the Odu Ifa are infinite. It is like asking 'is there a complete written copy of the science of the universe.' No such book could ever be written. However, that doesn't mean that there aren't books about science."[13]

One of my favorite contemporary books on Ifa is Iyalosa Apetebii Olaomi Osunyemi Akalatunde's *Ona Agbani: The Ancient Path: Understanding and Implementing the Ways of Our Ancestors*. She wrote,

Ifa is the result of thousands of years of painstaking research and observation of nature and human's relationship to it, as well as, human's relationships with The Divine and other humans. The information gathered in this research is compiled in the sacred oral scripture of Ifa known as the ODU and in the DNA of each melanated person as part of the "genetic library"; the storehouse of information passed from parent to child. According to the primordial observations of our Ancestors, all things are a part of the Divine Whole. "All things" includes objects that most would consider inanimate. There is no spiritual line of demarcation between the so-called sacred and the so-called secular. Everything that is granted the power to exist is wholly, a part of the Divine Whole.[14]

Akalatunde explained later in the book the presence of Eurocentric Christian elements—these being particularly visible in Santeria where Catholic saints with relatable traits were used as substitutes for Orishas to allow for a more public worship. She wrote,

With the Maafa in which millions of Afrikans were captured and placed in captivity, our ties to our villages were severed and the priests and priestesses were thrust together. This catastrophe forced them to merge all of their wisdom into one common practice. Maafa marked the beginning of Ifa in its current Western state. This form is known as Orisa Worship, Santeria "worship of the saints," Sango Baptiste, Lukumi, Macumba and a myriad of other names.[15] . . . Many of the practices also added Native American elements that were introduced to the practitioners on these shores. These new practices were also forced to include Euro-Christian elements which allowed the Ancestors to camouflage their practices and thereby survive in an environment created to destroy them.[16]

And so it went that Maafa exported Ifa across the Middle Passage in the most terrible way. Through the bodies and spirits of the slave trade. Tribes were mixed and mashed, and so were their belief systems.

Ifa had always been passed down via practice, DNA, and Odu, the oral tradition, but with Maafa, the necessity of an oral tradition became especially important. Testimonies and instructions once encoded in song and dance became whispers. Because of this, many words have a variety of spellings and pronunciations. Even in this chapter, so far you've seen *Vodou* and *Voodoo*. Other spellings are: Voudoun, Vodun, Vaudon.

The spirits, Lwa, sometimes Loa, too, go by many names. Sometimes Chango, for example, is Shango. Mixed up and redistributed, the words, spellings, and names may be different, but the concepts are largely the same. When we learn about Ifa, Yoruba, Vodou, we learn that they have much in common with the Western contemporary notions of paganism and Witchcraft that they no doubt influenced, or more likely, begat—herbalism, meditation, Earth- and sky-based spiritual systems, offerings, gratitude, manifestation, and the interpretation of dreams. But Ifa and especially Vodou have their faith woven into a complex and deeply public, personal, whole-life relationship with Lwa. Offerings are not optional. The Lwa must be paid. Lwa, also known by many other names, including Loa, *les mystères,* and "the invisibles," are the spirit realm representatives of the One: Olodumare, Bondye . . . the sum total of all consciousness. Some scholars speculate that it was an ancient, foreign misunderstanding of Olodumare, this notion of Oneness, that led to the monotheisms of what we know today as Judaism, Islam, and Christianity. Ifa predates these monotheistic systems, by some accounts, by ten thousand years.

Karen McCarthy Brown described Lwa as "both mirrors and maps, making the present comprehensible and offering directions for the future."[17] Messages are sent from Humanity to the Divine, via service, prayer, offerings of food and drink, dance, drums, and many multitudes of other thoughts and actions. Messages are sent from the Divine to Humanity through possession, visions, and dreams. But again the Lwa must be paid. A lot of the ritual of Vodou takes the form of specific offerings to specific Lwa—they each have their own tastes.

The necessity of oral tradition before and secrecy after Maafa means there is no one set of rules, spellings, names, or terms for gods. In her way, Karen McCarthy Brown preserves this oral tradition by transcribing Mama Lola's words exactly as Alourdes spoke them, phoneticizing her accent and filling the book with long swaths of Mama Lola's word for word storytelling.

Haiti is considered by many to be closer to its roots in Africa than many other colonial destinations and indeed has a truly remarkable history of survival, Magick, and resistance. Part of the reason Haiti was able to preserve these ties is that African captives led a successful slave revolution, a battle led by Toussaint L'Ouverture, fought from 1791 until 1804. For nearly a hundred years after this revolution, Haiti was largely isolated, evading the destructive colonial hammer for a little while. Legend has it that it was the Orisha Ogun who planted the idea of a revolt into the heads of Haitian slaves and Maroons—a term for Africans who had escaped from slavery, mixed with the Taino (Indigenous people of this land), and formed independent settlements. And it was Ogun a.k.a. Papa Ogou who helped them to victory in the Haitian Revolution of 1804. Yoruba tradition says that there are over four hundred Orisha, but most commonly you'll see seven major deities, and together they form a pantheon—each one is associated and identified with forces of nature. Very basically, Chango is fire, Ogun is the forest, and Oshun and Yemaya are the rivers and seas. Ochosi is animals or the hunter, Obatala is the sky. Elegua (or Elegba) is fate. So when an Orisha devotee wants to petition Yemaya, the devotee might go to their altar or straight to the sea to communicate with Yemaya directly.

In Yoruba Ifa, Ogun is said to have used an axe to clear a path on Earth for the other Orishas; he is a father figure and a great protector for those in battle. And so the story goes that it was Ogun who led the hearts and minds of the victims of the slave trade to their courageous and successful revolution.

Haiti would become the first sovereign nation in the Western Hemisphere to unconditionally abolish slavery in the modern era and remains the only state in history to have been established because of a slave revolt. But the power struggle in Haiti did not end with this revolution. French and Spanish oppression and Haitian rebellion continues spiraling around and back to the Haiti of 1936 and the birth of Mama Lola, a baby girl born Alourdes, with the bonfire of her people's history in her blood. From birth it was established that she would help and need help: Philo fell ill after delivering her daughter, so Mama Lola was breastfed by a local woman who had lost her infant child weeks before. As her first act of care, self and other, Lola and her wet nurse helped each other to survive.

Alourdes comes from a line of Healers, Manbos, and Houngan, and most members of her family have stories of trying to dismiss the call. But when Lwa or Orisha make contact, attention must be paid. They manifest in visions, coincidences, but most likely and profoundly through Dreams and even through possession, and, as Mama Lola found, they will not be ignored.

Her grandfather and grandmother, Philo's father and mother, were legendarily magical. Grandpa was prone to drunken rage and specialized in revenge magic. He only spoke to the spirits when he wanted something. The story goes that when he died suddenly in the street, Sina, Mama Lola's grandmother, said, "It is better this way. I know the spirits want me. Before I always said No. Now everything has changed. Now I will serve the spirits. They will take care of me. I do not need a man."[18] Perhaps a prophecy for the generations of women to come in her family line.

Philo's gift of healing at first showed itself exclusively through dreams. Solutions to problems came to her, appearing in her dreams as spirit messages. But the vocation of Healer, a job that—for her—could only be successfully performed upon receipt of a message in a dream that may or may not come, didn't exactly make for financial stability. Over time Philo honed her craft, eventually becoming knowledgeable enough that she no longer had to wait for dream-state instructions before counseling a client. She made a name for herself as a Manbo, at one point having future Haitian President François Duvalier a.k.a. Papa Doc as a client. But Philo's generosity kept her from attaining wealth. Giving money away, paying others' overdue rent, and feeding their children were common practices for Philo. Mama Lola's daughter Maggie said:

Work with the spirit run in my family—my grandmother, my mother. People coming in here to see my mother all hours of the day and night. She never too tired to see people. Just like my grandmother, always helping people . . . they don't ever have no money. They just giving . . . always giving.[19]

Mama Lola grew up in what was essentially a Vodou healing center, surrounded by women. Her father was not in her life, but his was also a family of Houngan so Mama Lola had magic on both sides of her family tree. Despite her DNA, Mama Lola was not immediately drawn to the calling. She claims to have "preferred secular dances to those for the spirits,"[20] but for Mama Lola, and for us at Beltane, there is room for all kinds of dancing.

At seven years old, Mama Lola had one of the most defining experiences of her life. Defining for her story, but not for her personally—she doesn't remember it at all.

One day Alourdes was badly bitten by the neighbor's dog. That night, leg carefully bandaged by her mother, Alourdes woke in a panic. Her head was spinning. Something was dreadfully wrong. She had to move. She got out of bed and walked and walked and walked. This frantic feeling, this need to escape was the last thing Mama Lola remembered about the incident. She went missing . . . in every sense. Trying to diffuse Philo's desperate fears, a friend joked that perhaps the spirits had taken Alourdes below the water. Maybe they wanted to make her a Manbo.

There are stories about the voodoo Lwa Lasirenn. That she will pull people down under the water, *anba dlo* (if you speak French you might understand this as *en bas de l'eau,* or under water), and force you to live there with her, connecting you through the water to all knowledge . . . all life. Karen McCarthy Brown wrote, "The stories have a common pattern. A person, usually a woman, disappears for a time—three days, three months, three years. When she returns, she is a changed person . . . She has gained sacred knowledge . . . Living below the water where spirits instructed her in the arts of diagnosis and healing. . . . I once met a rural priestess . . . When I asked her who had initiated her, she responded that no one had. Her instruction, she said simply, had come *anba dlo.*"[21]

At seven years old, Alourdes disappeared for three days. There are many other bits of evidence that suggest maybe Mama Lola gained her true title of Manbo *anba dlo* during those three days—an oddly placed comb, the demeanor of the dog. When, after a three day search, she was found, she was unharmed and playing by the water.

Mama Lola's first paying job at age sixteen was as a singer and dancer in Haiti's La Troupe Folklorique Nationale and not much is made of this time except that her singing career was well paid and ended when she got married. You'll recall that it was popular at the time for tourists visiting Haiti to want to see a "Voodoo Dance," so this was perhaps another prophetic time in her life. Not yet a Manbo, she was already performing the dance.

In Haitian Vodou, the dance opens a portal that allows possession by the Lwa. In fact, it's believed that each Lwa has its own set of movements that can be used to make contact. Many ancient dances still exist, like the *zèpòl,* a shoulder dance, and the *mayi,* a three-step pattern. There is also the *yanvalou,* a ritual dance from Benin, West Africa. This dance and others are Rele Lwa, dances performed specifically to summon the Lwa. The *yanvalou* is performed as a group prayer, the wild spinning and twisting, snake-like motions, long, fluid steps, and sweeping arms of the dancers invoke the trance state, allowing for possession to take place.

One of my oldest friends has been a dancer for most of her life. She started in the usual forms, tap, ballet, jazz, and in our teens we would root through her closet, pull out her hilarious old dance costumes, and wear them to parties for a laugh. The costumes were exuberant, glittering monstrosities of spandex and tulle, neon, sequins, and feathers. We paraded around, wearing them as armor to protect us from a world that took itself too seriously. As my friend matured, she continued to dance, eventually discovering contact improvisation or contact dance. Contact improv was created by Steve Paxton to inform and explore the human body in motion, both emotionally and mechanically—balancing, falling down, lifting, and being lifted. Touch, roll, collide, all while keeping an awareness of your own body and the body of your dance partner. Dance improv then becomes a physical practice as well as a spiritual one. It is an exercise in compassion and self-awareness, how we stand, pose, or take up space and what do those things say about our bodies and our minds? This awareness is healing.

The Sun Dance of the Indigenous people of the Prairies and the Great Plains of North America is also a healing dance. It can be a grueling test of spiritual and physical endurance for the dancers, with their pain and exhaustion serving as a sacrifice made for the health of their community. Like Vodou dances in Haiti, the Sun Dance was also outlawed in North America. It wasn't until the 1950s in Canada and the 1970s in the United States that the colonizing government lifted these prohibitions. Still today, many Indigenous people lack access to these sacred ceremonies, illegal for five hundred years.

For most dances, especially these ritual, ceremonial dances, the drums drive and lead the steps. Songs that have been passed down for uncountable generations, across the ocean and on to the island of Haiti, tell stories of the Lwa and teach their histories. Movements are communications, found deep in the DNA of every dancer.

Haitian dance is an integral part of ceremony and spirituality, and the complexity, power, and perseverance of these dances have led many anthropologists and choreographers to the island to learn about these movements. The year of Mama Lola's birth was the same year as anthropologist and choreographer Katherine Dunham's first visit to Haiti.

Born in Chicago in 1909, Katherine would become an incredibly successful dancer and choreographer—establishing and running the Katherine Dunham Company, one of if not the earliest self-supporting predominantly Black dance companies. She is hailed as one of the first African Americans to conduct anthropological fieldwork, and the first anthropologist to explore the function of dance in rituals and community life. All of her research informed her civil rights activism, raising Haitian dance out from behind the demonizing glare of colonialism and presenting it as a valid, beautiful, and intense religious and cultural artform. Her book *Island Possessed* tells of Haiti's history, how the island came to be possessed by the spirits of Vodou, and how she herself became possessed by Haiti—its people, its culture, its ritual dance. Katherine purchased a parcel of land there and adopted Haiti as her second home.

Like the Witches in this book, Katherine presented as fearless, and she used her bravery to change the world. In 1950 she was on a tour of South America with her troupe. Arriving at her prebooked hotel in São

Paulo, Brazil, she was refused service by the man behind the counter. Because she was Black. Because the dance company surrounding her was all Black. At this time there were no written anti-discrimination laws to protect Afro-Brazilians, but, undeterred, Katherine went the very next day to see a Brazilian attorney regarding the racist incident. As a result, Congressman Affonso Arinos de Mello Franco introduced a new anti-discrimination law. Katherine's refusal to allow herself to be treated badly, even as a guest, and her determination to make change, to battle racism in all its forms, ended with a law being passed to benefit Black Brazilians. It was the first law of its kind in their history.

As she got to know Haiti, its people, its customs, Katherine recognized that the vital and unifying spirit of Haiti came down to Vodou. She went to study the dance and became a partner in the dance. She learned that the dance of Vodou goes beyond the body, beyond art, and into the realm of the sacred. It was not just celebration, it was care. At one point she calls the days-long drum and dance ceremonies "bush psychiatry," connecting these rituals to the mental health of their practitioners. And this is a Beltane lesson that we can keep for ourselves. Dance. Because it is not frivolous or sinful, it is self-care, part of Nature's psychiatry. Eventually, Katherine was officially initiated into Vodou.

And so it also went for Maya Deren. When Katherine wrote her master's thesis on Haitian dances in 1939, Maya was her editor. She was an experimental filmmaker who, inspired by Katherine's work, first visited Haiti in order to make a film about ritual dances. She, too, found a truth there, beyond measure. She found a belief system that resonated so deeply within her Ukrainian-born heart that she, too, became an initiate. Maya saw the dance in all aspects of Haitian life. In her book *Divine Horsemen: The Living Gods of Haiti,* she wrote of the countryside as a "theatre in the round, where a lyric dance drama of prodigious grace and infinite variety is in continuous performance."[22] From the predawn dark, through the day, and back into the night, Maya described the "onomatopoeic rhythms and cadences phrasing"[23] of market-bound women, the percussion of a donkey's hooves. Beyond the ritual and ceremonial, Maya recognized the choreography of all life. Undulating waves.

She noted that a baby on his mother's hip, absorbing the beats of a ceremonial drum, will "know the drums' beat as its own, blood-familiar pulse."[24] And we Witches recognize this too—the beat of the drum, the beat of our pulse, the magic of dance in all forms: the natural molecular dance, the fun, "secular" dance, the sacred, metaphysical dance that, as Maya says, "is a statement addressed not to men but to divinity."[25] Divinity, for Maya, is the Loa. As she wrote, just as the physical body of a man is meaningless, material substance, devoid of judgment, will, and morality, unless a soul infuses and animates it, so the universe would be but an amoral mass of organic matter, inevitably evolving on the initial momentum of original creation, were it not for the Loa who direct it in paths of order, intelligence, and benevolence. The Loa are the souls of the cosmos.[26] The Lwa are the souls of the cosmos. So when we dance, we may dance in solitude, for our souls alone, we may dance with our soul mates, or we may dance as tribute to the souls of the cosmos. For Beltane, any form will do, as long as we are dancing.

Maya spent the late 1940s and early 1950s filming in Haiti, so she may have, at some point, run into Mama Lola. In the 1950s Alourdes was living on her own with two children in Port-au-Prince. She was looking for work, eventually gaining employment through the government-run tobacco industry. She told her biographer: "Let me tell you something. When you go to the office and ask for job, that man, the inspector, the one in the head office—if he say 'Yes I'm going to give you the job' you have to sleep with him first! You say no, you don't have no job! Sometimes they make love to you and you still don't have no job. Sometime when I think back I get angry. But that's life! I can't help it! That's life!"[27]

When she loses her job as a tobacco inspector, she's forced to sell sex more directly and frequently. Though she's quick to make a distinction between her role as a "Marie-jacques," more like an escort, and a *bouzen*, or street prostitute. She goes on "dates" with men—dinner, dancing, and then sex. Interestingly, she would approach payment in the same way she would later as a Manbo: she gives what she can, and accepts what is given in return. Back then there was no other way for her to buy food, or pay her rent or her children's school fees.

Sex work is not the defining moneymaker in her life, certainly, and I might have glossed over it if not for Mama Lola's own words to Karen McCarthy Brown: "You got to put that in the book. Because it's the truth. Right? Women got to do all kinda thing. Right? I do that to feed my children. I'm not ashamed."[28]

What sets Mama Lola apart and so often comes through in her telling of her life story is that she is not ashamed. Our society's relationship to sex is complicated and toxic, and it gets only more complicated and toxic when money is involved. Christian colonialism paints Sex and Dance as shameful, bodily acts. Shameful *because* they are of the body. Whenever I question the power of Dance, I remember that the movie *Footloose* was based on a true story. An American town really did put a ban on dancing. If dancing had no power, it wouldn't be outlawed. If colonizers did not believe that Dance had power, they would not have made it illegal. Remember that. Dance has power. Your *Single Ladies* kitchen dance has power. Your twerk is a weapon. It is Witchcraft.

But of course, sex work is nothing new.[29] One woman Karen McCarthy Brown met in Haiti joked that she was going to market to sell her land. When asked, "What land?" the woman hooted, pointed to her vagina, and grabbed her crotch, laughing, "I can sell my land anywhere!"[30]

When Alourdes was in her twenties, with two children in Port-au-Prince, life was hard. She had become pregnant for the third time, not by a client but by a dear and trusted friend and lover. He deserted her when he found out she was carrying his child. She said sorrowfully that she and her children went to bed hungry on more days than she'd like to remember. This third child, a son, William, was born with meningitis. Mama Lola took him to the hospital and was given a prescription for drugs she couldn't afford to buy. The lights turned off from nonpayment, she sat in the dark, cradling her sick child in her arms . . . weeping.

So when she asked her brother, who was living in New York, for a small loan, and he instead gave her the option to join him in America, she packed her bags. She left her three children in the care of her mother, Philo, and arrived in Brooklyn in 1962. Before she left she told her mother, "I'm going to that city!! Lotta stars! Beautiful! Oh boy! I don't think I'm gonna need no spirit in New York." She laughs in her retelling. "And I was wrong!"[31]

Even her first attempt to apply for a visa was greeted by the U.S. Embassy official with a sneer and a series of demeaning questions. Was she going there to work as a prostitute? Could she prove that this man she was going to stay with was her brother and not her pimp?

By December 1963 she was living in the United States, but she was dying. She complained of pain, she couldn't sit or stand. Struggling to breathe, she eventually made her way to a hospital on Prospect Avenue. On January 8, a priest arrived in her hospital room to give Mama Lola her last rites. Diagnosed with an infection in her intestine, Mama Lola was operated on, kept in the hospital for a couple more weeks, then discharged. Or as she put it, "I feel all right, then they put me out."[32]

There were some welfare systems in place, but no one told Mama Lola about them. No one at the hospital told her anything. But they did take down the address of her family in Haiti and asked that she return with her passport and alien card. Fear kept Mama Lola from returning to the hospital for follow-up treatments. She'd heard horror stories about enormous medical bills being sent to relatives in Haiti, or deportation if she could not pay the bills herself. Like many people who survive without socialized medicine, she was too poor and too scared to seek further treatment. Inevitably, she got sick again, was taken to a different hospital, and was again, for the second time, given last rites and expected to die. But once again, she felt all right, so they put her out. Mama Lola had been hospitalized, so during that time she was obviously not able to work. She couldn't work, so she had no money, so she couldn't pay rent. She couldn't pay rent so she was homeless.

The Lwa could see her value though; just by chance, walking the streets of New York, Mama Lola ran into a friend of her Haitian family, Yvonne Constant. Yvonne took Mama Lola home and fed her fish, rice, and beans, and gave her a place to sleep. Mama Lola was so tired. She slept and slept.

During her time at Yvonne's, Mama Lola was contacted by her sister-in-law Bebe. Alourdes had stayed briefly with Bebe when she arrived in New York, and the two did not get along.

Bebe had dreamed of a man dressed head to toe in denim, standing on a corner in New York City, waiting for the light to change. The light turned green and the man turned to Bebe and greeted her, "Hi Cousin," before asking if she knew Philo and if she knew Alourdes. Bebe replied that she did and the man gave this message: Tell Alourdes, if she dress like me, everything going to be beautiful![33]

When she awoke, Bebe, whose own mother spoke to spirits, understood the dream, and recognized her dream man as Kouzen Zaka. Kouzen (Creole for "cousin") Zaka is a Haitian Lwa. His color is blue, especially blue denim—the outfit of a Haitian peasant, and the outfit of the man in Bebe's dream. He is excellent to talk to about herbal medicine and healing. So when Mama Lola heard her sister-in-law's dream she also understood and knew what she had to do. She had to return to Haiti.

Mama Lola's brush with death conjures a fear beyond being deported or unable to pay medical bills. In the darkness we find fears, created and fed by xenophobic patriarchy: Witch, Zombie, Mummy, creatures pushed to populate our nightmares. Through fright tales and horror films, ancestors and their beliefs are turned into Monsters. To be feared, but not revered. But the fear does not stop at scary movies.

In her book *Haitian Vodou,* Mambo Chita Tann explained, the term "zombie" has come to mean either the soul that has been stolen and enslaved (before or after physical death) or the living person whose soul has been stolen and enslaved in such a manner.[34] So it's especially heinous that colonizers should enslave people and then demonize even the word that came to denote a soul also stolen and enslaved. A soul can be enslaved by any constant cutting down from the all-too-real world we live in. Living in hardship, peril, beat up and put down, sick, but too poor or too scared to seek treatment, so stripped of resources and self-esteem so that all strength or energy to care is lost, damaging a crucial piece of one's soul and one's brain. For the science-minded among us, let's cite an *Atlantic* article "How Poverty Changes the Brain." "[The Brain's] limbic system processes emotions and triggers emotional responses, in part because of its storage of long-term memory. When a person lives in poverty, a growing body of research suggests the limbic system is constantly sending fear and stress messages to the prefrontal cortex, which overloads its ability to solve problems, set goals, and complete tasks in the most efficient ways."[35]

Maybe we should be less afraid of being eaten alive by *Walking Dead* Zombies, and more afraid of all the ways a body, a mind, and a soul can be enslaved. Maybe the zombie apocalypse was/is colonial capitalism's reduction of People to Things. Machines without souls. George Romero's 1978 film *Dawn of the Dead* shows the zombie as mindless consumer. Consuming resources and lives without thought or compassion, the undead hordes retain their human greed, but lose their human care.

Lucky for Mama Lola—or as Zaka, Lwa, and Bondye would have it—someone did care. The woman who had saved her life, Yvonne Constant, saved her life again, paying Alourdes's passage back to Haiti when it was her turn for Hands. Hands was a community-based financial exchange. If there are ten of you, and you each put in ten dollars a week, then each week, for ten weeks, someone gets $100. In Hands there is no hierarchy, no pyramid, and no scheme. Just a circle of protection and love. Everyone climbs the ladder together.

When Alourdes arrived unannounced in Haiti, her mother saw her and promptly fainted. Philo had also had a dream about her daughter returning, broken, from the United States. Within a few days of Mama Lola's return, Philo had been possessed by Papa Ogou. Common among Manbos, the priestess becomes what's known as a horse, and the Lwa becomes the rider. Not completely dissimilar to the dissociation of the Zombie, but this is a temporary possession, not sinister, used only to deliver a message or instructions from the divine. This time the message was for Mama Lola. She said, "Papa Ogou come in my mother's head, and tell me I'm supposed see with card, you know . . . do spirit work . . . help people. That I don't like!! I say Oh boy! How I'm going to do that? Because to help people you got to know a lotta thing. I say, 'How I going to put all that in my head?' My mother tell me, 'Don't worry. You'll manage.'"[36]

Mama Lola followed this instruction and used an ordinary or extraordinary deck of playing cards as her primary tool for divination.

But first she had to be initiated. She had her instructions from Papa Ogun; he had told her mother that the sacred rattle, the *ason,* had been her father's family's tool for service and protection. Mama Lola would need to carry one as well. But initiation rites cannot start right away. Ritual garments must be sewn, and Mama Lola's family had to save up for offerings: food, drink, sacrificial animals. Drummers would be hired. Initiation is elaborate. Mama Lola's began with a simple head washing (*lave-tête*), and a promise on her part, to the spirits, that she would go back to New York, just long enough to save up the money she needed, and then she would return to Haiti to complete her initiation.

Mama Lola had been unsuccessful her first time in New York, but this trip was different. She got a job her second day back in the city. Slowly she built up her understanding of the spirits and their instructions. Slowly people began to come to her for help. Slowly she was becoming a healer with enough clients to quit her day job forever.

After two years of working in New York, she had saved the seven hundred dollars required for her initiation, and, as she had promised, she returned to Haiti. As part of her initiation, Mama Lola had to *kouche,* which is a prolonged period of isolation. Again, those of you who speak French might recognize this as *couche,* or to go to sleep. For her *kouche,* Mama Lola stayed in a little room for nine days. After her *kouche,* she was a Manbo and her training from her mother began in earnest. She spent a month in Haiti learning about the cards, how to communicate with spirit, learning about herbs. Everything that had surrounded her as a child, her grandmother and great-grandmother's service to spirit, all of that ancestral knowledge was coming back to her and she learned quickly.

Mama Lola made a powerful return to New York. She healed the sick, reunited star-crossed lovers, and conjured jobs for the unemployed with her guidance from spirit. "Some people got spirit in their family," she told Karen McCarthy Brown. "But when they grow up, they think they too big-shot to serve the spirit. They too ashame about that. But I'm not ashame at all, because I love spirit, because they help me. That's my belief."[37]

In 1965 she was finally able to bring her three children to New York, and by the 1970s, Mama Lola was a renowned Manbo, being called upon by people in need both in Haiti and in the United States, or by her initiates when a case proved too tough to crack. The Black mambo, dressed all in white, trekking across cursed fields and broken hearts with her pail of Florida water, limes, ashes, indigo, molasses . . . this is the Mama Lola that Karen McCarthy Brown met and studied. The first edition of *Mama Lola: A Vodou Priestess in Brooklyn* came out in 1991, and the book fueled Mama Lola's already growing fame. Each edition after the first would feature her proud, beautiful, wise, *do no harm but take no shit* expression. Mama Lola accompanied Karen McCarthy Brown on educational tours and fact-finding missions for years. She would continue to go back and forth to Haiti from time to time, from Brooklyn to Port-au-Prince and around the world. Speaking. Helping. Building her reputation. Building her power.

Her last trip to Haiti was in 2009.

A magnitude-7 earthquake struck Haiti on the afternoon of January 12, 2010. More than half a million people were injured or killed, with millions more being displaced. One more disaster in a country that continues to suffer from centuries of political, economic, and social injustices, and setbacks and inequalities. The earthquake was a disaster that would cause Mama Lola to claim she would never return to Haiti— her mother's home, holy space, and family altar destroyed . . . she said, "There is nothing left."[38]

In the new millennium Mama Lola took up practice at Voodoo Authentica, a Vodou shop, museum, and spiritual center in New Orleans, giving blessings and readings, and performing other Manbo-ly duties with her daughter Maggie and goddaughter Brandi. Brandi says, "Mama Lola just has this presence that says: I know who I am, and I am voodoo. . . . If you come to Mama Lola, you are a part of her."[39]

I reached out to the staff at Voodoo Authentica who told me that as of 2016, Mama Lola was officially retired and living with her family. She was no longer performing any kind of spiritual work or readings, at least, not for the public. On May 23, 2020, just as I was finishing this chapter, only a few weeks before our final deadline for this book, Mama Lola died in Brooklyn. I am comforted by the knowledge that if anyone can pass from this realm and into the next with grace, magnitude, and elegance, it is Mama Lola. For her, most certainly, Papa Legba has opened the gate.

We can't leave New Orleans Vodou without spiraling past one of its most famed practitioners: Marie Laveau. Marie was a midwife, herbalist, and famed Vodou priestess who was born in the French Quarter of New Orleans in 1801. She was referred to by Zora and many others as the Queen of Vodou, a legacy that lives on today. She was famously and stunningly portrayed by Angela Bassett in the TV series *American Horror Story*, and this portrayal brought even more interest to Marie and her tomb. Both Risa and I have visited her grave in Saint Louis Cemetery, New Orleans, on separate occasions, and while our experiences were quite different—I was there pre-Katrina and Risa was there after the flood—the power of Marie is steadfast. I was determined to see the tomb, so, undeterred by the locked gates, I climbed and jumped the stone wall, cutting my hand in the process. Another blood sacrifice to the spirits. At Marie's grave, there is always evidence of the faithful who have passed by before, leaving offerings, as I did, of tobacco, marijuana, crosses and cards, flowers or coins. At some point, drawing X's on her grave became the habit of those visitors seeking Marie's help from beyond, but this tradition damages the tomb and is discouraged by preservationists. In 2014, a restoration of her tomb was completed and as of March 2015, a large fine has been waiting for any visitor who attempts to write on the grave.

Let's spiral this story backward one more time to 2007 at the doors of a sprawling California starlet's mansion. And maybe as you enter you roll your eyes and wonder what Mama Lola is doing there. On this day, in this place, Alourdes might say to you, as she has said in the past, "I just do what I want. Nobody don't tell me my business! What they mean? White people can't have no spirit? Spirit for everybody!"[40]

You likely didn't expect to read the name Tori Spelling in this book, but magic knows no bounds and always disrupts our expectations. In

2007 Mama Lola appeared on Tori's reality show *Tori & Dean: Inn Love*, when Tori sought the Manbo's help in lifting a perceived curse.[41] While it's clear that Mama Lola's relationship with Tori Spelling deserves no more than a footnote in her rich history, we can't help but stop and marvel at the absurd balance that life and magic can produce. It's glorious to see Tori, the poster child for monied white privilege, trusting and recognizing the power of the Haitian Manbo. And maybe we can all admit to getting a bit of a postmodern thrill from watching Mama Lola pelt Tori with her special blend of herbs, oils, and ice-cold water. But the best part of Mama Lola's interaction with the star of *Beverly Hills* is the manner in which Alourdes replied to Tori's complaints: "It's cold," Tori shrieks. "It's not cold," Mama Lola states back matter-of-factly and with authority, as if her speaking the words quite simply makes them true. The water is not cold. Tori stops complaining. Mama Lola's words have changed reality.

Your words can change someone's reality. We know this. And we all need help sometimes. We all need to care and be cared for. In Mama Lola's life, as with all of us, she has been a giver and a receiver. Her story would not have been possible without her occupation of both roles. We should all aspire to a Mama Lola level of balance between caring for ourselves and caring for others. Don't be afraid to ask for help or to ask someone to dance. Bring your Beltane fire and your Maypole dance as you embrace the new world growing around you. Do not fear the changes. Even biographer Karen McCarthy Brown confessed in her afterword that Mama Lola once said, "I hate that book . . . because I change and it doesn't."[42] So keep writing your book. For many descendants of the survivors of Maafa, learning about Ifa and Vodou is a way to connect to their most ancient DNA. It is an anticolonial act. For descendants of colonists, learning about Vodou helps to uncover the lies that racism and colonialism tell, to debunk the lie of superiority that we've been taught to tell ourselves. We all must continue writing and rewriting the book. Learning, dismantling, and rechoreographing the dance.

As you go dancing about your Beltane, praise the souls of the cosmos and ruminate on the notion of care in your own healing journey. Check yourself for zombie bites, the festering bacteria of colonial thought in your bloodstream. Ask Elegba, safe keeper of Ashe, ruler of doorways, standing at the crossroads of Human and Divine, to bless you, and us, as we conjure up the scent of Florida Water and a quote from Mama Lola to carry with us in the bonfire of our hearts: "I help all the people. Big people, small people, poor people, I'm there to help anybody . . . anybody . . . And all the people I help become my friend. My family . . . Papa Legba, open the gate!"[43]

Ritual

We encourage you to not be shy or ashamed, but if you have to, go ahead and do this ritual in your mind's eye. The neurons that fire when we dance or when we *think* about dancing or *remember* dancing are almost exactly the same, almost as though spirit is dancing within us all the time. Like a jump rope always turning, waiting for us to run in and skip to the beat.

In a standing or seated position, close your eyes. In the silence hear your breath and beneath your breath, your heartbeat. Place your hand on your heart and feel the thumping bass drum that is with you all the time.

Bring your awareness down to feel that internal rhythm in your pelvis, in between your hips. Sway.

Imagine your hips are rocking side to side like a boat, safe in a quiet sea, beneath the vast dance of planets and stars. Imagine you are a tree in a summer wind. Sway.

Cross your arms in front of you and imagine you are holding a sleeping child in your arms. You are rocking an infant to sleep. Sway.

Wrap your arms around yourself. Feel the warm embrace of your imagined slow jam. Sway.

Breathe deeply as you sway.

Place your hands in a prayer position in front of you. Sway.

Slowly raise your hands above your head and spread your arms, saying, I am the fire, reaching toward the sky. I am the seed, stem, and bloom, reaching toward the Sun. I am the dancer, learning the dance. I am the tree in the breeze. I sway, I bend, but do not break.

Repeat as necessary.

INCANTATION

I just do what I want.
Nobody don't tell me my business!
I'm not ashamed.
I'm not ashamed at all.
But I'm not too big-shot to serve my spirit.
Life is a dance and I am a choreographer.
All the people I help become my family.
Open the gate.
The water is not cold.

5

Litha

This circle is led by Amy

LITHA FALLS ON THE SUMMER SOLSTICE, THE LONGEST, MOST BRILLIANT DAY OF THE YEAR. At this time, the Sun is unrelenting in its brightness and so should you be!

Feeling the Sun on your face is one of life's great simple joys. Knowing the Sun will rise and set is one of our great simple faiths. When we pull the Sun card from our tarot decks we smile and relax a little bit. It signifies vitality, fun, warmth, and success.

Think of all the metaphors that use Light to signify Truth, Hope, Salvation, new beginnings. The light at the end of the tunnel, shedding light on a subject, or the Greek philosopher Diogenes carrying a lantern, searching for an honest man. Litha is that light of Truth. Personal Truth. Self-esteem. Abundance. Growth. Possibility.

At Litha we take a moment for unapologetic self-congratulation. The seeds are sown, tended, and nurtured. Buds are flowering, still growing, and the Harvest has not yet begun. In this moment we can glance briefly backward to acknowledge the steps we took months or even years ago that have led us to where we are today. What we planted is now coming to fruition. A harvest, literal or metaphorical, can't happen without planning, hard work, and nurturing. As you watch your buds bloom (literally or metaphorically), take a moment to say, "I did that. I made that. I got here."

Litha is a time for gratitude and not just for the manifestations that you're about to enjoy, the awesome summer you're about to have. Litha is also a perfect day to give some of that gratitude to yourself, unabashedly honor yourself for getting through every single hardship in your year or your life. For tackling every challenge that has led you to this moment. Over, under, through, around. Put your face to the Sun and exchange vows of strength, courage, and persistence with that sacred light in the sky. You did it. You made it. You have risen and you will rise again. Now prepare for the next challenge. Because life doesn't stop, and neither can you. The Wheel of the Year keeps turning, and hurdles will inevitably arise, but at summer solstice we embrace our capabilities without doubt and our power without fear, and look to the future without anxiety. We meet the Sun with delight.

We are like the Sun. Powerful. Luminous. We can create and nourish. But we can also burn. We can scorch with our judgments. We can shame and exclude, set fire to our and other people's sense of self. To prevent this, we must temper our heat—not with self-doubt but with compassion. The warmth of the Sun is knowing that you are amazing. The burn is thinking you are better than anyone else. A confident person warms, lifts others up, nurtures, laughs at themselves first and hardest. A conceited person burns others down to empower themselves, and believes that different ways of living are an affront to their own choices, an insult to their lifestyle. They cannot be told they are wrong. My mother used to say, "There are two kinds of people, those who try to lift you up and those who will try to pull you down. Either way, everyone is just trying to bring everyone else to their level." To quote the almighty songstress Lizzo in her self-love anthem "Juice," "If I'm shinin' everybody gonna shine."[1]

Litha is all about not dimming your light—let them squint at your overwhelming brightness. Let their eyes adjust to your dazzling glow. You are like the Sun, allowing none to diminish your brilliance. Be intimidating. Speak your mind. Loudly. Love yourself in such a way that the love shines out from you and forces those around to enter and share your light. A light whose warmth they can feel lifting them to your level of authenticity, compassion, and self-worth. Or let them turn a blind, shielded eye, knowing that a luminance as bold as yours may compel some to draw their shades. They can't take the heat. Shine on, and live your truth. But be warned. Some won't draw their shades. Some will attempt to put out your light. With mockery. With violence. In a perfect world (that we are creating here together), everyone would be safe to express who they truly are. Radical. Queer. Different. Witch. In this society, the choice is yours: blend in or take the heat that comes with standing out.

Each of the eight Sabbats has a complement—an equal yet opposite, a perfect difference—that sits across from it on the Wheel of the Year. In the chapter on Yule, Risa wrote about her experience of giving birth to her daughter. At Litha, we ourselves are reborn. In a conversation about fertility, artist and scientist Jacqui Beaumont told me that, as a trans woman, she considers an aspect of her fertility to be giving birth to herself.[2] Creating a new person who needs nurturing and guidance to grow. Jacqui also works with cells in a lab. This work and her self-creation are done with what she calls "the medium of life."[3] Your life is the material for your art and experimentation. Litha is associated with maturity, full grown like the Sun on solstice, and there is nothing more mature than taking ownership and responsibility for who and what we are. In the long light of the summer solstice, give birth to yourself. Allow yourself to escape that womb of complacency or blame, society's or other people's expectations. Even if just for today. Even just as an experiment. Or make it a yearly endeavor and let it change your life.

For Litha we fly at the speed of light to Eastern Europe and invoke the spirit of Marija Gimbutas, a woman who shed light on human history. When faced with mockery and the rejection of her discoveries, she insisted that it might take decades, but eventually the value of her work would be recognized. She said, "I planted my seed as well as I could."[4]

From Lithuania we travel south through Poland and Slovakia to arrive in Hungary to meet Zsuzsanna Budapest a.k.a. Z. Budapest or Z. A woman who, blinded by her own luminosity, has perhaps taken self-assuredness too far.

Witches are a curious bunch, in both senses of the word curious. We are strange, and we have a lot of questions. A persistent asker of Why, a Witch (or a child or a dissident) is often dismissed with "because it's always been that way." Well, historians are here to say no, these pieces of thousand- or ten-thousand-year-old evidence say different. We were different. Things CAN change. Now, gentle reader, close your eyes and take that idea to its ultimate, where discoveries are made and theories are put forth that shift our very understanding of the world we live in, of the values of humanity! And in this world-shattering place, we find a woman who went digging and digging and digging to unearth new truths about civilization. In this place we find archaeologist Marija, a small, demure seeker, challenging our accepted history of human life on this planet.

Let's start this story as *faaaaaarrrr* back as we can go. Somewhere between eleven thousand and three million years ago . . . OK, maybe that's too far back—let's start this story in 1994 with the death of the great goddess excavator Marija, whose *New York Times* obituary read, in part, as follows:

> *Perhaps her most controversial thesis was that the world was at peace during the Stone Age, when goddesses were worshiped and societies were centered on women. Then, the thesis went, about 6,000 years ago a culture in which the two sexes lived in harmony was shattered by patriarchal invaders, and the worship of life-giving goddesses was replaced by reverence for war-like gods. Her studies and interdisciplinary approach also created a new field, archeomythology.*
>
> *Skepticism about her thesis was widespread among scholars, but her ideas were welcomed by many feminists and by Joseph Campbell, the mythologist. Writing about [Marija's book]* The Language of the Goddess, *Gerda Lerner, a historian at the University of Wisconsin, said that although Marija's theory could never be proved, it could "challenge, inspire and fascinate" simply by providing an imaginative alternative to male-centered explanations.*[5]

This is the legacy I want for us all.

May we challenge, inspire, and fascinate! Marija said, "All I ever wanted was to find the truth,"[6] and she dug deep, literally and metaphorically, to uncover the truth. What comes through most in Marija's writing, in her books, is her diligence. She lovingly and thoughtfully illustrated and catalogued every scrap and fragment of ancient history she found to a nearly overwhelming degree, but more important than the finding, she sought context, real-life values for the objects she unearthed. She wanted to know not simply what they were but what they meant and how they spoke to the society that produced them. Her confidence in herself and in her findings wasn't a gift from the goddesses; it came from her steadfast devotion to information. She didn't just believe, she knew.

In her early life in Lithuania, she was a child of means and this enabled her to pursue an education that was not accessible to many people, let alone little girls. Marija's mother had a doctorate in ophthal-mology from the University of Berlin and was the first female physi-cian in Lithuania. Her father was also a doctor who published both a magazine and a newspaper. Marija said, "If you do not have a vision as a person, you cannot see much,"[7] which almost feels like an inside joke once you know her mother was an eye doctor.

In 1998, in honor of Marija, Joan Marler founded the Institute of Archaeomythology. She was Marija's personal editor and has engaged with Marija's ideas and Marija the person perhaps more than any other contemporary scholar. In "A Tribute to Marija Gimbutas" in *Sojourn* magazine, she described how Marija's childhood in Lithuania, seeing people work in traditional ways, sparked her interest in the ancient. Marija told her, "The old women used sickles and sang while they worked. The songs were very authentic, very ancient. At that moment I fell in love with what is ancient because it was a deep communication and oneness with Earth. I was completely captivated."[8]

The songs of the working women inspired Marija and showed her the depth of connection between our traditions and the Earth itself, the conversation between song and soil. At that moment, she fell in love with what is ancient, and this love would direct much of her life. But perhaps War, more so than Love, charted her first course. Marija was forced to flee Soviet-occupied/annexed Lithuania during World War II. She made her way to Germany where she continued her education at the University of Tübingen, eventually earning a PhD. In Marija's lifetime, Lithuania was ruled by Russia, then Poland, back to Russia, then Germany, and Russia again, so it makes sense that she would go looking for something more ancient than the occupations and borders she grew up with. A time before political jurisdictions.

Marija was obsessed with information and context. As a result she refused to focus on one discipline. She studied archaeology, mythol-ogy, linguistics, ethnology, and the history of religions—a mixture that would inform the basis for her expansive cultural theories. Each depart-ment offered new clues to the solving of humanity's mysteries.

In 1949 she moved to the United States and started working at Harvard University. Because she spoke multiple languages and had such an interdisciplinary knowledge base, she quickly became valuable to the Harvard faculty. In 1955 Marija was made a Fellow of Harvard's Peabody Museum. She joined the University of California, Los Angeles faculty in 1963, serving as professor of European archaeology until her retirement. But her heart belonged to her motherland despite her new American home. Europe called, and Marija would direct five major archaeological excavations in southeastern Europe in her time at UCLA. She said to Joan Marler, "Life twisted me like a little plant, but my work was continuous in one direction." And this is a great lesson for Litha. Life may twist, but the work is continuous.

It's fairly straightforward to dig up an excavation site, find a pot or a fragment of a pot, and announce: These people made pots. But Marija and others like her wanted, needed to know more. To infer. To build a story from a fragment. So the question becomes, how to describe a culture, purely from the material goods you find? How to find a pot and discover a whole society. It's tempting to hear this and think that somehow our goods define us, to let it fuel our collective mania for consumption. But in Marija's world you'd be better off carving sigils into the stuff you already have. Because the things that Marija found were simple objects but not simply objects. If you understand their language, they tell a story.

In her gorgeous and encyclopedic book *The Language of the Goddess*, Marija wrote, "The amazing repetition of symbolic associations through time and in all of Europe on pottery, figurines and other cult objects has convinced me that they are more than 'geometric motifs'; they must belong to an alphabet of the metaphysical."[9]

Witches know that symbols have power, but that power is so often corrupted or transferred. The swastika is perhaps the most notorious example: a Hindu sigil of divinity and spirituality, used to denote good luck and glad tidings, was stolen by an army. Now it is a symbol of hatred and violence. We see this happen, too, with the Pagan symbols that populate our Christian holidays. Stars, candles, trees. They are not for Nature, but for Nativity. Not for the sky, but for Santa Claus. It is easier to keep the symbols and remove or change the meaning to suit our need to control—and so it was, as Marija's theory contends, when the culture of war invaded the culture of peace. The symbols of matriarchy became symbols of patriarchy. She wrote, "The bull is linked with regeneration. [Yet the figure] is not a bull's head, but the female reproductive organs. The similarity is striking indeed."[10] And so it was that a uterus and ovaries connected by fallopian tubes, a symbol of fertility, became the bull's head—a symbol of virility and charging strength.

Joseph Campbell, another man whose name we're more likely to recognize than the woman who inspired him, contributed the foreward to Marija's delicious volume of drawings, photographs, and analysis, *The Language of the Goddess*. He equates Marija's findings to the Rosetta Stone, that they serve as keys to unlocking treasures of ancient thought. Campbell saw Marija's book as a call for the transformation of consciousness, revealing a possible age of harmony with Nature and peace in accordance with creative energies. He also famously inspired George Lucas in the creation of the *Star Wars* series, and I love this interplay of Marija's contribution making its way into both ancient goddess worship and futuristic science fiction.

In *The Language of the Goddess*, Marija wrote,

The reason for the great number and variety of Old European images lies in the fact that this symbolism is lunar and chthonic, built around the understanding that life on earth is in eternal transformation, in constant rhythmic change between creation and destruction, birth and death. The moon's three phases—new, waxing, and old [full]—are repeated in trinities or triple-functional deities that recall these moon phases: maiden, nymph, and crone; life-giving, death-giving, and transformational; rising, dying, and self-renewing. Life-givers are also death-wielders. Immortality is secured through innate forces of regeneration within Nature itself. The concept of regeneration and renewal is perhaps the most outstanding and dramatic theme we perceive in this symbolism. It seems more

*appropriate to view all of these Goddess images as aspects of the one
Great Goddess with her core functions—life-giving, death-wielding,
regeneration, and renewal. The obvious analogy would be to Nature
itself; through the multiplicity of phenomena and continuing cycles
of which it is made, one recognizes the fundamental and underlying
unity of Nature. The Goddess is immanent rather than transcendent
and therefore physically manifest.[11]*

In Marija's view, we are part of Nature, immortal. All aspects of one
great force of life, death, and renewal. The things that connect us exist
now just as they did, as they do, as they will . . . the things we share, the
Moon, Sun, Earth, and stars, are the same Moon and Earth that was
honored by the earliest humans. And they are all free to behold. Free to
connect with. Life and Death and multiplicity. There's no admission fee.
While we impose meaning and rules and tariffs and borders that only
serve to divide us, there shines the Sun, in perfect equality for everyone.

We see the alchemy of combination so many times in Witchcraft
and throughout this book—Pamela "Pixie" Colman Smith with her
illustration and divination, María Sabina with her poetry and magic
mushrooms, Zora Neale Hurston with her pen and traveling bone. The
work of Marija requires a conversation between archaeologists, linguists,
mythologists, physical anthropologists, students of religion, ancient historians, artists, poets, scientists, and Witches. She called this mixture
archaeomythology.

*There is a belief that religion cannot be reconstructed, that it's a
waste of time even to speak of religion because archaeologists cannot
do it. Maybe this is because they are not really trained. They are not
interested in mythology at all and are just seeing the material culture. They don't want to see anything else; they think they are safe in
reconstructing the ways of agriculture or how pottery was made, and
that satisfies them. In our days there are no people with vision. They
cannot go across the border of their discipline. Archaeology now is
interested mostly in excavation techniques and they want to be very
precise; the computer is used and all that. Of course, you can reach
some conclusions using statistics, but if you do not have a vision as*

a person—if you are not also a poet, or an artist—you cannot see much. You will be just a technician, and this is in most cases what happens.[12]

In archaeological digs of sites from the Bronze Age (3000 BC–1200 BC), one typically finds burial sites of dominant males surrounded by weapons. Many excavations of Neolithic sites had been done, but Marija took the extra step to study each excavation report in its original language. She had many questions and found few concrete answers, but it was clear to her that something distinctly different from what she'd seen from the Bronze Age was happening in the Neolithic period. So she resolved to do her own research. She found a sense of peacefulness from these early societies amid the prevalence of female figurines and repeating patterns. Her travels to sites all over Eastern Europe strengthened her theory and her unapologetic use of the word Goddess.

If all this prehistoric goddess stuff is starting to sound familiar, maybe you've already read the Yule chapter and met Monica Sjöö. Monica and her *The Great Cosmic Mother* coauthor Barbara Mor were deeply inspired by Marija and mentioned her several times in their book. In one excerpt they discussed the prevalence of phallic imagery in relation to this prehistoric Goddess.

> *These are not aggressive or misogynistic phallic images; rather, they seem to represent the phallus serving the Goddess and the life process of all. This is really shown in the Goddess-phallus stones, with the Goddess figure carved on phallic-shaped bones or rocks; this phallic form of the Goddess is found continuously from the Paleolithic through the Neolithic and into the "proto urban period" in Mesopotamia. Marija Gimbutas sees these Goddess-phallus icons, deriving from the Old Stone Age, as suggesting the "androgynous nature" of the Great Mother. This is so. They also suggest the potential unity of the sexes, in mutual love service, before their disastrous splitting apart by patriarchal misogyny and puritanical sex-codes.*[13]

Marija found statues that had BOTH male AND female traits: clay sculptures of plump women with phallic heads and folded arms. They are amazing works of art indeed, resembling both the feminine, bottom-heavy goddess and, to put it bluntly, dick and balls. This helped Marija emphasize co-creation—that the Great Goddess is All so of course exists as androgynous, nonbinary. Everything. Everything all at once.

People are using the term "nonbinary" a lot these days and while you might understand what that means culturally, maybe you're not familiar with what the words themselves mean and how they're used. You've probably heard people say "smash the binary" in the same breath as "smash the patriarchy," so I think it's worth going off on a patented Missing Witches tangent to talk about the Binary and how it got worked into contemporary culture.

When we say binary we mean things that are opposites or set up in opposition to one another. Either This or That. Day, Night. Black, White. Good, Bad. In the language of computers' binary code there are only 1s and 0s. 1 or 0. Nothing else. But to view the world in only sets of ones and zeros, thises and thats is, as we've seen over and over again, easy, uncomplicated, and deeply Dangerous. It sets us up as Oppositional. Day and Night are opposites sure, but can we all agree that some of the most magical times are held in those blurred spectral moments between the two? The dusk, the dawn, the in-between times.

The binary we are almost always talking about when we use this term "Nonbinary" is Man/Woman. Some people feel trapped by society's expectation that we fit into one and only one of two, only two, options: male OR female. The binary says Red or Blue only, but I don't want to live in a world without purple. Purple is my favorite color. When I first learned about deconstruction theories and movement, I felt like I had found a name for the cultural dissidence I feel like I was born with. They ask: does this mean what we think it means or what we're supposed to think it means? Let's take this apart and see. And they proved with literary and cultural criticism that meaning, all meaning, is imposed by our reading. That Humanity, that Art, that meaning is not Yes or No, but maybe, maybe, maybe, what do YOU think? Not just What does it mean, but How does it mean and Why does it mean AND CAN it mean something different?

Ultimately, binaric gender expression rules are all a bunch of baloney anyway. Historically, manly men have worn everything from wigs to robes to kilts—the first high heels were made for men. Everyone has body hair (OK, except for those with alopecia—shout out to my hairless homies). Pink is for Girls and Blue is for Boys is a pretty recent marketing construct. So look how you want, wear what you want, be who you want, choose your own name, and impose *your* meaning onto the world. And MORE IMPORTANTLY, let's all strive to create a world where EVERYONE is safe to do so. When we bask in the rays of the Litha Sun, let us accept everyone as they are, give birth to a new self, but skip the gender reveal party. Gender essentialism is so passé.

Marija often emphasized the egalitarian nature of the society she was theorizing. To her, Mother-goddess-worshipping society is not the same as a matriarchy. Matriarchal hierarchy structures are the same as a patriarchal society, not the actual opposite—she wrote: an egalitarian society is without hierarchy.[14]

In *The Living Goddesses* she wrote clearly that while the female form seems to dominate, this is simply because Birth was a most sacred mystery. In fact one of her most important discoveries was a birthing room. Walls painted red. Marija was a feminist, certainly, but she was not, as some have accused, a skewed, man-hating revisionist. She wrote,

> *The female body, and particularly its generative parts—vulva and uterus or womb—are predominant. [Because] The woman's body was regarded as parthenogenetic—that is, creating life out of itself. The female body gives evidence of maternity while the male body does not give evidence of paternity.*[15]
> *. . . The male element in symbolism was significant—male animals and humans stimulate and enhance life, particularly plant growth. They are [seen as] an important part in the process of becoming but do not actually create life. . . . In Neolithic art and myth, the male deities appear as PARTNERS of the goddesses.*[16]

In Marija's thinking, the role of the father in the creation of life in prehistoric antiquity may not have been valued, *only* because it was not understood. Nonetheless, everyone was seen as having a valuable role. Jacqui Beaumont found it problematic that Mother Earth is given "feminine" attributes—that femininity is painted as soft, nonaggressive, compliant, but Mother Earth is as destructive as she is creative. As rigid as she is supple. As terrifying as she is nurturing. Witch archaeologist Vanessa Oliver-Lloyd reminded me that Matriarchy isn't synonymous with Peace. That an ancient matrilineal society of Québec's Iroquois people would capture men from other tribes to replace fallen warriors.[17] What Marija claimed to have found was not matriarchal or hierarchical, but Egalitarian. If we flip the binary instead of dismantling it, if the oppressed become the oppressors, we will have solved nothing. Us versus Them is tempting. It gives us a sense of power and superiority. But the Witch rejects this temptation, knowing that we are all One.

We've pondered so many times, on the nature of patriarchy and how it started and why. What happened??!!? It's just like some baffling decisions got made at some point in prehistory that people and the Earth should be conquered and subjugated. That women should be silent. And we've all seen some caveman cartoon of him whacking a cave woman over the head with a club and dragging her back to his cave. We've been led to believe that it's just always been that way. Man strong. Woman weak—the female of the species forced into servitude to pay for her Protection against a cruel world. Marija is perhaps the closest I've come to getting some kind of answer to our question: Has it just always been this way? Marija is here to say, emphatically, no, these pieces of ten-thousand-year-old evidence say different. It's a resounding No. It. Has. Not. Always. Been. This. Way. A peaceful, Earth-connected society is possible. An egalitarian society is or, at very least, WAS possible. In her Neolithic digs, Marija found thousands of artifacts but not one weapon. Not a single tool of war. A society that was herding animals, practicing agriculture, creating pottery and art, had NO USE for weapons. No concept of War.

Marija's work gave birth to a whole new incarnation of feminism and feminist spirituality. Science and history to back up the notion that we can live together in peace, equality, and harmony.

We always say, when you go looking for Witches, you find them everywhere. Wonderful, wacky, and wise Witches. You can't research a Witch without finding at least two more. I was delighted to stumble upon an interview with Marija conducted earnestly and eagerly by a woman named Starr Goode in a YouTube upload of a cable access program, *The Goddess in Art,* that ran from 1986 until 1991. "Dedicated to the Return of the Goddess, the series explored the legacy of this oldest tradition in art as well as feminist spirituality in contemporary art. The moderator, Starr Goode, interviewed scholars to uncover Her suppressed history and artists who were inspired by a radical re-imagining of the feminine."[18] The show is comical in its visual datedness but that's what's so fun about it. It's a time capsule that for me, as a child of the 80s brings magical crashing waves of nostalgia, but the content still resonates with me as a Witch of the twenty-first century. In the archaeology of digging through the infinite strata of the internet, there are many, many treasures to discover.

And *The Goddess in Art* series feels like an archaeological prize find to be placed among Marija's unearthed carvings in the continuing history of goddess worship. In her notes for the Marija episode, Starr wrote, "One of the greatest scholars of the twentieth century, Marija through her work as an archaeologist uncovered the symbolic language of the Goddess and provided a foundation for feminist spirituality."[19] In the interview/slideshow, Marija reminds me of my Eastern European family: stern, almost cold, but there is a warmth there, a determination in her voice as she says, "The image of death is combined with the symbols of regeneration. That is continuous through time for millennia."[20] Death is continuously combined with regeneration. In a way, Marija was the ultimate binary smasher. Male Female, Past Future, Life Death.

In the final chapter of *The Living Goddesses,* Marija returns to her homeland and the ancient beliefs of the people by the Baltic Sea. She considers the Balts to be the "last pagans of Europe" since Christianity didn't make its mark in that area until the fourteenth century. The Balts had a pantheon of deities, not entirely dissimilar to the African Yoruba Orishas, or the Greek gods and goddesses, each being connected to an aspect of Nature. One could connect with the deities through a rock. The goddesses were seen in the animals and in the stones.

In the customs she describes, one kisses the Earth as they would kiss their mother, in the morning and in the evening. And again, as with the Orisha, many deities simply changed form in order to sustain their devotees' beliefs despite Christian colonialism. The Virgin Mary became a stand-in for the pagan goddesses of the past. Marija made an extensive list of "surviving" goddesses in this final chapter, including a familiar name, Baba Yaga, known in Russian folklore as a Witch or even an ogre who eats children. In Marija's telling, Baba Yaga is a Slavic goddess of Death and Regeneration. Still a terrifying figure, but Marija reminded us that the Slavic word "baba" means "grandmother," which softens our perception. In Marija's list, the goddess who sings out to me is Ragana. She still exists in Lithuanian folklore. Degraded by the violent push of Christianity, she is the Witch, and her name remains a Lithuanian curse word. Ragana is, again, nonbinary—a goddess of both death and regeneration. She is lady, toad, bird, dog, and snake, singular and multiple. In some incarnations she appears as a beautiful nude maiden, at other times, a dangerous hag. She is the balancer of all life energy. She is the Witch who knows the magic of herbs. She is healer and destroyer.[21]

I think this description works for Marija too. Marija destroyed our old way of thinking, our old perceptions of what is ancient. She destroyed the Always Has Been narrative of the patriarchy. But with her work, she also healed that part in all of us that yearns to know that sometime, somewhere, peace was possible. Equality was possible. It is healing to know that if we lived that way once, we can live that way again. In harmony. With no need for weapons and no tools of war.

In the afterword to *The Living Goddesses*, editor Miriam Robbins Dexter wrote of Marija's impact:

In the last decade of her life, Marija Gimbutas' own ecological and spiritual beliefs found resonance in the growing spiritual and ecological movements in the United States and abroad. Her books, as well as her presence, became a strong focus in ecological movements—so much so that many people, without perhaps intending to, learned quite a bit of archaeology. Marija Gimbutas' philosophies—describing a world where men and women might live in harmony with one another and with their environment—found a home in the hearts of thousands of people, helping to shape the ideas of a new generation of ecologists. Women and men in the fields of ecological science, anthropology, folklore, and mythology, as well as archaeology have been touched and transformed by the works of Marija Gimbutas.[22]

Marija has had a lot of detractors over the years. Every strong woman is a Witch and she is always hunted, right? I've seen her work described as "off the wall," "eccentric," "hippie," and even "horsefeathers." As long as Marija was investigating the Bronze Age, she was a respected scholar. In her assessment of the Neolithic period, it became clear to Marija that femininity was valued and that Earth-based spirituality was central to this society, and she started using the word "goddess." These peace, love, and harmony theories made it imperative for the capitalist heteropatriarchy to dismiss and demean her other academic work. One of her biggest and most scornful critics was Colin Renfrew, a geneticist who claimed that such a large, ancient society as Marija suggested, based on her findings of recurring symbols throughout Eastern and all of Europe, was impossible. Turns out, it just took awhile for Science to catch up to what Marija already knew. We now have the technology to analyze DNA, to map and trace the movement of genetics. In 2017 Colin took to the stage at the University of Chicago and declared, "Marija's hypothesis has been magnificently vindicated."[23]

Marija was right.

She told a colleague that it might take decades, but eventually the value of her work would be recognized. In a letter she wrote to her old Lithuanian colleague and professor, she wrote, "I planted my seed as well as I could."[24]

And that goes for you, too, Witches, planting your seeds of crazy ideas! It might take decades. You may not live to see how you changed the world. You may never know how The Magic of You can ripple waves into the future. So plant your seed as well as you can. Live your truth, even if no one gets you right now, and take some advice from Marija.

Emboldened by that great sunny Litha spirit of self-assurance, may her words resonate with you, shake you out of preconceptions of prehistory, and thrust you headlong into your brand-new day on this ancient Earth: "Don't be sheep! Do what you want to do. It's very important to be mobilized, to have determination to do what is meaningful. If you feel a need to do something, you must do it!"[25]

I fully endorse Marija's message here and would add: If you feel a need to do something, you must do it . . . with compassion. Because our next Witch is powerful and brilliant, but I fear she is missing one of the key features of the modern-day Witch: radical compassion. Radical compassion manifests as deep love, an awareness of how our words and actions affect other people, that those effects can ripple through eternity. No change is too small. Maybe you smile at a stranger on the street, they feel good so they give their next server a really nice tip, then that person has a little extra money to get their kid a new shirt for school, then that kid has a bit of extra confidence so he talks to the new kid in class and they become lifelong friends. In my imaginary world those two kids go on to encourage each other in science and as a team, they cure cancer. All because you smiled. But the reverse is also true. Maybe you hurt someone, so then they hurt someone else.

Z. Budapest has been labeled and embraced the label of TERF— Trans Exclusive Radical Feminist—a feminist who doesn't accept that trans women are women. We at Missing Witches are not that. INclusivity is our mandate and our guiding principle, so I was disappointed to find more rot amid my ancestors' bones. In the spirit of Safe Spaces of all kinds, we want to make the Missing Witches Coven, in all of its incarnations, as safe as we can—a place where we can talk about issues from a core ethic of radical compassion. Where it's safe to ask questions, make mistakes, or respectfully disagree. Learn. Grow. Change our minds, change the world, name and shame the failings of our ancestors but retain the ability to separate the toxic from the healing.

Our goal is to learn from their missteps, why they happen, and do better, without throwing away the lessons they have to teach, recognizing how experience shapes point of view. As anti-racism author and activist

Layla Saad wrote of her work, "The loftier goal is to help us to become better ancestors for those who will come after us."[26] This is another link between the Witch and the artist, organizer, protester, dissident. We see the world as it could be, instead of how it is. This vision drives us. It drives us to heal the wounds our ancestors have inflicted or endured. The Witch and the Activist both believe that we can change the world.

This story got very personal for me, very fast. I read that in the aftermath of the Hungarian Revolution of 1956, Z. Budapest walked from Hungary to a refugee camp in Austria. And in the aftermath of the Hungarian Revolution, my father had walked from Hungary to a refugee camp in Austria. It's possible that this Witch walked beside my father on this traumatic road, and maybe they made eye contact, and maybe there was comfort in that. It makes me feel connected to her in the same way I feel connected to my own family. Those whom I love despite their shady politics and clashing personalities. I'm a child of a not altogether friendly divorce, my parents were constantly talking contradictory smack about each other.

In a way, it did me a small favor because I learned early to make up my own mind. To do my own research and draw my own conclusions, to accept the good and do my best not to dwell on the bad, to snatch the teachable from the jaws of the traumatic. Z. Budapest could have been my aunt; her brother and my father were both named Imre. So I'm approaching this story the way we do with distant and problematic relatives at weddings and funerals. . . . Agree on some issues, speak up when we disagree on others, connect based on what we have in common and what we admire about problematic Auntie ZsuZsu, without holding our tongues on the bad.

Once you learn her name, you don't stop seeing it. She pops up constantly in feminist documentaries and Witchy reading lists. As a lesbian radical feminist, she lit up the 1970s, manifesting the Witch as author, activist, journalist, playwright, and songwriter who was arrested for doing tarot readings and took that battle to the California Supreme Court. Love her or hate her, Z. Budapest is a firebrand and contemporary Witchcraft has felt her heat.

In her autobiography, *My Dark Sordid Past as a Heterosexual,* Z. Budapest recalled driving to a speaking engagement and passing rows of demonstrators bearing placards with phrases like "Death to the Witch":

> *I had been invited to the library to give a lecture about the Goddess. My need for political freedom had brought me from Hungary to the United States. My desire for religious freedom brought me to the Goddess, the cure for the fear of God, a cure that I have been talking about to anyone who will listen ever since. . . .*
>
> *But to a lot of people, the very concept of the Great Goddess is the greatest heresy, and the greatest threat to male domination of women. Once women discover what has been taken from them they want to reclaim Her. When women know their Goddess it is impossible to enslave them. Once again I was being hunted.*[27]

Every strong woman is a Witch and she is always hunted.

The staff at the library had noticed an increase in teens checking out books about Witchcraft. A friend of Z.'s worked at this library and had the idea to bring Z., a "real Witch," to the library to give a lecture and answer questions. She photocopied a picture of a black cat from Z.'s *The Holy Book of Women's Mysteries,* added the words "Witchcraft" and "Goddess Lecture" plus the date and time, and one teen took this flyer home to his militant Christian mother. And the mother took the flyer to her minister. And the minister thought the poster was, to quote Z., "a splendid opportunity for a crusade against Satan."[28] It turned out that many militant Christians saw this little library lecture as an event worthy of protest. *The 700 Club,* a Christian television show, organized buses to bring in protesters from all over Northern California. Z. wrote, "Their hatred was a potent weapon. By definition I was evil and it was God's will to destroy me. 'Thou shalt not suffer a Witch to live!' one of the posters proclaimed. To them, I was not a human being, but a dehumanized 'Witch,' much easier to hate."[29]

And this is how it works with all forms of prejudice. Once you have an Us and a Them, dehumanization is easy. Thinking that because someone is different than you, that they are *less than* you becomes easy.

Z. was born in Hungary in 1940 to a long line of nasty (in the Donald Trump sense—nasty meaning strong, bold, loud) women. Her mother was a sculptor of goddesses. Her Granny Ilona was a suffragist who gave motivational speeches and wrote for the national Women's paper, preaching Women's Liberation before women had the vote.

In *Summoning the Fates: A Generational Woman's Guide to Destiny and Sacred Transformation*, Z. wrote:

> *During the Hungarian revolution in October of 1956, I was on my way to a demonstration. When you are sixteen, being part of a collective uprising is very exciting. . . .*
>
> *When I finally crossed the bridge, I heard shots. That wasn't too unusual. It was a revolution, and people had been shooting off guns in celebration for days. But when I turned the corner to the plaza, everything was silent. Too silent. Instead of a crowd of cheering, shouting people, the plaza was covered with bodies. All those who had made it to the plaza on time had been shot down. The blood was still dripping onto the stones. I stood stock-still, realizing that I had indeed arrived too late—too late for the massacre.*
>
> *In Hungarian the Fates are* Sors Istennök, *the destiny goddesses. But their Latin name, the Parcae, means "those who spare," and indeed my life was spared by them that day. We all have stories about incidents during which that weird feeling, usually accompanied by fear or frustration, has come over us, and it turned out to save us in some way.[30]*

My father's take on the revolution, skewed by time and deeply personal experience, was heartbreaking in his retelling. He lived with me in his final years, and I still go searching for snippets of old conversations in bowls of chicken paprikash. . . . He had dementia so I'm working with the memories he lost. He told me the Hungarian revolutionaries managed to rise up, free political prisoners, hold down the Russian Army. They called out to the rest of the world, "come and help us, we have them! But we can't hold them down for long. Come help us out!!" And no one came. No one came and no one helped. So the revolutionaries, mostly university students, the young, bright future of Hungary, exhausted and outmatched, fled or were killed. That's how my father told it. Bitterly and with disappointment. Sometimes I think maybe a hint of that bitterness and distrust made its way into my Hungarian blood and manifested in an unwillingness to ask for help. I learned too early that it's infinitely easier to struggle alone than to ask for help and be ignored.

Z. Budapest wrote, "In our family, being a Hungarian was the Religion. You had to know your history, honor ancient feuds and treaties, and revel in being a Magyar. This was the best and most cursed of all nations one could get born into, but also the most magical. Situated at the crossroads between the steppes of the east and the nations of the west, we had been regularly overrun by bigger nations."[31]

I had to laugh when I read this. I heard that message growing up so many times. It was a point of pride that Hungary had been overrun so many times, but the language, the country still existed. Hungarian Hungarians persisted. And maybe there's something there that informs Z. Budapest's abject *stubbornness*. For better and for worse.

My mom was born in Southern Ontario, my father is Hungarian, his second wife was from Venezuela, and my husband was born in Scotland. And we live in the woods of Franco Québec. There's no room for nationalism in this family. It's crazy that my life exists at all. So I often wonder, is it fate? Or just a single random endpoint in the chaos of dispersion. Maybe people with dislocation in their blood contend more with the notion of providence than those with a clear and local history. Maybe being forced to leave her homeland fueled Z. Budapest's repeated consideration of destiny.

She wrote, "What rules our lives? Is it chance, or choice, or something else? Is it the stars, or that strange force people call Lady Luck, or Fortuna? Since the beginning of time, people have tried to figure out what determines their destiny. In Hungary we have a saying, '*Ember tervez, Isten végez*'—'Humans plan, God finishes.'"[32]

"*Ember tervez, Isten végez.*" Maybe it was being forced to leave but being Hungarian, and these northern Eastern European roots come up in her writing often. She is so fiercely Hungarian that she named herself after its capital city. Born Zsuzsanna Emese Mokcsay, she took the name "Budapest" and wears it as a badge of honor, defiance, persistence.

She wrote of the three maidens, the three fates, sitting by a deep well in a deep cavern in the mythology of Northern Europe. In Z.'s view, they are the source of all other triple goddesses and the pattern for the Maiden, Mother, and Crone. Beginning, Middle, and End.

When we summon the Fates, we call them out from their deep hiding place in the unconscious. . . . There are no guarantees with this force. But there are certain practices, a kind of etiquette of interaction with the Fates, that have worked for people before. We call it the technology of the sacred. "Sacred" means that we are speaking not of a technology of machines but of souls.[33]

In Austria, she finished high school and attended the University of Vienna on a scholarship. Landing in the United States in 1959, Z. Budapest studied in Chicago where she met and married Tom, the father of her children. After her two sons were born, Z. Budapest started using birth control and told this to a priest during confession. The priest flew into a rage and told her that this was an unforgivable sin.

Z. Budapest wrote, "This sounded a lot like what my father had said when he was guarding my virginity, only now it was my womb. 'I think you are a pompous ass!' I told the astonished Father Taylor. 'You know nothing about menstruating, or getting knocked up, or birthing children, much less raising them. You don't even know about sex!' 'The Church says—' he gulped. 'The men who run the Church say,' I interrupted. 'You say, you ignorant, self-absorbed, over-served men! You have nothing to offer women but grief. I will never come back to your Church.' As I left I lit a last candle for the Blessed Mother. 'Please, don't let them ever humiliate me again!' Then I left the church, and the Church, forever."[34]

On this day, she says, she became a feminist. For better and for worse, she solidified the bond between Goddess, Womanhood, Feminism, and the Womb, and a scorn for anyone without these organs who dared to tell her what a woman is or does or should be.

Her mother-in-law loved being a grandmother so Z. was often free to take small acting and modeling jobs. She learned improv at the famed Second City. Then the family moved to New York.

Fast-forward through run-ins with Johnny Carson, Harry Belafonte, TV, film, theater, her husband's affair, their divorce, and his remarriage, and Z. is on a bus to Toronto to hitchhike across Canada. Through the bus window, she watched as the city disappeared, convincing herself that this was just a short trip. Instead she went all the way west and all the way south, eventually landing in California.

At a certain point she realized: "Men just didn't deliver love to me anymore."[35]

By 1970 she was an out and proud lesbian and Witch living aloud in Los Angeles. In 1971 she founded the Susan B. Anthony Coven #1, a women-only, Witches' coven. If you female identifiers have ever planned a girls night, you might understand this feeling. A lot of women, especially at the time of Z. Budapest's early activities, were struggling to get their voices heard. They were (and are) breaking into male-dominated realms and dreaming of a place where they'd be less likely, maybe, to be interrupted, dismissed, ignored, talked over, or straight-up demeaned. Patriarchy is a hard slog. It is violent. It creates a culture of fear and capitalizes on that fear. Z. had seen this through a domineering father, a domineering state, and a domineering church—an oppression that she boiled down to one thing: men.

Even Wicca itself and the neo-pagan renaissance is largely credited to a man: Gerald Gardner. And elsewhere there are weird, ugly stories about unsettling, hierarchical, dogmatic, even exploitative New Age covens where ideas like Sexual Freedom were used to manipulate and abuse, rather than to heal.

Janet L. Jacobs did a study "The Effects of Ritual Healing on Female Victims of Abuse: A Study of Empowerment and Transformation" analyzing the effects of ritual healing on women who have been victims of abuse, incest, rape, and battering. "The study was conducted through participant observation of a women's spirituality group. The focus of the analysis is on the process of empowerment as it is experienced in a ritual context that provides a means for cathartic expression as well as participant identification with female symbols of power. The findings of this study suggest that women-centered rituals are effective in reducing fear, releasing anger, increasing one's sense of power, and improving the overall mental health of those who have experienced the trauma of victimization."[36]

It's from this perspective that Dianic Wicca was born.

First problem. Z. Budapest named the coven after Susan B. Anthony, who is another great example of a person who goes in the *welllllllllll* category. Yes, Susan B. Anthony worked tirelessly as a suffragist, but her quest for women's right to vote in particular contained extremely racist rhetoric—a reaction to the prospect of Black men being given the vote before white women. But Susan B. Anthony was also an abolitionist and anti-slavery activist from the age of seventeen. We could go back and forth all day. But what we find is another problematic ancestor who, like many "heroes," did some great stuff and said some terrible shit. In these two, we find women who rank humans in their quest for equality. Women arrested for acting on their beliefs. Susan B. Anthony and Zsuzsanna Budapest have a lot in common.

Z. Budapest will go down in history as the last person to have been arrested and tried for Witchcraft in the United States. She was arrested for doing a tarot reading in her own shop, the Feminist Wicca, in 1975, and tried and convicted. Z. Budapest appealed her conviction on the grounds that tarot readings are a form of spiritual counseling for women within the context of their religion. It took nine years in courts, but she was acquitted and better yet, the laws against "fortune-telling" were struck down. So if you are an entrepreneurial Witch, you can thank Auntie ZsuZsu for blazing that trail. The formal establishment of the Susan B. Anthony Coven was also a reaction to the charges—her defense team called her the first Witch prosecuted since Salem. Their tactic was to establish Dianic Wicca as a bona fide religion, making Z.'s conviction explicitly unconstitutional and in violation of the California Freedom of Religion Act.

Z. was also instrumental in the creation of Take Back the Night marches. I remember attending a Take Back the Night march as a teen in my hometown back in the '90s, and even then I remember arguments over the fact that men were allowed to attend the rally, but the march itself was for only women and children. It was a symbol of Women's Power, what we were capable of doing and being on our own, even in the face of fear. More than twenty years later, that conversation has become even more complicated, more nuanced. We as a culture are moving toward a place where binaries no longer make sense—or maybe back to a place where we recognize that binaries never made sense. Binaries beget hierarchies. They are an easy and lazy way to classify and label people—at best, incomplete and, at worst, dangerous.

"All Women" or "Women Only" sounds fine in a healing context until we have to decide what a woman *IS*. We are all so much more than just the sum of our parts. Here's what we know: Z. has been explicit about her denial of trans women into her Dianic, all-women's coven. In her view, trans women do not fit the genetic, biological, or experiential prerequisites for womanhood. But we also know that at the time of this writing, 2018 was the deadliest year for assaults against transgender Americans since the Human Rights Campaign began keeping records.[37] Transgender deaths by fatal violence have increased during each of the last three years.

AND we know that the Gay Panic defense is a real thing. A trans woman named Islan Nettles was beaten to death in the street by a man whose friends had mocked him for flirting with her. The killer confessed to killing her, pleaded guilty to manslaughter, and was ultimately sentenced to just twelve years in prison. The mitigating circumstance being that Nettles was trans, and her killer just freaked out. This happened in 2013. It's not a history lesson. It's Current Events and Islan's is just one story of many.

It costs nothing to welcome a trans person into a Coven, into womanhood. But to exclude them in this society is deadly. To exclude people keeps them on the outside and allows for the type of thinking that allows the panic defense. When you exclude someone, you make them a freak, which means it's totally normal and righteous to be freaked out by them, and by extension, totally normal to react to that fear with violence. Exclusion is deadly.

Things came to a head for Z. at a public pagan convention, PantheaCon, in 2011, when she held a Ritual for cis women only. Pagan

writer Peter Dybing led a protest and later wrote: "It is time for compassion in this discussion, time for the Trans community to sit and listen
with open hearts to the pain of women who have suffered abuse at the
hands of men, time for the Dianic community to listen with open hearts
to the Trans communities experience of violence and exclusion. I believe
all of my sisters have the ability to tap into the energy of the divine and
approach these issues with respect, compassion and the intent to heal."[38]

There is no one, singular, shared experience of being a woman. It is
different for Every One. We as humans are condemned in a way, to live
our lives from our own perspective, but when we listen to other people
and look to them for their *difference* of experience, this is how we expand
our world view past the boundaries of our own vision. It is astral pro-
jection of perception. Listening to people with differing experiences is
fucking MAGIC. We can listen and be transported out of our narrow
field of view. We can connect on what we share *and* what we don't! We
can say with eyes wide: I never thought of it that way!!

I was raised in a very gynocentric environment. I had a sister, my
mother had a sister, my grandmother had a sister. My father moved out
when I was six so I lived much of my life surrounded, almost entirely, by
women. And I was raised feminist. So despite the fact that I am six feet
tall, have a deep voice, broad shoulders and body hair, thick eyebrows,
androgynous clothes, and a bravado that one woman after seeing my
rock 'n' roll band said was "like a man" (for the record and in her defense,
English was not her first language and she meant it as a compliment and
I took it as one) . . . despite the fact that I often get misgendered (called
"Sir" on the phone or in shops) or have my sex, the status of my genitals
questioned by curious children and men, I myself, personally, have never
questioned that I am a woman. I don't know how it feels to be trans. I
don't understand what it truly means. But I don't need to understand.
I don't need empathy to have compassion.

We as a society need to get to a place where our differences are revered
and not feared, where we can love WITHOUT understanding. But that's
easy for me to say. The dumb luck of being born white, middle class, cis,
het, and Canadian. If I was hurt or sick, I had access to free health care.

My public-school teachers were mostly good. The system was set up, for the most part, to protect me. The world, for the most part, IS my safe space. Little things that add up. I can kiss my partner in public without fear of judgment or attack. My identification matches my identity. Most people just see me as a "regular" woman. I do not take this for granted.

I respect so much the need and desire for safe spaces, especially for people who feel alienated by the world at large. A place free of judgments and devil's advocates. Free from scorn or the threat of violence. A place where you are One and not The Other. So I understand why Zsuzsanna Budapest felt compelled to create a Safe Space Coven for Women. I do not understand why she feels she gets to decide what being a woman is, what it means and, most importantly, who qualifies. In *The Holy Book of Women's Mysteries,* she wrote, "That is a definition of the Female. A definition of Womanhood: strength and beauty combined."[39]

And in her invitation to the now infamous PantheaCon ritual, she invoked "the beauty and grace of the feminine form in all of her infinite variety."[40] Infinite variety. As I look at her and at my own problematic ancestors, I worry that all her good legacy work will be lost to her stubbornness on this one issue. Is it that same laudable stubbornness that fueled her decade-long state Supreme Court battle to legalize Witchcraft that is also fueling her shameful trans exclusion? And if so, what do we make of this stubbornness? . . . It's almost as if nothing, no one, no single quality even, is inherently good or inherently bad. We are defined more by *doing* than *being*. And in the opposition of Good and Bad, we are all nonbinary.

When asked about her choice to name her coven after Susan B. Anthony, Z. Budapest said, "We chose her name because [she] was a suffragist whom we all respected. She had her limitations. She was not perfect. And neither are we."[41]

Well Z.'s darn right about that. None of us are perfect. But we must consider: what will our legacy be?

Z. Budapest is alive and well, continuing her practice and boycotting PantheaCon. So what is the message here? To segregate ourselves until we are alone? To curate the people around us to the point where we have only a mirror? To take Witchcraft and Womanhood back to the dark corners because we can't agree on who is allowed in? Funny me, I thought the whole point was that we are all One. Patriarchy divides, I thought, Witchcraft Connects. Patriarchy is competition, I thought, Witchcraft is collaboration.

I told you this shit got personal, so what does it all mean for me? I went looking for the Witches I'd been missing, I went digging in Hungary for my geographical Boszorkány[42] heritage of goddess and craft and destiny and roots, and I was so excited to find this feminist force of nature and Fate who had shared part of my father's history. Who had walked the same traumatic path as my own father. I went digging and I found Z.

Years ago, I took my father back to his hometown in Hungary. This was after his dementia diagnosis, after he had come to live with me. Every day, sometimes every hour, he would ask, "When are we going to Szeged?" I knew it wouldn't be long before he'd be incapable of travel, so I took all the money I had and poured it into plane tickets to fly to a place I had never been, so I could go for the first time, with my father, to the place where our blood came from. Over dinner on our first night in Hungary, my father's brother, my uncle, went on an insulting, sexist monologue about my mother, whom he hadn't seen in over thirty years. He claimed she wasn't a good cook, and she dared to have a job, so she wasn't a good mother. I loudly announced that as a working woman, I would pay for dinner.

We left the restaurant and I cried in the streets of Szeged. The feeling I had was similar to the feeling of discovering some of Z.'s politics: Why? Just *why*? I came all this way to see you. I was so ready to connect . . . Healers and scientists can harness the power of natural poisons and turn them into medicines. It's a very Witchy thing to do. We make medicine from poison, Art out of grief, grab calm from inside a storm . . . So what do we, as Witches, do with these disappointments? These poisons hidden among the flowers? These thorns among the roses? We harness their sharpness and power to carve a Welcome Sign and hang it up on our doors, on the Missing Witches' door and in the doorway of our hearts.

Come inside. Join our circle. You are welcome here.

If you, like me, are the lucky bearer of Cis/Het/White Privilege, then you also carry the shame of our shared colonial history. When we dig up our ancestors' bones, sometimes we find rot. In these times, we thank our ancestors for their service in bringing us into creation. Then we can leave ancestor *worship* behind and focus on the real act of love: ancestor *healing*. Being better ancestors. Our healing work becomes taking on the education of ourselves and others, doing the labor of making things right.

It is our duty to balance the scales in any way we can: donate, demonstrate, celebrate, LISTEN. To use our privilege to erase our privilege. Jacqui Beaumont told me, "The best thing we can do is just to listen . . . If we're more actively listening, we're seeing things deeper than what they are on the surface."[43] If the Witch has one goal, it is to see things deeper. Like Marija, the depth of our vision can dictate the breadth of our contribution.

We are like the Sun. Powerful. We can produce and nourish. But we can also burn. Our power isn't true power unless we can control it. Otherwise we might hurt people without even knowing the pain we have caused. Because what we say has power and cannot be unsaid. What we do has power and cannot be undone. Every action has a rippling effect, for better or for worse. The tiniest act of kindness or unkindness can make waves into the farthest unknown parts of the universe. At Litha and always, no love is too deep, and no change is too small. We hold in our hearts all the potential of the Sun. To create, to nurture, and to destroy. What will our legacy be?

Ritual

Before you begin, stand in front of a mirror. Look into your own eyes and say out loud, "I love you." If you feel you don't believe it, say it again and again and again. Say it until you are laughing.

Use the light of the Litha Sun, the strength of the solstice, to see yourself. See your heat. See how you glow. See your own incandescence as you smile.

Now, with this self-love in your heart, create a self-portrait. This can be done as a drawing or a poem or point form notes—you can even use your phone to take a selfie.

See that you are made of elements: Earth, Air, Fire, Water, (bone, breath, energy, blood) working together in the meaty electronic system of your body.

Now transform your portrait. You can write on top of your poem with a different colored ink, you can paint over your drawing. You can burn your portrait or submerge it under water. If you're using your phone, do not burn or submerge it (safety first). Instead, use an app to digitally draw or write on your selfie. See how you can be transformed. See how you can transform your very self.

This ritual can also be done as a group with your coven (friends). Express your love of each other, then draw a portrait of one of your coven members. Make sure everyone is both an artist and a muse. Now take the portrait of you and transform it as instructed above, or use your imagination to change it in any way you can think of! See how you can transform yourself beyond the perceptions of how people see you.

Since Litha is the longest day of the year, you may have time for another ritual. If so, consider calling the corners and writing down your own personal definition of success. This, again, can be done alone or as a group. Blessed be your Litha.

Speak these words outside, loudly with your face to the Sun, at noon if you can. (Litha is not the day to be concerned about what the neighbors think.) If you are reading this from inside the broom closet and being loud isn't safe for you, then whisper, but do make noise loud enough for at least your own ears to hear:

INCANTATION
I am here.
I am shining.
I am whole.
I dig for Truth.
I plant my seeds as well as I can.
I dim my light for no one.
Today, I recognize my own value and the value of others.
Eventually, everyone will.

LITHA CAROL

D
Thank you, Sun!
A
Our thanks to the Sun!
D
Thank you Sun!
A
We give our thanks to the Sun.
G   A   D   G
You shine shine shine shine shine and so do I
G   A   D
Glory Litha time!
D
Thank you, Sun!
A
Our thanks to the Sun!
D
Thank you Sun!
A
We give our thanks to the Sun.
G   A
Summer Solstice
D   G
is powerful and so are we
G A
Joyful Litha
D   G
Light the way for us to see
G A
Oh merry Litha
D   G
shine shine shine and so do we
G   A   D
All Glory to the sun!!

You can listen to a recording of this Solstice Carol on missingwitches.com.

6

Lughnasadh

This circle is led by Risa

IN THE HEAT OF SUMMER, BALANCED BETWEEN THE SOLSTICE AND EQUINOX, WE CELEBRATE TOGETHER AGAIN. We take pleasure in the feeling of the season at its height, and we begin to feel the pull, tipping gently back toward the dark as the days creep a little shorter and the cold whispers in at the edges of the evening. At Lughnasadh, or Lammas, we feel the throbbing life of the Earth around us most palpably. This is the time to stretch our strong roots into the world around us that is our body. On the cross-quarter days between solar events, we can sanctify a space for our lunar mind—communal mind, just beyond the grasp of our ego in default mode—to remind us that we are connected to that Earth body all the time. And on Lughnasadh, as the light of summer is harvested, we can harvest and ignite our own power to heal and protect it.

Once, on Lughnasadh, we made a fire that licked three feet above our heads and consumed an entire birch tree—a full foot around—that had fallen, rotten, across our beach. We roasted fresh corn in husks in the fire. When we shucked the corn we tied the golden husks into the shapes of men.

I had recently escaped a con man to build a home. And finally, for the first time in my life, I felt safe. I was with a group of good men: queer and straight, Witches and amenable atheists. The two are not mutually exclusive—Witches and atheists—and good men have always fought and celebrated alongside feminists of all genders for a world without the violence done by patriarchy to us all. Good men have always been there, fighting the choking saddle and bridle of patriarchy's limited roles for them—provider, warrior, weapon, tool—that wants to break the tender shoots of their own lunar minds and ride them into the ground. Queer people have always put their bodies on the line—sometimes by choice and sometimes by necessity—to defend the sacred idea of a safe space beyond the domination of simple, brutal binaries.

That Lughnasadh, around the beach fire, everyone brought their own sorrows and triumphs to the act of twisting, burning, and releasing. The corn figures symbolized acts of cruelty, disrespect, betrayal, injustice. They symbolized the way greed and ego make puppets, poppets, steal souls. We threw them one by one on the fire, in silence, and watched them burn.

And then we made more, laughing and eating corn, and we burned them all.

Finally, we crowned the towering pyre with the handmade, blue wool slippers of a con man. Someone who had—months before—torn up my life. We lay the tired, knit things on the raging flames, and as they were consumed, we made up a song of thanks to the grandmother who had made them.

We free ourselves by sending love to the people who stitch.[1]

We call out to the endless weaving that continues right alongside the rent and the tear.

Lughnasadh is a pagan holiday, with Celtic origins, celebrating the grain harvest. On August 1, you reap your grains and corn, make loaves of bread from the living body of the Earth and thank them for their death, and know and pray that the grain will rise again next year and that you'll be there to see it. Then with your bread and corn you might gather together by a bonfire and honor Lugh, the craftsman god, iron smith, master mason, and builder, maker of the tools that built a home on the land.

Though actually, the mythological origin of this Celtic holiday was a day Lugh dedicated to honoring his foster mother Tailtiu. Tailtiu, who died of exhaustion after clearing the plains of Ireland for planting. She is the goddess figure who stands in for all the women who cleared the ground and left all their strength in it.

In her *The Blue Jay's Dance: A Memoir of Early Motherhood,* Louise Erdrich described the way the land beneath us is layered with laylines of loss, strength, and history. In her story, her old farmhouse house is itself a haunted body.

Deep in the foundation of the house she hears a wail, and without thinking or telling anyone she crawls under the house. "Water flowed through invisible pipes around me, hitched and gurgled. It was like being dead, or unborn. I hadn't thought about it then, but now I could clearly see part of me, the husk of myself, still buried against the east wall: a person sacrificed to ensure the good luck of a temple, a kind of house god, a woman lying down there, still, an empty double . . . How many women are buried beneath their houses? How many startling minds, how many writers?"[2]

Our houses, like all our loved and broken land, carry the bones of people, animals, and trees. We hold these in our pantheon of the Witches we've been missing; the caretakers who had some pathways of their potential, some shoots of the wild and glorious minds, sacrificed to the unpaid labor of the home.

My grandmother helped fight Nazis when she was a terrified and ferocious teenager in Copenhagen during World War II. She'd earned a spot on the Danish Olympic swimming team the year the Olympics were canceled by the war, so she channeled her frustration into smuggling gun parts in the bottom of her school bag.

After the war ended, she fell in love, and adventured across Europe with her husband and three kids strapped precariously onto a motorcycle and sidecar. They came to the Canadian prairies to teach and survive in a house without electricity and six months of snow that piled and towered above the roof. Despite speaking and writing four languages, she couldn't get qualified to teach. When they finally arrived at a private school in Ontario with their teenage kids and gained a little breathing room financially, she collapsed inward for a couple years. There were yawning, creeping months when she didn't seem to move at all.

When she died, we went through boxes of her photographs and found an album from this period. An album that consists entirely of the same photo of the beach taken over and over again, with the date marked below, moving through the seasons. A sad, gray chronicle of days dripping slowly across the lake and trees.

So she did get up from the couch, I guess. Enough to walk to the door, down the path to the water. To think about the water, take its picture, and walk back home again.

Our family can't agree on the roots of this long depression because we've all heard different stories. She was blurred by bipolar, her mind runneled by her grief after my grandfather died and moved to frequent contradiction by a wicked sense of story, and her life story fragmented into hard-to-piece-together revelations. About things that happened during the war. About having been raped on a train or alone in that house. Or both. We share the versions we had heard from her at different times late at night in pieces; and we live out our own cycles of depression, addiction, abuse, and storytelling spiraling from that haunted core.

When I was little, she gave me a painting she had done of the house on the lake where she had taken pictures. I keep that painting hanging in my own lake house now. I have good memories of being there with my grandparents, a few good summers spent picking blackberries before my parents split. I also keep it as a monument to the women and children who left a piece of themselves buried in those walls. We build their bones into our homes, whether we want to or not. If we honor them and tend to these sunken shadow gardens, maybe we can become the generation that breaks out of these old spiral curses and harvests some healing.

I bought my house on a lake five years ago in an act of lunacy or magical thinking or mad optimism or prophecy. I did not have a license or car, or any way to get there. I lived in an apartment in Montréal with a boyfriend who had brought a bunch of his belongings over but had never moved in and would periodically disappear.

My mother told me she had a small amount of money set aside for my wedding, but since it didn't seem like that was happening, she would contribute it toward a condo in the city if I wanted. While I can see the appeal of the condo—a clean, new, windowed box downtown—what called to me was something else entirely. Somewhere we could go to swim, to listen to the wind in the trees. To spread out the fine nervous tendrils that I could almost see fritzing like a radio halo around my mother, my sisters, and me.

I had bookmarked one hundred houses without doing much about it, but when I found mine, we went to visit it the next day. The owner, Claudette, welcomed me and my mom. Claudette was nervous and lovely and wringing her hands. She and her husband had built the house up from a tiny three-season cottage in a series of DIY renovations, like the metal spiral staircase half-embedded in a wall to take you down into the basement where they had added a painting studio. She was the painter. Views of the lake in winter adorned the walls, alongside queer little fairies peeking out of wildflowers.

175

She served us tea on the screened-in porch that leans like a boat over the lake and, as we listened to the loons, she and my mother spoke of their anxiety, of how this place could be a balm.

The homeowner told us that her husband Yves had lived with bipolar. Thirty-five years ago they had moved from a small town nearby to seek haven permanently in the woods. She had filled the garden with herbs, local flowers, and berries, but since he died and her knee went out they'd all gone wild. The garden below was a riot of disorder flickering like a hallucination it was so full of bees and butterflies.

Claudette told us that after her husband's funeral, she had sat in the darkening house alone. As she spoke she moved her hands and breathed heavily and we could feel in the air between her words how something dense and unexpressed had mounted, heaped, and choked around her. It had been raining that night, and she was mourning so many things she couldn't express as the rain pounded on the metal roof and the dark came down. Finally she couldn't take the pressure. She ran outside to the path into the woods in her bare feet in the summer rain. Only there did she break down and sob, soaking the forest in.

Somehow this story sealed the deal between us. We held hands and knew that we would be the ones to take this house, and let Claudette go on to the bright little condo she'd been dreaming of.

The day I signed the papers—having scraped together every cent I owned and could borrow—my mom came with me and we went to visit the house. We didn't have the keys yet and Claudette wasn't there, but we peeked in the windows and saw what she had left: the beds were made, the cupboards full of plates and mugs, and her painting of the lake hung on the living room wall. She had shed it all like a perfect shell and left the whole lovely thing for us to step into. My mom had bought a pie and a six pack of beer at the corner store, so we had a picnic and went skinny dipping, and my mom yelled, "We are beautiful!"

By the next summer we'd started to uncover the rot in the DIY walls, and the truth about the lover who had never quite moved in came out. The whole messy truth was everywhere like black mold: the money he had emptied from my credit cards, the countless scammed investors, the other women he had "lived with" and betrayed in Toronto, New York, and Boston; the pathetic mess of it all was spread like an ugly wasteland across my life and sense of self.

The rot in the walls and in that person I had put my faith in are forever tied together for me in a lesson I go back to when the light is waning: the hero, the fortress, the perfect life is an illusion. The truth is more difficult and much more rich with magic.

When we emptied out Yves's workshop we found stacks of matchbooks hidden in mugs and tins all bearing the logo of what we figured out—with a little asking around—had been a discreet gay bar, Le Clandestin, in a nearby village. And with them we found a handwritten note, scrawled in a shaky hand that said, in French, "I will love you eternally."

I don't know what kinds of sorrow are soaked into the walls of this house, but I can guess. In my own sleepless nights here—as I sweated out my identity-hangover from being conned—I sometimes saw Yves standing on the lawn. He wasn't watching me, and it wasn't scary. He was a dream, or a pattern of energy burned into the dirt, or a ghost, or a figment of my always overactive imagination. And I knew what he was watching, over and over again, was Claudette. Her barefoot night run in the rain. I could see, in the sleepless dark, the way love—the strange and unique forms it takes for each of us—leaves pathways and monuments. Unseen but all around us in the earth, veined through our foundations.

Louise Erdrich wrote that "grief blinds us to itself, plunges under, moves through our arms into the earth, and surfaces in moments out of time. Grief is alchemy by which living memory changes the daily lead and silver of our loved one's existence to purest gold."[3] In my experience of pouring grief, fury, and regret all the way out, raging with a fire at Lughnasadh, I felt it move through my arms into the earth. I shed its weight like a husk. And slowly, I felt the lead within me change. Our traumas aren't gifts, but the burning does make the gold that is already within us more apparent. In every version of what happens to us there is a version of ourselves that can rise to meet it. As the days get dark we can more clearly see the brightness in ourselves.

Perhaps one secret missed by the alchemists, wealthy men work-ing on state-sanctioned magic while Witches burned, is to study grief and love alongside fire and metals. To consider love in all its life-giving forms. To see beyond the material world the golden waves and roots that tie us to our homes, to the Earth, and to each other.

Accept new forms of life
and talk to the dead
who drift in through the screened windows, who collect
patiently on the tops of food jars and books.
Recycle the mail, don't read it, don't read anything
except what destroys
the insulation between yourself and your experience
or what pulls down or what strikes at or what shatters
this ruse you call necessity.[4]

There is a fourteenth-century Kashmir Shaiva Tantra poet—a woman who in many times and places would have been called Witch—who offers inspiration in this season of the shedding of our husks. A woman who left an abusive family and walked out into the world singing. A mystic who saw the illusions of the necessary dissolve and who shared a vision of the entire world lit up with love.

The soul, like the moon,
is now, and always new again.

And I have seen the ocean
continuously creating.

Since I scoured my mind
and my body, I too, Lalla,
am new, each moment new.

My teacher told me one thing,
live in the soul.

When that was so,
I began to go naked,
and dance.[5]

In the poems of hers that survive, Lal Ded teaches that dying to the illusions of necessity can let us see the only truth: there is no difference between you and me and rich or poor or God Themself.

Now I saw the hearth ablaze,
Now I saw not fire nor smoke.
Now I saw the Pandava Mother,
Now she was but a potters' aunt.

Centuries after she "began to go naked and dance," Lalla had many names; we choose to align ourselves with the ancient language of the common people who call her Lal Ded, which colloquially means "Grand-mother Lal," and "more literally it means 'Lal the Womb' a designation that connects her to the mother goddesses whose cults of fecundity and abundance form the deep substratum of Indic religious life."[6] Down here in the foundation of our homes we find the grandmother and the womb and they are one, endlessly birthing a world beyond sectarian, binary violence. Lal Ded devoted herself to her studies of kundalini yoga; to Shaiva Tantra philosophy; to the mounting power of mantra and of her own breath; and to sharing her clear-eyed wisdom with the people. Her words shine a wry, transcendent, humanistic light in a world that was and still is torn.

The Lord has spread the subtle net of Himself across the world.
See how he gets under your skin, inside your bones.
If you can't see Him while you're alive,
Don't expect a special vision when you're dead.

Lal Ded left the constraints of existing religious language behind to speak her spiritual truth in the common language, Kashmiri. She put poor and working people at the heart of her message about the divinity of all. And she rejected the differences between Hindu and Muslim:

Shiva pervades at every place and thing;
Do not differentiate between Hindu and Muslim
You are intelligent enough to recognize your own self;
That is the true acquaintance with God.[7]

Lal Ded inspired generations of people and poets on both sides of the conflict in Kashmir. She has been celebrated as a Hindu *bhakti* saint, a shining light of Kashmir Shaivism, an elite Sufi mystic, a pious Muslim woman, a syncretic saint embodying Kashmir and its people, and a poet authoring the first known verses in modern Kashmiri. In her multiplicity and her authority, she can be a doorway for us in our workings toward peace.

> *On the one hand Lalleshwari gave new life to Kashmiri Shaivistic spiritual tradition, and on the other hand, she brought it close to the approach of common individuals by articulating its tenets in the language of the common people, thus making it an effective tool not only for individual emancipation but also for social unification.*[8]

Witches and mystics are dangerous because they claim their own authority to access the magic—the Spirit—that is woven throughout the Earth and in our own bones. We reject illusion to see the fine net of the world all around and through us—all of us. We take the sacred fire and return it to the people.

The most often repeated origin story about Lal Ded and the revelation of her power is the parable of the water.

Married at the age of twelve and abused by her new family, Lal Ded would slip down to the river and wade across the water to study and meditate in the tradition of Śaiva-Śakta Tantra. She learned to use mantra and the power of breath and sound. One day, when she was returning from one of these escapes with the water for the household balanced on her head, her mother-in-law flew into a fury over her missing hours, and Lal Ded's husband caught his mother's rage and hit Lal Ded. As the water jug she carried tumbled from her head, Lal Ded let the jug fall, but held the water . . . quietly hovering over her . . . contained by nothing at all.

She emptied the water into the containers of the household and then poured the remainder out onto the land, creating a pond that still bears her name. "This episode created a sensation in the whole countryside. People started coming from far and near . . . it became impossible for her to remain confined within the four walls of her house"[9] and so she left. "Lalla is said to have lived long in divine ecstasy preaching the gospel of love and tolerance . . . there is no monument to mark the place where her mortal remains were either cremated or laid to rest, though she was equally claimed both by Hindus and Muslims . . . It is said that a flame of light shot forth from her body and vanished into the void leaving not a trail behind."[10]

On Lughnasadh we can let our feelings—loss or love or rage—become a conflagration. Become one with the flame of light we all are. Become ourselves a glowing beacon to mark the place of the grandmothers in our own traditions who have cleared the ground to get us closer to the goals of unity and peace.

We are, as the placards shout, the granddaughters of the Witches you could not burn. We are the granddaughters of mystics, painters, and poets who shed everything to listen to their own breath, choose their own teachers, see the goddess in the potter's aunt, go naked and dance.

Western esoteric traditions can feel like a hodgepodge of variously understood Eastern philosophies, treading a wavering line between cultural appropriation and theft. On the one hand, we want to empower you by saying go ahead and dig into the traditions that inspire you, keep what resonates, and leave the rest. On the other hand, we know that in doing so we run the risk of stacking our shelves with half-truths and superficial knowledge. And worse, that we contribute to the erasure and commodification of culture and knowledge from Black, brown, and Indigenous communities. We may find that we end up with all dust jackets and no books, that what we retrieved from our spiritual journey is only the trappings of Spirit, without any connection to Spirit itself. We have to keep asking, do we come with humility and hard work to these teachings, do we put blood and skin in the game that threatens the lives and land and wisdom of these teachers? Or do we traipse over them, just another settler colonizer profiting from what we don't quite understand.

In "The Goddess and the Great Rite: Hindu Tantra and the Complex Origins of Modern Wicca," Hugh Urban credited Doreen with at least having an honesty about the inspiration taken from Hindu Tantra by early creators of the modern craft.

> *While [Gerald] himself only referred occasionally to Tantra, his most important student and collaborator, Doreen Valiente, did so openly and repeatedly. Indeed if the connection to Tantra is largely implicit in [Gerald's] writings it becomes quite explicit in Valiente's . . . Unlike [Gerald], Valiente is also more forthcoming about her sources and influences, both textual and artistic. For example she mentions an exhibition in 1971 sponsored by the Arts Council of Great Britain, focused on the art "associated with the eastern cult of Tantra . . . which has served to awaken a lively interest in tantric ideas among occultists and other seekers for truth."[11]*

Rather than consume and commercialize other spiritual traditions for our own profit, we hope to take guidance from the Witches we've been missing to do the work required to honor the traditions and people we have the privilege to learn from. We want to include Lal Ded in our pantheon of Missing Witches to honor the fact of her desire to connect, of her generosity. We want to bow to the power in her poetry, and to the lineage of Tantra that made its way into Western esotericism and Witchcraft and planted seeds there that continue to unsettle the settler mind today. We want to be part of a movement to expand who can see themselves in a Witch tradition, who feels safe here, who feels welcome. That's what the circle is for. And we want to lend our labor—flawed as it may be, and blinkered by our perspective and our privileges—to the work of many powerful healers, mystics, and Witches of color who have safeguarded and shared knowledge, and resisted the grasping misappropriations of the white New Age. In the spirit of Labor, it's become a tradition for us to donate our Missing Witches earnings every May to the Native Women's Shelter of Montréal. It's a beginning.

We also want to disrupt the subtle racism of reading colonized cultures as always-victims, only pillaged, perpetually plundered. Because the truth is, spirituality is a conversation with an ancient history of influence and interconnection.

Thinking about esotericism in terms of... historical encounters would allow us not only to examine the intersections of Kabbalah, Hermeticism, and Christian mysticism in European esotericism, but also to examine the intersections of Greek and Arab thought in Islamic mysticism; or the intersections between Chinese, Indian, Arab and European forms of alchemy; or the intersections between Indian thought and Romanticism... Esotericism might then be re-imagined as neither "Western" nor "Eastern" but rather as a series of knots or nodes that lie within more complex historical networks that circulate through the religious, social and political order.[12]

There have always been people—seekers, Witches, poets, mystics, and potter's aunts—who have engaged in the kinds of loving conversation that dissolve illusion and duality. This book is humbly dedicated to them.

To include Lal Ded in a history of Witches is not so much of a stretch. According to most historians, she practiced a right-handed version of Tantra that rejects animal and human sacrifice, but "for most native Indians, Tantra stands for scary Witchcraft and ghoulish Aghoris . . . idolatry, magic potions, debauchery, and the talisman."[13] In India, and most places, a spirituality that rejects dominant patriarchal control of body, property, education, mind, and soul, is dangerous. "What makes Tantra interesting in modern times is the potential rediscovery—yet to be widely disseminated—that Tantra stands for social revolution."[14]

Tantra and Witchcraft represent a revolutionary idea: "while Tantra may endorse liberal values, it does not establish secular values, but just the reverse, it spiritualizes all modes of experience."[15] The fundamental revolution in Tantra is that the individual can find and know the divine within themselves and in their own experience, spread out like a net all over their own world. Access to knowledge is broken away from the hands of the powerful. The spirit sings to us directly and we can hear her and harmonize. When all things are spirit, all divine, then every action we take toward each other and the Earth needs a different kind of decision-making equation than capitalism is equipped for.

This tradition understands the power of our own voice as being connected to the original and ongoing creation of the universe. This is one idea from the vast philosophy of Tantra that becomes deeply integrated into contemporary Wicca and Witchcraft, and it is inherently revolutionary.

Ipsita Roy Chakraverti is a Wiccan Priestess from Kolkata, India. One quote from Ipsita unlocked something in us and became a constant touchstone for our work: "Every strong woman is a Witch and she is always hunted."[16] Ipsita in her life's work and writing allied herself with the women who are hunted. In a time of active violence against women in the name of Witch hunting, she put herself out front, claimed the title for herself and for all of us who are strong. This electrifying philosophy shapes her life and is her message to a world that was and is still profoundly unequal.

> *In Tanzania alone, it is calculated that more than 5,000 women a year are murdered as Witches, some macheted to death, others buried or burned alive. In some countries, like the Central African Republic, the prisons are full of accused Witches, and in 2016 more than a hundred were executed, burned at the stake by rebel soldiers who, following in the footsteps of sixteenth-century Witch finders, have made a business of the accusations, using the threat of a pending execution to force people to pay. In India, as well, the murder of Witches is rampant— especially in the "tribal lands," such as the land of the Adivasi, where large scale processes of land privatization are underway.[17]*

Land and property disputes, the rejection of sexual advances, and family feuds recur as motivating factors in calling Witch, and infuriatingly it's often a male Witch doctor who gets to make the conviction, consolidating his power in precarious times.

Witch hunters rape, physically torture, and disfigure women's bodies in contemporary Witch hunts. This gendered violence increases in a complex relationship to poverty and capitalism, and colonialism and nationalism, and when famine in West Bengal brings it to a head again in the 1980s, the Witch hunt changes the course of Ipsita's life.

Ipsita was born on November 3, 1950, in India, but spent much of her early life in Montréal. She read books on all kinds of esoteric thinking when she was young, especially Indian mysticism. She says she was inspired in part by the ways she stood out in Canada. She was always asked about where she came from, and that made her think about the philosophical and religious traditions of home in relation to Western thought.

She was lovingly supported in her interests and independence by her parents, in a way that's still out of reach for many of us, no matter where we come from. She says her mother was a kind of feminist, and maybe even a Witch, in the sense that all strong women are Witches. She was protected by the extreme privilege of her family and her class, and she knew it and used it.

You could be called a dayan *and burnt alive, or you could be called an enchantress and enlighten an audience on the art of Wicca. Ipsita is the latter, and she has used her social and economic padding to make others* listen *to her.*[18]

Ipsita makes us listen to a message about the world that is singing disruptive truths all around us: "I have gleaned wisdom from the old trees on Mount Royal, from the megaliths of Brittany and from the mysterious rocks of the temple of Konark at Orissa. I know for a fact that other dimensions exist, that we have other senses, which are in constant communication with higher planes of knowledge and being. The inanimate lives. The dead do not die. We are immortal."[19]

At fifteen, Ipsita encountered a group of women who met in drawing rooms across North America and Europe, "mental Amazons" she calls them, including a famous Broadway actress and a widely respected Egyptologist and more whose identity she keeps secret.

This mysterious school—the Society for the Study of Ancient Cultures and Civilizations—gets talked about a lot in articles about Ipsita, but even before her acceptance into this secret order (or study group or coven), she describes visiting the Kahnawà:ke reservation outside of Montréal where she stayed with a Kanien'kehá:ka family, and was given insight to another tradition, another window into the complex power in the natural world.

She wrote,

One evening we talked of power. What it meant. True power.
Sources of power, how to find them. And objects which could be made
and used to draw in power. My friend Mini's grandfather went into
the cabin and brought out things he had made or which had been
given to him by his ancestors. He told me,

    "Understand them for yourself, your mind must always be free
as Eki the Eagle. Experience from your own heart. Wisdom comes
from within." He held out a long white eagle feather, which gave
out sparks of light in the dark—and in a copper box there lay two or
three of the loveliest crystals that I had ever seen. Mini's grandfather
smiled. "I am glad you like the gems of Yellow Woman. These are used
to ward off her bad temper. She is whimsical—like a storm in the
desert sands . . . to the Native North American Cochiti tribe she is a
predator, a force which devours. But to some people Yellow Woman
may show a smiling face and be a bride, a benefactor or a heroine. To
the Keres she signifies the total woman. I picked them up one night
near Punished Woman's lake in South Dakota, after a screaming
coyote-like storm . . . Yellow Woman came in the form of lightning
and gave them power. And I have given them power by saying the
chants of father sky and other earth over them. They can heal. Or they
can destroy. But then power always has two faces does it not?"[20]

In a clearing shaped like a teepee or a cone of power in the woods, Ipsita learned a Sun dance, drawing energy from the Earth, renewing her cells and breath and sinews.

Her great-grandmother had also prayed to the Sun God. She had dared to sing a prayer that Ipsita tells us was not meant for women. The song of the Sun was taken by her, taken into her, generations before Ipsita learned the Sun prayers of another tradition.

Part of Ipsita's repeated message in her book and in her life is that strength and even arrogance in women bring us close to the goddess—to our own goddess being—and set us free: "I love arrogance in a woman, it is the one quality that sets her at par with the Goddess."[21] Arrogance can help clear the ground, burn the illusions of necessity, the husks of convention and control and caste and duality, to claim a place for ourselves and our children and grandparents in the Sun.

Mini's grandfather told her, "Stand on a spot where you feel the spirit resides. Then crouch and dash your two arms behind you expelling your breath. Draw energy up from the Earth as you breathe in. Close your eyes. Steal that energy. In your mind's eye see a yellow coil of fire ascending. That is what the wolves guard. It must be stolen."[22]

For all who have been colonized or violated, take this wisdom to heart. You do not need permission from any authority to access your magic, or the magic running hot and ready for you in the Earth. See the yellow coil of fire. Take it back.

When Ipsita returned to the city the summer after she learned the boldness required to draw the power from the ground, she was summoned to join the Society for the Study of Ancient Cultures and Civilizations. Not just to "study about the incredible and the unknown, but to live it, to experiment with it, to become it."[23] This is the invitation of the craft: to go beyond learning from authorities, to conduct our own experiments and become the incredible. To be free in our own minds and lives and thereby to embody the spirit that moves the universe and brings new life out of rot and ferment. Ipsita wrote, "The studies, the discipline, the explorations into the tangible and the intangible set free the mind into the limitless. The universe opened out, timeless and ageless . . . And in the final analysis I think that is how we should lead our many lives, as players and scholars."[24] And so she consented to go.

One of the core principles of magic is "as above so below, as within so without." Another statement on the illusion of duality, this one comes from the *Emerald Tablet,* a fifth- or sixth-century document that is the origin of hermetic philosophy. Isaac Newton spent a lot of time thinking about this text, and his translation goes like this:

Tis true without lying, certain & most true.

1. That which is below is like that which is above & that which is above is like that which is below to do the miracles of one only thing.

2. And as all things have been & arose from one by the mediation of one: so all things have their birth from this one thing by adaptation.

3. The Sun is its father, the moon its mother, the wind hath carried it in its belly, the earth is its nurse . . . [25]

It goes on. Some have claimed this is a recipe for alchemy, that encoded in it is a recipe to transmute lead into gold. Some have spent their lives and lost their sanity working this text trying to find wealth or immortality.

What resonates for me today is the miracle of oneness. All things arose from one, nursed in the belly of the Earth. In our fractal multiverse we echo and hum with the divine that is nothing and everything.

One of the ways nonlinear meaning makes itself known, and one of the ways magic works and winks to us of its oneness and its working, is through synchronicity. If you are at all Witchy minded, it is encouraging to take pleasure in the ways the universe sometimes seems to rhyme.

For example, I have spent my life missing these grandmothers, mystics, feminist philosophers, and activists, so I went looking for real-life Witches. And I found Ipsita—she wasn't lost, she is a respected healing priestess, elegant warrior, gentle healer—but she was missing from me. Finding her was like getting hit with a wave of light and power, and there she was telling stories of growing up in my hometown. She said, "I went to school in Montréal, with its apple orchards near Snowdon,"[26] and those apple orchards were on the grounds of my high school. She studied in a house in the Laurentians with crumbling stucco, and the lake house I bought with my mom, tucked in the foothills of that exact same small mountain range, is caked in crumbling stucco too.

After buying that house, finding rot, feeling loss and fury moving out from my arms into the earth, then getting hit with the astonishing magic of new good love, getting pregnant, and moving to the woods, we tore down the extension Claudette and Yves had built. Beneath the stucco you could push your hand through the sodden beams. Digging out the rot in the ideas I have bought into is part of how the universe has been teaching me through rhyme.

Ipsita's lake house had six gables and in the center an exquisite rose window suggesting maybe it was built with a rosy cross connection— maybe the nonsectarian, nonreligious version of Rosy Cross that pre- dates Christianity and the secret brotherhood of the Rosicrucians, a Rosy Cross where "the cross represents the human body and the rose represents the individual's unfolding consciousness."[27] Inside, there were rooms for study and ritual, and one room with a thousand crystals. In this sanctuary, Ipsita received a crystal skull and an introduction to the crisscrossed histories and mythologies of the thirteen crystal skulls.

She described a "red indian"[28] legend of thirteen ancient crystal skulls the size of human skulls, which store knowledge of the origin, purpose, and destiny of mankind. According to the crystal skulls mythology, all thirteen skulls will one day be rediscovered and brought together. One skull was discovered in the ancient Maya city of Lubaantan in Belize, one was in the Museum of Mankind at the British Museum, one has a large ornate crystal and gold cross fused to it, altered from its original state to show the dominance of the Church. There are rumors of a crys- tal skull kept in the vaults of the Vatican. Some are rumored to move on their own, some heal and bring wealth, others to destroy the lives of their collectors. Some legends have it that there are twelve planets in the cosmos inhabited by humans, and there is one skull for each. The thirteenth is a kind of key.

I love a story of sacred secret interplanetary communication, but I have almost twenty years' hindsight since Ipsita wrote *Beloved Witch,* and more research has been done on these skulls that mysteriously appeared in collections in the nineteenth century, revealing the rot in some of the mythmakers who spun their stories.

Recent electron microscope analyses of skulls by the British Museum and the Smithsonian Institution revealed markings that could only have been made with modern carving implements. Both museums esti- mate that their skulls date to sometime in the mid to late 1800s, a time when public interest in ancient cultures was high and museums were eager for pieces to display. A British Museum study in fact pinpointed the manufacture of most of the skulls to an area of Germany famous for manufacturing intricate quartz and crystal designs in the late 19th century. The crystal is said to be found in Brazil or Madagascar and thus inaccessible to pre-Columbian indigenous civilizations. Its examinations and the fact that no such skull has ever been uncovered at an official archaeological excavation led the British Museum to extrapolate that all of the famed crystal skulls are likely fakes.[29]

One of the prominently quoted sources for the legend of the skulls is Claude Harley "Swiftdeer" Reagan who—aside from being a notorious fabricator—is not actually Native American.

In 1991 Tim Giago, editor in chief and publisher of the newspaper *Indian Country Today*, published a column "Phony Indians" in the *Baltimore Sun*, calling out false profiteers across North America, notably Claude Harley Reagan:

> *All the traditional people of the Cherokee Nation were mortified the night Harley "Swift Deer" Reagan made his Home Box Office television debut in a program "Real Sex." The tribe denounced Mr. Reagan, saying he had disgraced the Cherokee Nation, and demanded an on–air apology from HBO. Of course, this never happened. The Harley Reagan segment was aired as part of the national "Real Sex" series. His presentation consisted of naked men and women engaged in various forms of embracing and touching, which "Swift Deer" claimed were ancient Cherokee sex rituals. "Swift Deer" was quickly exposed as a fraud by the principal chief of the Cherokee Nation, Wilma Mankiller.*[30]

The list is long of white people pretending to be Indigenous to sell a half-baked spiritual solution, and the results range from ridiculous to deadly. Theft of culture and violation of bodies are choking weeds with the same root; or maybe it's more accurate to say they emerge because of the same missing root. A missing rootedness that makes people into profiteering puppets, missing their souls. To learn from those who have been choked by these weeds, let's shed distortion and fight exploitation to keep clearing the ground.

Beyond the lurid and appealing mythology of crystal skulls, I wonder if there is a deeper wisdom here that Ipsita only hints at sharing with us.

We go down detours and through halls of mirrors as we jolt and stumble toward new ideas. Witches use illusion, drama, and masquerade to evoke that open, decentered, communal lunar mind and draw the seeker toward new ideas. Ipsita said, "I believe that long ago a few women in the Laurentians knew much more about the science of crystals than do the most specialized instruments today."[31] Maybe sometimes it takes ornate crystal skulls for us to think about the energy and original consciousness in simpler pieces of stone.

Queer Wiccan leader, gentle solitary Witch, and author Scott Cunningham wrote, "The common, everyday stones you see lying on the street or dug up in your yard, those tumbled up on river banks or beaches, or lying scattered as if a giant hand threw them onto the countryside, are possessed of powers and can be used in magic just as can those of tremendous commercial value."[32] Let's add this to our kindling pile of husks shed for the early harvest: the idea that expensive stones, mined and hoarded with colonial violence, have more power than the ones we find along the unique pathways of our own lives. There are stones all around us that speak to us about the places where we live. Every stone offers a piece of the consciousness of spirit and a profound stillness that is available to us if we listen.

It turns out that "as traditional attempts to explain consciousness continue to fail, the 'panpsychist' view is increasingly being taken seriously by credible philosophers, neuroscientists, and physicists."[33] One interpretation of panpsychism holds that "any system is conscious—Rocks will be conscious, spoons will be conscious, the Earth will be conscious. Any kind of aggregation gives you consciousness."[34]

We add layers of love and meaning and pain to these aggregations when we build them into our homes and temples and lay them on our altars. There is an emergent something that looks into us, and can help us in our craft and in the work of healing the world. "In magical thought, the human body is the 'microcosm' (small representation) of the earth, which is the 'macrocosm.' The earth is also the microcosm of the universe. In other words, we are pictures of the essence of the planet and thusly of the universe. As such, when we change ourselves, we change the earth and the universe."[35]

Ipsita learned to love, thank, and receive energy from trees as a student in the Laurentians. She wrote that "according to the Egyptians and the Celts stone and wood have thoughts and a certain kind of comprehension,"[36] and she described experiences in the Grand Canyon and at the Konark Sun Temple in India where the mundane world thins. As woods dwellers, we relate to this. When I was scared to make the move from the city, Amy told me that since moving to the woods she'd never been lonely and I've found it to be true. Here in the woods on unceded Anishinabewaki, Huron-Wendat, Omàmiwininiwak land, we are relearning how to listen.

With help from our elders and our children, with meditation or collective song, with a blessing from something in the rock and sea and geometry of place, the electricity in the air changes. Something that's always there can reach you for a second, across the divide of an imagined (and therefore real) duality. The consciousness out there can recognize that we are recognizing it.

For Lughnasadh, this season of shedding illusion and harvesting ourselves and our light, follow Lal Ded and Ipsita to the oneness beyond a separateness of self and other. Because the truth is both: We are unique and we are One, everything is divine and Nothing is. We are the animals and the stones and trees, and they are us. In order to suppress the trauma of the many genocides of late capital—industrial animal slaughter, the burning of the Amazon, the desertification of the prairies, the bleaching of the reefs—certain kinds of spells have been used to lull and distract us. But when we dig into our histories, we find simple spells of our own. And we find each other.

In certain society circles throughout the 1980s, Ipsita became known as a Wiccan, and some genuinely tortured people came to her for healing, while others came with less pure ends in sight. She got sick of seeing this side of human nature. "I hated to be confused with a miracle peddling godwoman or guru. I felt contaminated. My power had been given me by a Source which did not stoop to doling out favors to the greedy and ignorant."[37] So she stopped her sessions and decided to go to the villages of Bengal and Odisha "the interiors which most city dwellers chose to read about, not to visit."[38]

The summer that I went to Purulia the sun blazed down and the temperature soared to 48 Celsius in the shade. That summer was a grueling one . . . A social welfare organization had asked me to accompany them to the rural areas of Bengal where there had been some cases of alleged Witch hunting. I was asked to talk to the women accused or to their nearest kin. My job was mainly one of counsellor and investigator.[39]

She built trust with the women in the community, and they began to tell of women who have gone missing. Witch accusations had been mounted against women who rejected sexual advances, or widows finally able to own their own land. Accused, raped, disappeared, their lands now owned by their accusers. It is infuriating and blatant.

Witch hunting in Indigenous, rural communities in India repeats patterns we recognize from the European Witch hunts of the fifteenth century. A dominant culture takes control not just of land, but of definitions of who is human, who is civilized, and which traditions are sacred.

Witch-hunting was closely linked to the colonial administration's effort to extend political and juridical domain; missionaries' zeal to "civilise the pagan"; and ethnographers' and anthropologists' ardour to primitivise the adivasis [the Indigenous].[40]

In an environment where Witch hunting was (and still is) actually violently happening, Ipsita went to the national press and declared herself a Witch. She gave herself over to the public eye and over the course of dozens of interviews, she explained what Wicca is, where she learned it, and gave insights into her beliefs and practices. By the 1990s she was directly addressing the reality of women being branded *daayans* or Witches, and India's Witchcraft-related violence.

I have tried to bring succor to women branded "Witches" or "dayans" who are still today being molested and killed for what they are believed to practice. I have brought their cases before the authorities and the press in an attempt to show up the hypocrisy of their persecutors—mostly men—who are trying to denigrate this ancient

branch of learning in order to wreak revenge on these women for
some very personal motives.[41]

She was protected by her class and wealth, and she used her position to force a conversation. "India is very patriarchal, even today. When they saw me, standing up for those they were trying to brand and destroy, and saw that I was helping these women by calling myself a 'Witch,' these lobbies erupted with fury. These were vested interests which could not tolerate me because I was saying that a woman who was an individual had her own rights."[42] She tied herself to vulnerable women and challenged the status quo just by asserting their individual rights. And she bound us all to an ideal of female power that transcends borderlines.

I follow a tradition which encompasses the goddesses of all cultures,
east and west. After all, the Wiccan tradition spans something which
is beyond barriers of land and people . . . we follow the goddess cul-
ture, we acknowledge the Indian goddesses Durga for strength, Kali
for detachment and power and Saraswati for learning and the quest
for knowledge. All these goddesses seem to have western counterparts;
hence we look upon the goddess power as one, whose manifestations
are many.[43]

As all manifestations of the goddess are one, all women are bound together in Ipsita's vision.

The men who tortured and burnt innocent women in medieval
Europe live on in other places, in different guises. Witch-hunting
never stopped. It just took on a more deceptive mask. Of course in my
experience with thousands of women who have come to me for help
I would say that every strong woman is a Witch and she is always
hunted. It goes against the nature of most men to tolerate a woman
they cannot dominate. Witch-hunting is present not just in rural
Bengal, Bihar, Orissa, Uttar Pradesh or Madhya Pradesh. It pre-
vails everywhere in the world where women stand up for themselves
and what they believe in. It is there whenever women refuse to be
the pawns or playthings of a callous society.[44]

Elsewhere she wrote, "In a society which batters and bruises its women, physically and mentally, in home and in the workplace, every woman is a Witch."[45]

Us, too, Ipsita, and me too. And me too.

What I have actually striven for, is a few pickings from the vast harvest of truth which lies beyond, and if I continue to use my arrogance against society it is because I deplore its hypocrisy.[46]

Ipsita burns with a strength that is completely at peace with her own powers and beauty. There is humility and arrogance both, nestled comfortably right next to each other. At the time of writing, Ipsita and her daughter lead a Wiccan Brigade and the Young Bengal Brigade, an open access community of study in Kolkata that explores comparative religion, philosophy, and psychology, ancient scriptures, and mystical traditions. She still strives to find and share from that vast harvest of truth, and she brandishes her own truth like a brilliant shield, unafraid. She has transmuted the experience of being hunted into being huntress—Durga and Diana—and for her, that is the Wiccan path. I wish it for all of us.

Picture a summer in the 1950s. Teenage Ipsita is invited by a friend to visit Elvis Presley. They hang out at Graceland for a couple days, just swimming and talking with the young musician and his parents. The scene is sunlit and innocent.

Elvis told Ipsita that when he was younger he had a healer's touch. He would be asked to lay hands on a child in pain and the pain would gradually go away. He doesn't do it anymore or talk about it, knowing how it would seem.

"You know, most people think I'm selling sex. They say my attitude and movements are indecent. They seem to think the only commodity that is saleable and earns money is sex. But I know for a fact that's not so. People want healin' not sex."

"Maybe you're healing through your music and your songs," I said.

He looked at me as if I'd just said something he'd been trying to say for a long time . . .

We were both possessors of an alien energy that didn't have a name. I knew that his phenomenal attraction was misunderstood by people . . . and I knew that his time with this special energy was short. It would leave him about the time his mother passed on. From that time onward he would return to the mundane world dimension and life would be a struggle as it is for most people.[47]

Ipsita saw Elvis's magic from that sunny innocent verandah, she heard a healing in music that some said came from the devil. And she saw how it was fundamentally tied to the gentleness and love of a mother who anchored him in grace.

I think there's something for us here, in the hot summer at Lughnasadh. An opening in the fire to glimpse beyond arrogance versus humility, sex versus healing, music versus prayer, self versus other, man versus Nature. We can see the consciousness in stones, and see our own selves in the weave of the world all around us.

We can turn the lead within us to gold and strengthen our magic: not with expensive implements; not with the power that comes from using others for our own ends but with that still-mysterious energy in our own bodies and minds. "From the creation of the universe to the production of sound in the human body Tantrism stresses the importance of sound as a divine substance and vehicle for salvation . . . Shakta Tantra assumes that the same movement that has produced the world as macrocosm is represented within the human body in miniature as microcosm in the production of sound."[48]

Our own songs are divine vehicles for salvation. Our breath and voice produce the world.

Ritual

Witches inherit the power of going skyclad directly from Tantric rituals and philosophers. Hugh Urban acknowledged that "[Gerald's] own term for the preferred method of working naked in the Wiccan circle is similarly drawn from South Asian traditions—"skyclad" as they say in

India'—referring to the Sanskrit term *digambara*."[49] This is one twist in the weave, one idea from the great conversation about spirit, one part of the song that has traveled the Earth.

Witches believe that there is power in stripping ourselves of what has seemed necessary in order to feel closer to the elements. We have hope at least that it is possible to shed our husks and dissolve the boundaries between us and the Earth.

If you are someplace where, for Lughnasadh, you can go skyclad, I hope you will. Whatever the state of body or environment you are in, you can let your mind dance by a fire in the warm night air for a moment without pain or fear, with the heat and sweat on your skin.

Feel the trappings of the world slip off you, feel your bond with the Moon and with the Earth and the plants ripe for harvest, feel the power of the age you are and all the ages you have been and will be. Feel sacred spirals of seekers dancing with you, lending you their strength.

For every ritual we look to welcome the elements. For Lughnasadh, make this a celebration of your body in the greater body that is all around you.

Sing and feel the graciousness of every breath and watch the gentle movement of the wind. Hold a glass of water and see its journey to you, through the lake and seeping Earth and weeping sky, then drink it down, knowing it waves and thrums with the tides deep inside us. Sink your feet, bones, and the roots of our minds into the Earth where all our power and our safety come from. And then the spark. A wooden match, a beeswax candle, a bonfire.

1. For your ritual, make a burnable figure out of corn husks, paper, or leaves and, in a safe place, light them up. This can be at home, baked in your oven. Or lit with a Bic in your sink. Make a simple ageless figure and then fill it with your bitterness, frustration, and fury, and then watch it burn. Do it again.

2. Glory in your feelings. Turn your ugliest emotion up to eleven like a flame catching. Let it ravage. We have spent too long frozen, now it's time to feel the full power of our rage and

sorrow; it's ours to ride. Find your loudest raging, screaming voice, even if it's poured into a pillow.

3. Continue to burn the puppets who have hurt and held you, and burn away the strings and traces of the puppeteers.

4. When you are done with this burning, go skyclad if you can. Shed your husks and feel your own heart beating with the thrum of raging in midsummer.

5. Sink yourself down to the Earth—or down onto the linoleum— and let the Earth reach up to hold you. You can hold each other actually; she could use it.

6. When you get up, breathe in and out. Pour a cold, clean glass of water. See its molecules in your mind's eye taking a shape that represents freedom for you. Each drop a perfect self, containing the whole of the Whole, singing.

7. When you feel yourself breathing in resonance with that singing whole (go slow), then gulp it all down. So joyfully, so thirstily it might half spill all over you like a goofy, messy, self-love baptism. Touch its coolness to your eyes, and breathe.

It is summer. It is August and the land is hot and dry and thankful for the rain.

INCANTATION
We are beautiful
We are beautiful
We are arrogant and brave
We have been the hunted and the hunter
And the hunt will come again
But the illusions which divide us
Will dissolve in grief and love
We are one
We are one
We are one

7

Mabon

This circle is led by Amy

MABON MARKS THE AUTUMN EQUINOX. Light and dark are equal. Both hemispheres of the Earth sharing light and dark in perfect balance. But the darkness is growing. Make your last harvest. Gather. Reap what you have sown, knowing that nothing grows again until spring, except, for Witches, within our hearts and minds.

Much of our lives, internal and external, are determined by the presence of light, both literal and metaphorical. The moon is ever changing in her cycle but has a solid planetary form. All that changes is the reflection of the Sun on her face. All that changes is our perception. Whether you tend to think literally or metaphorically, for humans, for objects, shadows give dimension and depth. A circle drawn with shading becomes a sphere.

Our Mabon conjures mysteries, the Moon and the world's first poet. Conjures phases and shadows, multiplicity and immortality. This Mabon is about signing your name to your life and your Self, but never fear. Don't be intimidated. Mabon is one of the weeklong Sabbats, beginning on the autumn equinox and continuing through the last week of September, so we've got plenty of time to solve our inner mysteries before the darkness takes over and we slip into its embrace.

Here's a warning: I'm going to be using extremely coarse language in this chapter. Cover your eyes, little ones, because I'm going to say "cunt." And I'm going to say it a lot. And I'm going to talk about menstruation. I'm not going to imply that the fullness of a woman's power comes from bleeding, because I think that's misogynistic, reductive, and transphobic. Plus it hurts my feelings. As an AFAB (that's assigned female at birth) cis woman whose "female" organs never worked properly and were ONLY a source of misery, pain, and disappointment, you'll never hear me say that menstrual blood is the only life, that giving birth is the only path to womanhood, or that having kids is the only mode of fertility.

Those of us without biological offspring aren't concerned with making the world a better place for only our children, but rather, for all children. We are there to pick up the slack for children without parents, for parents without time. We don't begrudge the new parents' insistence that having a child is the greatest love a human can possibly experience;

rather, we greet the gushes with love and enthusiasm. A friend of mine, a mother, told me once in one of my more vulnerable childless moments, "Don't worry, Amy, you've taken MDMA. You've felt the greatest love of all." And we laughed, knowing that the highs and lows of parenthood and drug abuse have much in common. Yearning, paranoia, exhaustion, and sometimes, total, indescribable ecstasy.

But there's a reason that we've labeled *Missing Witches* as a feminist project, and it goes back to our podcast's tagline: Through a murky history of defamation and erasure, we go looking for the Witches we've been missing. Because women's contributions have been so largely erased from human history that we HAVE TO go digging to find them. We've found over and over that amazing women have been swept under the rug of domesticity and pushed into the footnotes of collective consciousness. The work has become almost an exercise in speculative fiction. What might the world have been, in what kind of culture would we be living today if women's ideas had been nurtured, if women had been allowed to have an equal voice in creating the zeitgeists that formed our contemporary society?

The fact is, we cannot know and we cannot change the past, but we can imagine, and better yet, we can raise our voices, our radical, femme, queer, colorful voices. We *can* change the future. It's what Witches do. And we can look to the past to find women who changed their world, in spite of it all.

The earliest known author of written literature was a woman named Enheduanna who lived in Mesopotamia more than four thousand years ago. You'd think that as the first named and known author in human history, Enheduanna would be a household name. But I have a Lit degree, I love trivia, and I had never heard of Enheduanna until I went looking for the Witches I'd been missing. While she lacks the fame I feel she deserves, her legacy and her name have persisted. Enheduanna, *En* meaning "lady, high priestess," *hedu* meaning "ornament" and "An" the god's name An. Lady Ornament of An. We know her name because she signed her name.

Astrophysicist Neil deGrasse Tyson once said that by adding her name to her poetry, Enheduanna achieved immortality.[1] She can never die. So, at autumn equinox, with the world darkening around you, I want you to sign your name to your life and stake your claim to immortality. For Mabon's guide on how to be a lover and a warrior, in perfect balance and embracing our shadows, we turn to her, the world's first known poet, High Priestess at the Moon temple of Ur in what we now know as Iraq. Come with me and quote the poetry of Enheduanna as she wrote about her Goddess, Inanna: "SHE / in the midst of havoc / shouting over the din / begins her sacred song."[2]

Because I'm a Witch, I watch for signs. I pay attention to synchronicity, and as I learn about these Witches, I'm always considering how their story wants to be told. These are human lives and the themes that might emerge in their retelling are potentially infinite. What part of this story wants telling? What aspect of the spirit of Enheduanna sent me to find her name? As I was reading Betty De Shong Meador's devotional analysis of Enheduanna's life and poetry, *Inanna: Lady of Largest Heart,* I also[3] heard about *Cunt: A Declaration of Independence,* by Inga Muscio. I never thought there'd be so much overlap between these two titles, but there I was, unwittingly reading not one, but two books on the exhalation of the Cunt.

The Goddess Inanna sings to her lover in Meador's translation of Enheduanna's poetry: "peg my vulva / my star-sketched horn of the dipper / moor my slender boat of heaven / my new moon crescent cunt beauty."[4]

There are men who have cunts, who menstruate. And for those trans or intersex men who bleed, I think you'll agree that there's a lot more to being "male" or "female" than menstrual blood. And this whole gender essentialist conversation completely erases intersex people who, by the way, I'll say again, do exist. But whether you're a bleeder or a breeder, if you've got big-dick energy or yoni power, or prefer not to discuss your genitals with strangers, I think we all need to take a moment to unflinchingly look at menstruation and its connection to the cycle of the Moon, and to our earliest known symbolic structures and our earliest known poet. Because there's no one here to say *Ewwww* or *Uuuugh, not at the dinner table, Amy.* Here, we can see blood without wincing.

I'm not trying to exclude anyone by momentarily focusing on menses. I am a woman who does not bleed (in the monthly sense—to misquote Shakespeare, if you prick me, I will bleed). I know that womanhood and menstruation are not synonymous. And I can't wait for the day when sexism doesn't exist, pronouns are ungendered for all, and everyone is treated with justice and without prejudice.

When we talk about human history, though, women are largely missing. In fact, anyone who exists outside of the tiny slice of the gender spectrum that is *cis maleness* is missing. The erasure of gender diversity is the categorizing of gender, of people, into "cis man" and "everything else," and so this "everything else," this vast and colorful spectrum of gender variation gets chucked into the "woman" bin. That bin, as we've seen, is more easily thrown away. Stuffed in the back of a closet to be unseen, disregarded, and forgotten. Tossed out to be burned with the trash.

This is not only an issue of sexism or transphobia, it's also an issue of colonial racism. Many other countries and cultures acknowledge more than our oversimplified two genders. India, for example, legally recognizes more than three genders, including *aravani, jagappa,* and *hijra,* who are considered by many to be sacred people. The *hijra* are often hired to bless and celebrate the birth of a child. It's considered lucky to do so. That said, *hijra* also experience violence on par with trans violence in the United States. So often fetishization overlaps with demonization. Both serve to dehumanize.

The Zapotec civilization of Mexico recognized three genders: male, female, and *muxe*. The Buginese, or Bugis, people of Indonesia accept five or more genders. Some tribes of the Americas First Nations saw in their people up to seven genders. The laws of Judaism contain words for six genders. The list goes on and on. I spoke to Jason Sikoak,[5] an artist from Nunavut who told me that the Inuit didn't have gendered pronouns until the white men brought them. No He or She, only They for everyone. It will be interesting to see, in the future, how languages like French for example, which has no UNgendered pronoun, no They—*il/* he, *elle/*she, *ils/*he (plural), *elles/*she (plural)—will navigate our blossoming nonbinary consciousness and invent new words.

Because Witches know that words are spells, capable of creating or changing a reality. Witches also know that we are so much more than, as we saw in the Litha chapter, merely This or That. In discussions around contemporary spirituality, I have seen the words God and Goddess replaced with GoddETC, coined, I believe, by artist and self-described "queerdo" Maria Molteni, and I think that's a perfect description. What we, as humans, can imagine of that which is beyond. Etc. And so on. Plus more.

I reached out to Maria to ask her about this neologism. Up to this point I had often seen the more standard use of the letter X to replace a gendered suffix. Think Latinx or Filipinx instead of Latino or Filipina. Maria told me that the X is a No, a healthy and powerful No to Gender Essentialism, but the ETC in GoddETC is a Yes to Everything, healthy and powerful in a different way. For most of recorded *colonial* human history, the ETC of Gender is Missing. Women are missing. The Plus More is missing. Not just missing, but erased, squelched, deliberately left out of our stories of how culture was built. Cunts are missing.

Inga Muscio wrote, and I'm onboard and I hope you are too, that *it does not matter if they are biological, surgical or metaphorical. A cunt's a cunt.*[6]

Plus we have *RuPaul's Drag Race* that, despite its imperfections, contributed to our language another definition of CUNT, a winning combination of *Charisma, Uniqueness, Nerve, and Talent.* If you're reading this book, we're going to assume that you either have, or are, a bit of a cunt. We are Witches, after all, and the words Witch and Cunt have quite a lot in common.

Witch, it is thought, once meant Wise One. Now it's a synonym for ugly, old, mean, or evil. Similarly, both Betty De Shong Meador and Inga Muscio unpack the origins of the word "cunt." Inga said that "cunt" is related to words from India, China, Ireland, Rome and Egypt. Such words were either titles of respect for women, priestesses and Witches, or derivatives of the names of various goddesses.[7] Betty said that the word "cunt" took on derogatory connotations in modern times.

Deriving from the Indo-European base "Ku-," "cunt" is related to a variety of Germanic words meaning "a hollow space or place, an enclosing object, a round object," and so on; *kunt* or *kunte* meant vulva and made its way into Middle English as *cunte*. In the *Woman's Encyclopedia of Myths and Secrets,* Barbara Walker said "cunt" is a "derivative of the Oriental Great Goddess as Cunti, or Kinda, the Yoni of the Universe . . . also cunning, kenning and ken: knowledge, learning, insight, remembrance, wisdom."[8]

So for Mabon, we stand in perfect balance with our light and shadow to shout over the din of shame and scrutiny that our bodies and minds are subject to and to sing a sacred song of being, or having, literal or metaphorical, Cunts. Our cunning is a hollow space, filled with etceteras.

Performance artist Phoenix Inana[9] used to have a different stage name, until one night, she performed her version of the story of Inanna at a show called inCUNTations.[10] Bathed in sweat, glitter, and spotlights, in that moment she took on the name of her goddess. As with Enheduanna, there is power in a name.

Phoenix, who was born in Egypt and grew up in Kuwait, is a person who, to me, embodies a contemporary version of the goddess Inanna, more than just in name. Queer, gender-bending, gender nonconforming, a gender and sexually fluid creative who utilizes cabaret art such as burlesque, drag (performing as a Drag "King" and "Queen"), vaudeville, and belly dance in her work, Phoenix is also a trophy-snatching honorary member of ballroom pioneering House of LaBeija.[11] I interviewed Phoenix for this book, and we discussed which pronoun to apply for the purposes of this chapter. Phoenix said,

> *I think women are often seen as incapable of War or aggressive thinking—I think people think that women are best for breeding or soft things. Inanna wasn't about that, she wasn't about procreation, she was not a reproductive goddess, she was a goddess of Sex and War, and these are things that are commonly associated with masculinity. And it's just another example of how she breaks these boundaries and subverts our expectations of what the hell masculine and feminine look like.*
>
> *She just doesn't fit into any of those boxes. Even describing her with the "She" pronoun, it almost feels limiting, but I think it's important to describe her as a female goddess with "She" pronouns*

even though she has all this androgynous nature and requirements
for worshipping her, because there is something incredibly power-
ful about someone identifying as Female and exhibiting what we
understand in society now to be masculine traits. That is also subver-
sive and gender-bending. For this, I will follow in Inanna's footsteps
and claim a nonbinary She/Her pronoun.

Before we had anything, we had the Moon and stars to behold. The Sun would rise and set in a perfect and predictable order, but the Moon had a dance. Her veil of darkness slipped on and off. The Moon was ever changing, even in its steadfast routine. A Moon cycle, from New to Full and back to New, is about twenty-eight days, and the human menstrual cycle is also about twenty-eight days. In *Ianna: Lady of Largest Heart*, Betty De Shong Meador cited the book *Blood, Bread, and Roses*, by Judy Grahn, when she wrote: "The numinosity of the correlation between the moon's cycle and women's cycles has been observed in rituals of many cultures. . . . Judy Grahn attributes the origin of ritual, and even the beginning of culture to our ancestors' discovery of the correspondence of the menstrual cycle with the phases of the moon. [… Women were] obligated to observe the practices that would contain and harness the immensity of this power."[12]

I guess the forces of patriarchy, determined to strip Women and Witches of their power, figured you can't erase menstruation. But you can demonize it. Call it dirty and shameful until even those who bleed are embarrassed to talk about it with their closest friends. You can market tampons based on their invisibility, so tiny they fit in the palm of your hand so no one can see your secret, monthly shame.

Colonialism, religious, capitalist hetero-patriarchy breed shame and exclusion and seek control over bodies, minds, and behaviors. Under colonialism, there is ONLY one correct way of doing things, and anything else is abomination. You can't be queer, you can't be polyamorous, you must be white and cis, you can't express your thoughts or needs, you can't be a slut, you can't be a prude. You can't be weird. You must fit neatly into every box. Every authentic bit of you that doesn't jibe with the status quo is shameful and must be hidden. Kink-shaming, body-shaming, slut-shaming, "shame! shame! shame!"-ing, because keeping you ashamed of being *different* is a great way to make sure you're always dimming your light. Keeping hidden your shining sun of multiplicity and otherness. It's easier that way. Easier for them.

They can pretend there's only one way to live, and they operate as if you just don't exist. Out of sight, out of mind. And it's easier for you too… keep your head down, don't rock the boat, don't attract attention, don't make eye contact. Slip by unnoticed. Don't incite violence by existing… Be desirable but not too desirable. Be socially acceptable. Blend in. Be likable. Be lovable. But be careful. Or… say fuck it and be a Witch. Change the rules and Shine. Glory be the stink of your hard-earned sweat. Glory be the blood.

It's tempting to say that shame isn't real, because it is not a law of physics, it's not gravity. It's not measurable or countable. Perhaps that's where it gets some of its power, from the fact that we are too ashamed to even speak its name. On the small patch of land that I'm rewilding, stewarding for the Universe, dandelions are always the first blooms to burst into color. They are the first source of pollen and nectar for the birds and the bees. They present themselves as the Sun in full bloom, the Moon as they turn to white, and stars as they scatter their seeds. They are life itself. And yet, I worry about letting them run free. I worry that the neighbors will think I'm just lazy. I worry they think my wildness will contaminate their immaculate, manicured gardens. Somewhere in the recesses of my settler mentality, it is better to destroy the ecosystem than to contend with what the neighbors might think.

Shame is a great force, capable of controlling large patches of our environments, our bodies, and our lives, and it is created to be WEAPONIZED. Under patriarchy, and religious capitalism, shame is a commodity. It makes you hide. Makes you buy things you don't need. Products to fix problems that don't exist. It's the thrill that *The Simpsons* cartoon bully Nelson gets when he points and cries "ha, ha," coupled with a profit margin. It's the opposite of compassion. The conversations we have with each other, the learning, the writing we do create a shield against this shame weapon. When Enheduanna wrote, she laid herself bare, saying in her exaltation to Inanna, "I shall give free vent to my tears like sweet beer!" At Mabon we give free vent so as not to carry our tears with us into the coming darkness.

I spoke to artist, scientist, and biohacker WhiteFeather Hunter, who told me that because of its unique proteins, menstrual blood can be thought of as a healing elixir.[13] And it makes me angry that speaking to WhiteFeather was the first time I heard this idea. It angers me that society raised me to be sheepish and humiliated when I should have been empowered. Because telling women that they are gross or unclean isn't just psychological rhetoric. This shame puts bodies in peril. I remember seeing advertisements, and if you're old enough you might too, where a concerned mother asks her adult daughter in a whispered tone: do you ever feel *not so fresh*? And the thought of a fresh vagina never occurred to me until these advertisements showed up on my screen. They wanted me to buy their douche.

A douche is a prepackaged mixture of water and sometimes vinegar, sometimes iodine, sometimes baking soda that you kind of squirt into the vagina to, I guess, rinse it out? But most doctors recommend that women do not douche. . . . Douching can lead to many health problems, including problems getting pregnant. Douching is also linked to vaginal infections and sexually transmitted infections (STIs).[14]

So the products that we are shamed into buying to solve health and hygiene problems that don't exist can and do actually cause actual health problems. Blood, and honesty, and darkness. These can be Witches' tools. Beautiful and shameless.

Enheduanna's public priestly duties were focused on Nanna and Ningal, the Moon Couple—Lord of the Moon and his Lady Consort. Part of the job of Sumerian priestesses was to dress the statues that represented the gods, record the offerings given to them, and, in the case of Ningal, to chart her and Inanna's menstrual cycles. So we can assume that this was also one of Enheduanna's responsibilities. Some believe that Enheduanna's poetic reference to the lunar cycle, coupled with Inanna's destructive and creative force, is itself a metaphor for menstruation. Betty De Shong Meador wrote, "The correspondence of women's menstrual cycles to the phases of the moon became the focal point of ancient religious ritual, expressing the containment of dark and light. . . . The menstruating woman, particularly at menarche, was equated with the dark moon and the absence of precious light or consciousness. In the menstrual seclusion ritual, the women confirmed their ability to approach the dreaded state of darkness and chaos and still return to the light."[15]

Witches know better than to dread the darkness. We all come from a long line of Witches who returned from the underworld. As Phoenix reminded me in our conversation, "Inanna is the original rise again from the dead story—before Persephone, Jesus, before Dionysus, before Horus. Inanna went to the underworld, knowing that no one had ever returned, but also knowing that she would be the exception to the rule. She was defiant." As the story goes, Inanna attempted to overtake the underworld and was put to death for her excessive pride. Three days later Enki sent two Androgynes to rescue Inanna and she arose. Defiant.

In a cycle, we are both temporary and eternal. We take many forms: a seed buried in black soil or a dark womb, we grow and change, reaching upward and downward at once, becoming root, stem, bloom, flower and eventually, we return to become soil itself. Such is life. And we, as empowered Witches, can learn so much about this ebb and flow of our lives and our own selves from the Moon and from Enheduanna's poems about Inanna.

Because the Moon is an icon of beauty in both light and darkness. Inanna, by Enheduanna's telling, is equally beautiful in all her forms. Inanna is a Goddess of both Love and War who can change a person from male to female. Betty De Shong Meador explored Enheduanna's poem "Lady of Largest Heart" and there discovered what she called Inanna's four spiritual paths: Warrior, Priestess, Lover, and Androgyne.

In Enheduanna's writing, each of Inanna's aspects or spiritual paths seem to entirely dismiss meekness, servitude, and other domestic labels that have been thrust onto the female form for centuries. As the Warrior, the goddess is "keen for battle" and "fighting is [her] play." As the Priestess, Inanna is holistic, equally comfortable "to worship in lowly prostration" or "to worship in high heaven." As the Lover, Inanna covers the spectrum of relationships, naughty and nice, "to have a husband, to have a wife, to thrive in the goodness of love," but also "to spark a quarrel within love's lusty delight." She will guide you to love then keep that love interesting. As the Androgyne, Inanna is all things. This isn't just a metaphor for our fluid, nonbinary existence, rather Inanna and her worshippers were known to do Drag or, to use an older turn of phrase, to cross-dress as an important and some say requisite part of their devotion.

Betty De Shong Meador wrote that cult personnel of ambiguous gender performed within the boundaries of the temple ritual. So contained, this tearing of the fabric of reality enables worshippers to contemplate the fragility of their constructed reality and to make a place for instability within their predominantly stable world.[16] And I think this applies to modern Drag shows. These are spaces where we are safe and free to violate social rules, to tear up politics, gender, and the status quo and use the pieces as confetti. A Drag King or Queen takes the stage, and we question everything we thought we knew about gender, about the world. Witches are not light switches; we are dimmer wheels—the whole spectrum is ours.

In our interview, Phoenix said of Androgyny, "The theme of this generation's exploration is gender and what exists beyond the gender binary and how can we cross genders and what can we learn from that crossing? I think it's so meaningful to be able to cross any boundary safely, and learn from binary views, expand them, and explode them."

An androgynous person is, by definition, ambiguous, and ambiguity is *the quality of being open to more than one interpretation*. So, as Warrior, Priestess, Lover, and Androgyne, equally comfortable in each role, Inanna is the embodiment of paradox. But in this paradox there is no tension, no struggle, or no opposition. Inanna exists as the Moon—gender and conceptually fluid. Inanna exists as Mabon—an equal balance of light and shadow, blending, all parts, all phases revered and respected. And us too, Witches. So can we. It's amazing to see how a radical acceptance of ourselves can leak out into radical acceptance of others. The Moon in fullness shines. The darkness of the New Moon simply allows the surrounding stars to shine brighter.

Mesopotamia is a geographical term—Greek for "land between the rivers." Sumeria/Sumer was a civilization that existed in Mesopotamia. The Gods of Sumer are connected to the planets and other celestial bodies observed by Sumerians. Sumer is credited with inventing written language: cuneiform is an ancient writing system of wedge-shaped marks on clay tablets, and is the oldest known form of writing, older than Egyptian hieroglyphics. The word cuneiform "derives from the Sumerian 'kunte' meaning female genitalia [and] consists of arrangements of pubic triangles or Vs, which is the ancient Paleolithic symbol for woman."[17] Sumerians were also likely the first astronomers. Because of their devotional observation of the sky, ancient Sumerians were the first to adopt the twenty-four-hour day and the sixty-minute hour, developed from their calculations of degrees in a circle. The modern seven-day week originated with the ancient Babylonians of this same region for whom each day was associated with one of the seven planetary deities.

Sumerian spirituality was polytheistic, as we have seen with most ancient religions. But it differs in that the primary pantheon of gods coordinate with specific planets, rather than aspects of Nature here on Earth, as we see in Yoruba Ifa or neopaganism. The three most important deities in the Mesopotamian pantheon during all periods were the gods An, Enlil, and Enki. An was identified with all the stars of the equatorial sky, Enlil with those of the northern sky, and Enki with those of the southern sky. Beneath them are the seven planetary deities that gave us our seven-day week: the "seven gods who decree": An, Enlil, Enki, Ninhursag, Nanna, Utu, and Inanna. Inanna was believed to be the planet Venus, Utu was believed to be the Sun, and Nanna, Enheduanna's original patron god, was the Moon.

It is heartbreaking and mind-bending to live in a place and time when Arabs are demonized, painted by Westerners as being guided solely by violence. With hearts broken but eyes wide, it is especially important to note and to understand that the ancient people of the land between the Red Sea and the Persian Gulf, the Euphrates and the Tigris rivers, were likely the first poets and the first mathematicians. Math and

Poetry. These are the achievements we give as evidence of the astound-ing ingenuity of humanity itself, and these keys to civilization may have been cut in what is now called Iraq.

Phoenix is uncomfortable with the term Middle East(ern), preferring the acronym S.W.A.N.A. (South West Asian/North African). She said,

> *The term "Middle East" centers Western Culture. Middle East to whom? To where? That doesn't make any sense and it doesn't repre-sent our cultures at all, it doesn't show any commonalities. It always puts us in relation to the West. There is always a Self and an Other and we are always Othered just by using the word "Middle East" so a lot of people have been reclaiming the term S.W.A.N.A. I prefer this because it includes more people that also have links with each other. It includes anyone that was hit by the Ottoman Empire, and that reaches South Asian folks, Turkish people, Iran, a lot of places.*
>
> *So I think it's more appropriate to use this term because it draws us together, rather than putting us in relation to our oppressors. And if I'm being specific about people then I use their specific terminology that describes them, such as Persian if they are from Iran, Arab if they iden-tify as Arab but a lot of Arabized countries don't fully identify as Arab and prefer to be called by their national titles or their Indigenous titles.*
>
> *For example in North Africa we have Amazigh people who were previously called Berber, but Berber is an Arabic word that comes from another language that was also colonizing of the Ama-zigh. So they chose their own name: Amazigh, which means "free people." Calling all these people Arabs is like saying all white people are French. So, speaking clearly and respecting people's identities is super important. It requires a lot of research and it requires listening and following people you don't know much about to learn.*
>
> *African is another word that I personally love to use for myself as an Egyptian person. I claim Arab identity and I claim African iden-tity, and it's important for me when I break down what it means to be Egyptian to be able to classify myself as Arab African.*

There is power in a name.

Enheduanna was the daughter of a king—the great King Sargon of Akkad who is often credited with establishing the Earth's first known empire, ruling over more people and territory than any known conqueror before him. The legend of Sargon's birth might sound familiar to you. His mother is said to have been a high priestess who gave birth to Sargon in secret, placed him in a basket of reeds, and set him afloat down river where he was rescued and raised by a gardener. Does any of this ring a bell? If you have any background in the Old Testament, you might be picturing Moses right now, whose story is remarkably similar, despite post-dating Sargon's birth by about a thousand years.

Sargon would rise through the ranks to become the King's servant, eventually planning that King's death, and ruling his kingdom with expansion in mind. Sargon's goal, as it is with any king, was hegemony. Control. But it seems like it wasn't Sargon's implicit desire to simply conquer and destroy, but rather to unite and govern. He made little attempt at the kind of destruction and erasure of tradition and language that we see in later empires, and instead, chose to mix Akkadian and Sumerian beliefs, seemingly preferring symbiosis to annihilation. But really, what's the difference? In the United States, culture is called a "melting pot" where all the crayons are heated up and mixed together to, in theory, form a whole new color: American.

Of course what actually happens is that anything other than white, Christian, hetero, capitalism gets heated up and mixed together to form: Not American. In Canada we call our society a cultural mosaic! This sounds a bit better, right? Each piece of culture is added, undiluted, unmelted, into the larger picture of Canadian identity that we form together. Beautiful. Except that those bits of mosaic tile that aren't white Christian hetero-capitalism are pushed down to the bottom of our framework. Lit up for photo ops but otherwise largely ignored. We can't be sure whether Sargon was aiming to melt or mosaic the people of his empire, but we do know that under his rule, systems that had varied from area to area, weights and measures for example, became standardized across Sargon's territory, systems that remained in place for over a thousand years. It's worth noting that, though the system has changed, the global standard for numbers is, and has been for a very long time, Arabic numerals.

Nanna was an important god and the patron deity of the large city of Ur, just north of what we call the Persian Gulf. Nanna's temple was among Sumerians' holiest locales, so Sargon's appointment of his daughter as High Priestess was not only a religious act but also a political one. And Enheduanna was not only a great poet but also a brilliant strategist. She had been born into these immensely creative times: the birth of math, the birth of the written word. She spoke many languages and traveled between the temples of the kingdom, acting as both Priestess and ambassador. Among her most well-known and best-preserved work is a collection of forty-two hymns, the *Sumerian Temple Hymns*, written for each of the forty-two temples of her father's empire. Sargon had entrusted his daughter with an enormous responsibility.

Enheduanna would be the High Priestess of the largest, most important temple in his kingdom. This was not a mere figurehead position. Enheduanna had real power to shape and construct her society, and was tasked with the *unification* of the people. But as Benjamin Foster wrote in *The Age of Agade: Inventing Empire in Ancient Mesopotamia*, "Some read the princess-priestess Enheduanna's work as part of a heavy-handed effort to integrate the Akkadian with the Sumerian pantheons, thereby seeking to force religious unity on the realm. Some see resentment of an alleged promulgation of a comprehensive royal theology, or anger at the Akkadian ruler's assumption of the right to appoint high priestesses and other cultic personnel."[18]

Enheduanna's appointment was controversial. There were constant uprisings but King Sargon continued to triumph and is said to have bragged that the number of rebellions only served to show his might in victory. Both Enheduanna and her father recognized that religion and language were two key ingredients for peacekeeping, on one hand, and war-winning, on the other. Can a war ultimately be won with poetry? I like to think so, and the length of Sargon's rule would suggest that the composition and distribution of Enheduanna's forty-two temple hymns may have helped to unify the Akkadians and Sumerians of Sargon's empire.

But Enheduanna's role as High Priestess at the Temple of Ur also meant that she oversaw the temple's large financial endowment. Temples controlled the collection of taxes and the all-important distribution of grain. Despite these obvious monetary and political advantages, Enheduanna's very real devotion is made clear in her poetry. I do not believe that Enheduanna wrote these poems or performed her duties without faith, like some politicians who appeal to the religious strictly for power, but without any genuine belief or reverence. It was her job to attend to Nanna, but when things got real, as we'll see, Enheduanna turned to her goddess, Inanna, whom she saw as being the owner and bearer of all things, from the material to the divine.

To turn a man into a woman and a woman into a man are yours, Inanna.

Desirability and arousal, goods and property are yours, Inanna.
…
Observation, choice, offering, inspection, and approval are yours, Inanna.

Assigning virility, dignity, guardian angels, protective deities and cult centers are yours, Inanna.[19]

Enheduanna begged: "Precious Queen / Rekindle for me / your holy heart." Rekindle your holy heart. This is a mantra that I have adopted for myself. When it feels as if the flame in my soul is down to embers, I speak to myself Enheduanna's words. Rekindle your holy heart. I take a deep breath and with Enheduanna's words in mind, every exhale acts as bellows, and in this breathing my little heart coals begin to glow. Much like our bravery, our instincts, though when left unattended or unacknowledged may fade, are always there, awaiting rediscovery, so too is that Holy part of you. And every act of compassion for ourselves and others is kindling for our holy hearts.

And so it is too that when we revel in the unknown, when we bask in the darkness, when we cast aside our society's drive to concretize everything, when we value the unknown as much as the known, we release the burden of expectation. Who am I? is a much more loaded question than:

who might I be today? Embracing your emotions and your potential rekindles your holy heart.

Before Enheduanna, Priestesses were subservient to Priests, but Enheduanna was a Princess, the daughter of a King, so she was subservient to no one except her goddess. There is a beautiful play in her poetry between her clear sense of her own royalty and her vulnerability and submission when entreating her goddess. Like Inanna herself, Enheduanna was more than just an archetype, and her poetry allows us a glimpse into how human emotions, our being, our essence, has changed very little in four thousand years.

One of my favorite assessments of Inanna comes from Roseane Lopes who wrote, "Inanna provides us perhaps with the most complete portrait of the Non-Domestic, Non-Homebound and Non-Maternal Divine Feminine of Antiquity . . . Perhaps the best way to examine Inanna's femininity is in the light of what She is not in comparison to traditional models of femininity and roles played by women in society."[20]

And this description of Inanna rings true for us Witches too. As Pam Grossman wrote in her book *Waking the Witch:* "[The Witch] is perhaps the only female archetype who is an independent operator. Virgins, whores, daughters, mothers, wives—each of these is defined by whom she is sleeping with or not, the care that she is giving or that is given to her, or some sort of symbiotic debt that she must eventually pay. The Witch owes nothing. That is what makes her dangerous. And that is what makes her divine."[21]

Inanna owes nothing, beholden to no one, but is everything, is capable of everything, and that, too, makes her dangerous. Enheduanna appealed to not only the loving aspects of her goddess but also the ferocity and rage. She wrote about her goddess Inanna as a goddess of Love, but also and equally a goddess of War and Destruction. Like Inanna, like Nature itself, we are not confined to social order. We do not naturally fit into the wanton filing and ranking that patriarchy designed and fetishizes. We, as people, as Witches, as parts of Nature are more verb and adjective than noun. We are not just one thing. We are nebulous, paradoxical, contradictory. We seek descriptors, not labels, wisdom over knowledge. We are whole. And Holy. And at Mabon we can celebrate this being of all things at once by regarding the day's perfect play with the night.

Phoenix said, "It's also a decolonizing act to worship and recognize and honor Inanna because she proves that queerness existed long before Europeans came to the so-called Orient. Our toxic shame and conservative, homophobic, transphobic ways are inherited by being so colonized by the Europeans who came into contact with us. So that's a reclamation for me, saying, 'No, you did not start Queerness, no, we've been Queer.' Our own people tell us, 'You're being like a foreigner by being Gay, you're denying your own history.' I tell them that's not true." Just with her name, Phoenix Inana says so much. Names have power. If the one your parents gave you doesn't fit, choose a new one. Sign your work.

I read the first line of Enheduanna's poem "The Adoration of Inanna of Ur," "Queen of all the ME, Radiant Light," not knowing that in Sumerian mythology, a *ME* is one of the gods' decrees that make the civilizations of humanity possible. The MEs are the Sumerian understanding of the relationship between humanity and the gods. A ME is a world-ordering power.

My English-speaking brain took awhile to get over ME not meaning Me, Myself, I. But I find it a delightful and useful mistake to keep making. A declaration that makes all life possible? That's Me. The human condition? That's Me. A world-ordering power? That's Me. In the battle against Shame, it is beneficial to think of oneself as being fundamental to the understanding of the relationship between humanity and the gods. Queen of all the Me.

Relatedly, Enheduanna is the first known author in history who wrote in the first-person narrative. The first writer to say "I." To be self-reflexive instead of just telling a story. We find tales of Kings and Gods, but Enheduanna wrote about herself, her feelings, her fears. Enheduanna is the first known, written Me. The first poet. The first "I." The priestess wrote: "I, I am Enheduanna,"[22] and though her poetry is dedicated to the goddess Inanna in both intention and content, Enheduanna includes her own deeply personal emotions throughout. Not just those feelings of awe and devotion, but also fear, loss, and anger.

Most of her poetry was in exaltation, hymns to temples, gods, and goddesses, but it is, ironically, in "Exaltation of Inanna" that we learn the most about the poet herself.

Let's go back to our Beloved Ipsita from the Lughnasadh chapter who said, "Every strong woman is a Witch and she is always hunted."[23] And so was also the case with our beloved Enheduanna. Despite her power, despite her lineage, despite her intellect, she too was, for a time, exiled. "Exaltation of Inanna" is a poem written in distress. Uprisings were not infrequent, but one particular revolt was almost successful in deposing Enheduanna from her Temple. Four-thousand-three-hundred-year-old historical records are, of course, spotty, so we are forced to puzzle her exile together with pieces missing. Enheduanna first refers to him as "that man" but later names her attempted usurper: Lugal-Ane, which translates as "Great man of heaven," but who was he to her?

In his doctoral thesis "Pagan Queen: Jung, Individuation and the Goddess Inanna,"[24] Bernard Butler theorized that Lugal-Ane was a priest-to-be under Enheduanna's tutelage and that Enheduanna developed a crush on her student. Other sources say he was a rebelling Sumerian king. Enheduanna wrote, "Lugal-ane has altered everything and has stripped An of the E-ana (temple). He has not stood in awe of the greatest deity. He has turned that temple, whose attractions were inexhaustible, whose beauty was endless, into a desolation." Forced to roam the wild mountains of exile, Enheduanna felt she had been ignored or betrayed by her God Nanna, and so turned this plea toward Inanna.

My Nanna has cared not for me.
In the rebellious land,
they completely and utterly destroyed me.
Has he spoken it—does it mean anything?
Has he not spoken it—does it mean anything?
After he stood there in triumph,
he expelled me from the temple.

She proclaims Inanna's power, rage, and might, while documenting her turn from her old God, writing, "I have not said this of Nanna / I have said it of YOU / my phrases glorify YOU."

I Proclaim!
That you are wide as the earth
Proclaim!
That you crush rebellious lands
Proclaim!
That you shriek over the land
Proclaim!
That you smash heads
Proclaim!
That you gorge on corpses like a dog
Proclaim!
That your glance flames with rage
Proclaim!
That your eyes flash like jewels
Proclaim!
That you balk and defy
Proclaim!
That you stand victorious.[25]

Enheduanna had previously described Inanna as having a bountiful and radiant heart, but in her exile, it is Inanna's destructive power that bends Enheduanna to sing her praises. Conjuring all the blood, pain, fear, and creative potential of her existence, Enheduanna wrote: "Suffering bitter pangs / I gave birth to this exaltation / for you my Queen / what I told you in the dark of night / may the singer recount at noon."[26]

May what is in the dark be brought to the light, may what is secret be made known, may what is deemed shameful become our source of pride.

And it seems that Enheduanna's prayers to Inanna were answered, as the rebellion was squashed and military victories won. Enheduanna was restored to her rightful place at the head of the Temple of Ur. In total, Enheduanna held this position for forty years.

Betty De Shong Meador reminds us that in exile, Enheduanna "loses her position, her status, her influence. However, she does not lose her voice."[27] And that is true for all of us. One of the greatest voices of all time, Ella Fitzgerald, was homeless before her debut at the Apollo Theater. Having nothing, no material possessions, she never lost the creative power that lived inside of her. Your voice doesn't have to be a singing voice, like Ella, or poetry, like Enheduanna. Your voice can manifest in volunteer work, how you spend your money, journaling, protest, baking, dance, science experiments, or architectural designs. Your voice can be heard in a painting, how you raise your child or treat your pets, the planting of a seed or the knitting of a scarf. This is, to me, Enheduanna's greatest lesson: to speak your truth and sign your name.

But maybe that's too easy to say. How do we speak our truth if we're not sure what that truth is? Like anything else, the self and the truth require personal investigation. Mabon is the balance of light and dark, but we are moving toward and into the darkness. Inspired by Inanna's fullness, her lover self and her warrior self in perfect balance, Mabon becomes the perfect time to explore our shadows, get to know ourselves, and, hopefully, answer the question of What Is My Truth? The list of MEs that represented all of civilization included such positive ideas and characteristics as Scholarship, Music, Art, Sex, and Peace, but the list also includes some of the darker aspects of human life: Terror, Lamentation, and Falsehood. For the ancient Sumerians, both light and shadow were essential components of humanity. And so it is for you and me and all of us Witches.

Our shadow isn't our evil twin, it's not some Dexter-like serial killer waiting in the undisturbed recesses of our personalities to be uncovered and released. You are not Pandora's box. Your opening up releases miracles. Like a piñata, there are treasures deep inside. At its simplest, the shadow is the unknown, so the shadow self is the unknown self. It's a concept largely credited to Swiss psychoanalyst and psychiatrist Carl Jung, whose work would reverberate through many disciplines from Religion to Literature to Archaeology, including the scholarship of our

Enheduanna writer Betty De Shong Meador who refers to herself as Jungian. Jung famously said: "If you don't make the unconscious conscious, it will rule your life, and you will call it fate."

So when we do "Shadow Work," we are attempting to know the unknown by asking ourselves tough questions, and by reframing our existing notions of good and bad, right and wrong. The shadow isn't only the unknown, it is also the unacknowledged. Those bits of anger, emotion, trauma that we have buried down deep within our souls. We think that if we don't acknowledge these aspects of ourselves, that they will cease to exist, but like mold in a basement, the unchecked shadows can grow, throwing sickly spores into the air upstairs. Like the great goddess Inanna, by accepting all aspects of ourselves, the Warrior, the Lover, the Priestess, the Androgyne, by accepting and acknowledging both the shadow and the light, we allow ourselves to fully rejoice in our being and begin our own personal exaltation. Witches do not fear the dark.

At Mabon, as the shadow grows and covers the land, we must get comfortable with our own shadows. I asked my friend, Witch, shadow worker, and forensic archaeologist Vanessa to help me to understand this concept. She said,

> *Shadow work to me is an essential part of knowing one's self. It means taking the proverbial good hard look in the mirror at patterns and ways of dealing with things that are hurtful to you or to others. The reason that these keep showing up when you don't deal with them is because they are part of your Shadow. If you are fluent with tarot cards, the Shadow would be the Devil card, those thoughts and patterns that bog you down. You can feel there is something a little slimy in that darkness and you don't want to go there. But in not opening the drapes to let the light in, you are only letting that slime settle in.*
>
> *I believe all people who work with magic have a responsibility to work with their Shadow (mind you, you don't heal your Shadow, you learn to live with it and/or you heal the consequences of your*

Shadow). If you don't do shadow work then your love and light message is empty because it glosses over the most intricate of self-knowledge. Also not understanding one's shadow could definitely lead to dangerous or negative spellwork. As Witches, whenever possible, we are responsible for our energies coming from a place of empathy and not of hurt. A very black-and-white example is if you are making a hexing spell against someone because they made you feel jealous—then you are not addressing the shadow and being unethical. If you open the drapes and shed some light into why you felt that way and then you made a spell to reinforce your own self-worth, then you have healed the consequences of your shadow. Your Shadow stays there. Shadow work is always ongoing.[28]

When I was growing up, no one taught me how to ride a bike. I tried to teach myself once, but a neighborhood kid made fun of my training wheels and then I fell and scraped my knee. Bruised, bleeding, frustrated, and humiliated, I tossed my sister's old bike back into the depths of the garage and vowed never to try riding again. I was so ashamed that I didn't know how to ride a bike that I lied to my friends and told them I could. I spun masterful webs of excuses to avoid the embarrassment and mockery I was certain telling the truth would elicit. I learned to ride a bike in my late twenties, and I'm proud to have acquired the skill. But if I had been honest about my shortcomings to myself and to my friends, I could have learned two decades sooner. I missed out on a lot of fun and adventure because I was too afraid to admit that I didn't know how to do something.

We lose out on a lot in life by hiding our shame, refusing to acknowledge or reveal the unknown. Self-described "Bad Witch" Carolyn Elliott wrote that Shame is the magic killer.[29] I would add that Magic is the Shame killer. Witches view ourselves as a part of Nature, where even chaos has an order, and the wheel turns without judgment. We extend the compassion we feel for others to ourselves as well. We are the Moon, beauty and power in darkness and light. We are Inanna, equal parts Lover, Warrior, Priestess, Male, and Female. We are Mabon, in perfect balance. In our universal acceptance, there is no room for shame.

In Enheduanna's homeland, people continue to abide by the cycles of our closest celestial neighbor, the Moon. The dates of Islam's holy days of Ramadan and the two Eid festivals are based on the first sighting of the Crescent Moon that follows the new. Fasting and feasting in perfect balance, just like the light of the Moon.

Enheduanna's successful reign began a tradition of kings appointing their daughters to the role of High Priestess, a tradition that would live on for hundreds of years after our beloved poet's death. Her writing style is said to have influenced the form and content of the Hebrew Psalms that inhabit the Christian Bible.

In 1922 the British Museum and the University of Pennsylvania Museum partnered to excavate a mound of sand in southern Iraq that they theorized was covering the ancient city of Ur. Years of sifting through sand amid sandstorms bore fruit in 1927. While excavating what would be confirmed to be the Temple of Ur, British archaeologist Sir Leonard Woolley found a round like the full Moon, relief-carved gypsum object, now known as the Enheduanna calcite disk, depicting Enheduanna and three other people. The inscriptions on the disk identify Enheduanna, plus, presumably, the three most important people in her life: her estate manager Adda, her scribe Sagadu, and my favorite, her hairdresser Ilum Palilis.

The disk reads: "Enheduanna, zirru-priestess, wife of the god Nanna, daughter of Sargon, king of the world, in the temple of the goddess Inanna." What survives of Enheduanna is that alabaster disk, inscribed with her name and image, housed at the Penn Museum in Philadelphia, and her poems, copied and recopied for thousands of years. In 2015 the International Astronomical Union named a crater on Mercury after Enheduanna. She will live forever in the galaxy, in the planetary dance that begat her goddess. Immortalized on Earth and in Space.

For us Witches, too, there are many ways to become immortal. One of the best is to tell your story and sign your name. If you question your value, or the power of your words, remember that Anne Frank was just a teenage girl who kept a diary. Phoenix said, "I am hearing people speak Inanna's name and I know she is becoming part of the consciousness." Names have power. Stories have power. Rekindle your holy heart. And sign your name.

Ritual

You'll need two small apples and two small candles. Birthday candles are best for this. NOTE: if you're currently lacking in resources, skip the candles and speak your truth into any fruit or vegetable or nut or bean. Cut a single banana in half if that's what you've got, and use one half for the past and one for the future. Even two cups of water would work. Remember: Magic is flexible and doesn't require you to spend money you don't have—this is about your ritual, and we always encourage you to personalize your practice as much as you can.

Today, Mabon, the autumn equinox is the balance of light and dark. The seeds we planted in the past are harvested in the present to prepare for the future. Their growth required both the darkness of the soil and the light of the sun.

Pull out the stems of your apples and poke a small hole in each apple to hold your candle (an apple makes a great candleholder—or pipe—in a pinch).

One apple represents the past, one the future. You are the present.

Take a few deep breaths. Invoke your favorite Witch or goddess, call the corners if you like, or just take a minute to breathe.

Light the candle that represents your past. Speak over it. Talk to the apple about the blessings and traumas of your past. Be honest and vulnerable.

Light the future candle. Talk about your fears, hopes, and dreams for the future. Speak your plans and goals. Let the candles burn out or blow them out.

NEVER LEAVE BURNING CANDLES UNATTENDED.

If you decide to blow out your candles, take a big, intentional inhale and blow that concentrated power, extinguishing your flames with decisive purpose. Remove any stubs or wax from the apples.

Hold your "past" apple and thank the past for getting you to this moment. Then eat the apple. Taste your past. Feel it between your teeth and tongue. Chew it up and swallow it. Let your past go through and out of you as the apple quite literally passes through your body and out of your system.

Now take your "future" apple, thank the future for what it holds in store. Make a promise to your future self.

Bury the apple or put it in the compost or under a tree at a park. Somewhere it can feed the Earth and the bugs. If you don't have access to dirt, or can't stand the idea of wasting good food, we hear you. You can cut up the "future" apple and feed it to someone younger than you—ideally, a child. Again, make sure apples are free of wax, and use birthday candles for this since we know they are food safe.

Now you have processed the past and contributed to the future. Walk boldly into the coming winter, and sign your name to your fate.

INCANTATION
Proclaim!
I am _____ [your name], High Priestess of my Life.
I am wide as the Earth.
I am Beauty in all my infinite forms.
I accept my light.
I accept my shadow.
I kindle the flame of my holy heart.
I sign my name to my choices.
I balk, defy, and stand victorious.
I give birth to exaltation.
Observation, choice, offering, inspection, and approval
are mine.
I sign my name to a life of my creation.
I rekindle my holy heart.

Bonus Ritual: Shadow Work

For Mabon, with its darkening skies and soft chill whispering from the distance, we climb under our blanket of consciousness to explore our Shadows. I learned this technique from a personal session with astrologer and Shadow Worker, Monefa Walker.

Grab a pen and paper and center yourself in a comfortable, quiet place. With your eyes closed, take a few deep breaths, embracing the darkness that your lowered lids provide.

Ask yourself these questions and write down your answers:

What was the last thing that made you laugh—like, really laugh?

What was the last thing that made you angry—like, really angry?

What do these two events have in common?

By answering these questions we begin to understand the ME in all things.

8

Samhain

This circle is led by Risa

SAMHAIN SITS IN THE SPACE BETWEEN ONE YEAR DYING AND THE NEXT BEING BORN, AND IN THAT TIME WE GET A GLIMPSE INTO AN UNKNOWN COUNTRY.

The word means "summer's end," and it is a window ledge. A lintel on the doorway, a liminal evening through which we are leaning into the darker half of the year. It is a festival of death. A festival of meeting our dead as well as our ideas about death. Where other seasonal solar and lunar festivals are tied to the harvest, Samhain is the time when shepherds gather their flocks. It is a time of finding out who among your beloved will come home, and who will remain wandering in the upland pastures. It is a time for encountering the knowledge that this comes to us all: stepping out off the edges of all maps. "In our travels through the underworld, Witches become map makers"[1] wrote Amanda Yates Garcia, Oracle of Los Angeles. Meeting death is beautiful and horrible, inspiring and the most terrifying, and so we dress up to meet this specter in ways that hide us or empower us, disguise us and amplify us.

In past years Amy and I have celebrated this season together. She'd get dressed up in full glorious drag and we'd give out candy for hours, or I would throw a party for hundreds of masked revelers, playing one of my favorite roles: lurking in the background in black, making my magic unseen, and Amy would roll in just in time to win the costume contest.

But this year, at the time of this writing, death looms and hangs around us all like spiderwebs. We are midpandemic, the coronavirus counter jumps by tens of thousands every day. My parents are in self-isolation awaiting testing. A friend is separated from her children, working twelve-hour days in the intensive care unit; others from our coven are on the front lines in grocery stores, or supporting women living in unsafe quarantine homes. Another loses her daughter to cancer and can't collapse into her parents' arms. A friend's sister dies of suicide. My great-aunt drives herself to the hospital rather than tell anyone she is sick and risk infecting them, and dies of the coronavirus there after dedicating decades of her life as a principal in the toughest schools in New York City.

We are weighted with loss and afraid for our elders and afraid for the future. By the time this book comes out, the world will be different somehow. We usually look to the future with a certain kind of confidence that things will progress rationally, gradually, but the future itself is that unknown country. It is a box in which we are both alive and dead, and we know it now more than ever. The borders have closed and people sing to each other from their balconies trying to remember the touch and friendly crush of crowded bars, of a joyful hug, of a sloppy two-cheek kiss on the street. Maybe by the time you hold this book, we will have all rushed back into each other's arms again.

> *Our minds are still racing back and forth, longing for a return to "normality," trying to stitch our future to our past and refusing to acknowledge the rupture. But the rupture exists. And in the midst of this terrible despair, it offers us a chance to rethink the doomsday machine we have built for ourselves. Nothing could be worse than a return to normality. Historically, pandemics have forced humans to break with the past and imagine their world anew. This one is no different. It is a portal, a gateway between one world and the next. We can choose to walk through it, dragging the carcasses of our prejudice and hatred, our avarice, our data banks and dead ideas, our dead rivers and smoky skies behind us. Or we can walk through lightly, with little luggage, ready to imagine another world. And ready to fight for it.*[2]

For me it turns out that the best way to face death, and to prepare to walk through this portal lightly and to fight for a new world, is to continue to do this work. To slip into this writing room with its tilted walls hung with Witch art and paintings of animals, and to invite these histories onto the page. To see you all here with me, the great circle we make with our sympathy and our hope.

This work of prying open the stories we've been told—not just to include the spectacular and heroic lives of women, and Witches of all genders, and gender-nonconforming magical beings, but also their shocking and glittering ideas—is healing work. Together we disrupt a death spiral that has tried to erase what is magical in all of us. Together we cast a circle, keep a portal open, and we help each other through.

At Samhain in particular, we ritualize the knowledge that death is close but also that our lives matter. That this present moment is always a portal, a circle of white flame that holds space for things wildly new and very old. All our work is ancestor work, and in the great fertility tradition of Witchcraft, we are the womb and the tomb, we sit on the edge of life and death, calling new possibilities into the world.

The fact of your own death and the death of all your loved ones is a constant truth. On Samhain we're called to sit with this, to sit with them, in order to clear our eyes and reveal the incredible power of this exact moment, ripe with fear and gentleness and everything.

Sit and listen to death and to what she whispers to you.

The guides we've chosen for this season are iconic tarot artist Pamela "Pixie" Colman Smith and elusive and problematic trailblazer H. P. Blavatsky. In different ways, both offer us a message about standing in a dark doorway, facing the unknown.

H. P. Blavatsky has been called the mother of modern spirituality and one of the greatest explorers of the nineteenth century. She spoke Russian, Georgian, English, French, Italian, Arabic, and Sanskrit. She was a much-maligned philosopher and activist, and founder of a world religion that she never wanted to be a religion, rather wanted it to be just a means of investigating the wisdom of the gods. Theosophy. She was one of the first Westerners to convert to Buddhism, the first Russian woman to gain American citizenship, and the first Western woman to make it into the sacred fortified Himalayan nation of Tibet where she lived and studied for years. Probably.

She was certainly fiercely independent. A chain-smoking, not-quite-vegetarian. A celibate philosopher medium. A spectacular synthesizer of Eastern and Western philosophies.

H. P. Blavatsky remains deeply divisive, in part because she was intentionally elusive her whole life. As Witches before her have known: if you are different and powerful, sometimes you'll choose to hide or obscure parts of yourself to survive. Costumes, disguises, fashion itself is a powerful magic, a way of painting our minds on the outside of ourselves to alter how we can move through the world. Sometimes we wear the full regalia of Witch and it amplifies us, and sometimes we dress to slip unnoticed through cracks and past sentries. "We're all born naked and the rest is drag."[3] H. P. Blavatsky donned a kind of drag—especially when traveling long mountain roads to forbidden places in the 1800s—and conjured a new way of looking at the world.

H. P. Blavatsky wrote dozens of books and hundreds of articles that traced a worldview and history of the universe that she claimed was channeled directly from her Masters. These Masters may have been real teachers she had met, and maybe they could speak to her directly through her mind and across space and time. Or maybe they were a useful illusion, just a deft composite of people she'd learned from and books she had read. A disguise that allowed her to give her words more power while also keeping some mystery, and keeping some people who were politically vulnerable due to their revolutionary activities out of the firing range of the public eye.

Whatever the source or sources, her insights touched a nerve with thinkers across the globe, and the Theosophical Society she founded is active today, with headquarters in dozens of countries and dedicated to three core principles: to form a nucleus of the universal brotherhood of humanity, without distinction of race, creed, sex, caste, or color; to encourage the study of comparative religion, philosophy, and science; to investigate unexplained laws of nature and the powers latent in humanity.[4]

Whatever else she said and wherever else her words were taken—sometimes to horrible places—this is the stone I want to polish. The magic words to carry forward from H. P. Blavatsky into my own community building: to form that nucleus without prejudice and from there to investigate and study together.

The overwhelming body of her writing and thought is fiercely against injustice in all its forms and devoted to stitching ideas together to find a truth that could uplift and ennoble humanity. Her ideas have a world-changing impetus in them in a way that directly threatened colonial rule. "Gandhi first came into contact with Theosophy in London in 1889, when he was studying law and generally trying to adapt himself to

Western, specifically British ways. He believed, as many educated young Indians did at the time, that his people should give up their old ways, and strive to be like the English . . . reading Blavatsky inspired Gandhi to study Hinduism and to reject the notion, taught by Christian missionaries, that his nation's religion was mere superstition. It was this belief in the value of his own tradition that sustained him throughout his career."[5]

H. P. B., as she preferred to be called, was a White Russian noblewoman in the nineteenth century who had groundbreaking ideas about the universe, and space, and time, as well as religion, race, and sex. She had a mind open to philosophies and spiritualities from people of color, and worked to take herself to a place where she could be a student and a conduit for those ideas.

Though illuminated by this labor and love, her thinking was also distorted by the intensely racist discourse she moved through and benefited from. She took up a concept of "root races" and tried to theorize epochs in human history dating back hundreds of thousands of years. In doing so, she wrote things that contradicted her own often-repeated belief that "all men have spiritually and physically the same origin" and that "mankind is essentially of one and the same essence."[6]

In the most terrible footnote she wrote, "No amount of culture, nor generations of training amid civilization, could raise such human specimens as the Bushmen, the Veddhas of Ceylon, and some African tribes, to the same intellectual level as the Aryans, the Semites, and the Turanians so called. The 'sacred spark' is missing in them and it is they who are the only inferior races on the globe, now happily—owing to the wise adjustment of nature which ever works in that direction—fast dying out."[7] Vile. H. P. Blavatsky wrote racist things that were picked up and passed around by subsequent generations of "thinkers" trying to find justification for violence and injustice, and ended up in the hands of Nazi "theorists."[8]

So at the end of this book and before the next turn in the cycle, we go back to this crucial haunting question: should we choose to tell her story and keep her alongside other problematic ancestors in order to learn from their mistakes as well as their wisdom, to hold out a little hope for not repeating the same old tragedies again and again? Honestly I'm still not sure. In a season of death these are ghosts we have to reckon with.

Male philosophers of her time certainly have been kept and redeemed even in the face of their manifest mistakes and cruelties. Carl Jung tells a horrible story that begins: "A bushman had a little son whom he loved with the tender monkey-love characteristic of primitives." Leo Tolstoy, Karl Marx, Charles Darwin, Henry David Thoreau, Friedrich Nietzsche, and Mohandas Gandhi all said problematic things about race (to put it mildly) and have all been challenged and largely redeemed, or at least picked apart and sold for parts.

The nineteenth century was dominated by systems that needed to justify slavery and colonialism. This was the air they breathed, or, more accurately, the blood they drank. This is a hand so heavy it can make its nasty way into your language and behavior, and you can find you are a puppet to it just when you thought you had cut the last strings.

We live in a world where racism still pulls with its grim hand on our systems, bending them away from an equal justice. Where capitalism presses down on our fears and needs and makes it hard to see each other kindly and clearly. Where the goal of a universal brotherhood, sister-hood, nonbinary Witch-hood is a more glowing and imperative goal than ever.

So I want to see what I can learn and keep from the woman who wrote: "Hast thou attuned thy heart and mind to the great mind and heart of all mankind? For as the sacred River's roaring voice whereby all Nature-sounds are echoed back, so must the heart of him 'who in the stream would enter,' thrill in response to every sigh and thought of all that lives and breathes. . . . Hast thou attuned thy being to Humanity's great pain, O candidate for light?"[9]

As Witches we are called to listen to the suffering, to the river, to the ghosts beyond the veil, and to be changed by what we hear. We work and craft to be tuned like instruments so that our voices rise and resonate.

O candidate for light, on dark pandemic days, on days like Samhain that take us to the edge of the portal between life and death, can we tune ourselves to hear and weave true, missing stories into the fabric of our lives?

H. P. Blavatsky lived life as a portal, like María Sabina she opened the book.

> *As early as 1970, in an article for* McCall's *magazine, the novelist Kurt Vonnegut dubbed Blavatsky 'the Founding Mother of the Occult in America.' These days she is mostly vaguely remembered as a charlatan, when she is remembered at all. So it goes.*
>
> *Yet those who are aware of her, and of her contribution to Western thought, have a different view. Like the historian of esotericism Christopher Bamford, they wonder why she is not, as Bamford believes she should be, counted with Marx, Nietzsche, and Freud and one "of the creators of the twentieth century"? . . . By the time of Blavatsky's death in London in 1891, the Theosophical movement had spread from New York to India, Europe, and beyond, and included among its devotees some important names, such as Thomas Edison and Mohandas Gandhi . . . and Jawaharlal Nehru, India's first prime minister, who was initiated into the Theosophical Society by Annie Besant, the socialist and freethinker who converted to Theosophy after meeting Blavatsky, and who, as president of the society, helped India win its independence. Even Albert Einstein is said to have kept a well-thumbed copy of Blavatsky's magnum opus,* The Secret Doctrine, *on his desk.[10]*

The stories go that Einstein kept H. P. B.'s writing close, and would dip into her book in bed at night or when stuck on a physics problem. These are unverified. But I love the idea that the almost unbelievable leaps taken in theoretical physics at this time are somehow linked to a woman who traveled the world alone. That our understanding of the physics of the world and universe was opened wide by transmissions received from that great listener to the beyond, H. P. Blavatsky, who introduced the idea, in *The Secret Doctrine,* that the Eternity of the Universe is a boundless plane, "the playground of numberless Universes incessantly manifesting and disappearing."[11]

H. P. B.'s influence on the emergence of our modern mythologies extends beyond the math of universes into the core stories of magic in the silver-screened New World.

The Emerald City, the Yellow Brick Road, magical slippers, a brave farm girl protagonist, and, of course, the good and bad Witches are all now seemingly timeless icons from what some have called "the first American fairy tale" . . . a great many of them can be traced to the influence of [Lyman Frank Baum's] mother-in-law, the suffragist and equal rights pioneer Matilda Joslyn Gage. Gage was a follower of Theosophy, the nineteenth-century gnostic religious movement that brought Eastern mystical thought to the west. She would have been familiar with the ideas that one can go on a spiritual journey up the thirteen golden stairs to find enlightenment at the Temple of Divine Wisdom, and that one can reveal the ultimate truth behind world religions by metaphorically lifting the veil of illusion (or peering behind a curtain perhaps).[12]

H. P. B. is an ancestor of the Wizard of Oz, Dorothy, the White Witch, and the Wicked Witch of the West. While some of her ideas are deeply offensive, and her life story holds all kinds of conspiracy twists and turns, and her writing contains more creative leaps than I can wrap my head around, I do want us to see and keep this:

In the second half of the 1800s, a young woman heard the world sing to her across unseen planes. She sought out spiritual teachers her whole life to try to understand what she heard and what happened to her. Her transmissions from those teachers sent a wave across the world. Traces of what she heard and shared still run through our modern fairy tales and scientific and spiritual theories today.

On a day of Death let's be electrified by the way our lives live on. For Samhain, when the world is thin and we sit face to face with the unknown, we ask how we can be a portal, taking guidance from all ancestor Witches—flawed and brave. We ask to be tuned to the great river of sorrow and joy and otherness as it courses through the universe, and through ourselves.

After a childhood introduction to Tibetan Buddhism, shamanism, and Freemason secrets through her grandfather and other teachers, H. P. Blavatsky read and photo-memorized thousands of obscure spiritual texts and learned enough to get by in many languages.

According to her sister Vera, by the age of fourteen H. P. B. would dream awake and out loud, sharing a near constant stream of visions. Vera wrote, "For Helena all nature seemed animated with a mysterious life of its own. She heard the voice of every object and form whether organic or inorganic, and claimed consciousness and being."[13]

As a teenager, H. P. B. ran away from a marriage to a much older man and traveled the world alone seeking spiritual knowledge. For ten years. We know little about this time.

Almost 600 (!) biographies have been written of Blavatsky, but the details of her life, especially the years 1848–1873, remain sketchy all the same. Most of the authors have been either devoted disciples or sharply critical adversaries. Some interesting and well-documented facts, however, can be determined. She was born to a noble Russian family in present-day Ukraine, married at 17, ran away only months later, traveled widely and spent time in Cairo, among many other places, where she supported herself as a medium. In the category of details considered doubtful by her detractors, we find Blavatsky's claims to having studied voodoo in New Orleans, crossing the prairie in the company of native Americans, and spending seven years with the "Masters" in Tibet. Her adversaries' claims about bigamy, an abandoned infant, and charlatanry are equally contested by pro-Blavatsky writers.[14]

In the 1850s, after deciding she could safely return home without being forced to follow through on the marriage, we do know she returned to her family and started a business rafting logs. She noticed a fungus on the trees that could be used as a touchwood for fires. She knew and noticed wisdoms in the woods. Then things start to happen around her again. Raps in the walls, windows, and doors, furniture moving of its own accord. "She had acquired a reputation in Tiflis and other places as a magician, a seer, and what we would call today a 'psychic' and healer. By this time, she had given up answering questions by raps, which was tiring and time consuming, and taken up giving spoken or written replies. She later told A. P. Sinnett how she could read people's thoughts by seeing them emerge from their heads as a kind of spiral of 'luminous smoke' that formed pictures and images around them, and she remarked that often these thoughts find a home in the consciousness of other people. She had, it seems, begun to learn to control the strange phenomena happening around her."[15]

Just as she's beginning to get a handle on the way the unseen made itself known to her, H. P. Blavatsky had an encounter with Death. She was drawn *d'en bas de l'eau* like Mama Lola, and like her, this passing through attuned her hearing and honed her power. "In 1864, in Mingrelia, on the shore of the Black Sea, HPB was thrown from her horse. She fractured her spine and entered a coma that lasted for months. . . . She said that while in this state she had no idea who Helena Blavatsky was and that she seemed to travel in a far-off country. . . . Like many other esoteric figures—Steiner, Jung, Gurdjieff, Swedenborg—HPB had passed through what the historian of psychology calls a 'creative illness,' and had come out a changed person."[16]

Returned to her strength and electrified by her new vision and power, she traveled giving music recitals and studying kabbalah in Italy and Transylvania. Her travel diary mentions Odessa, Syria, Lebanon, Jerusalem, Egypt, and Greece. In 1867 she was in the Balkans, Hungary, Venice, Florence, and Mentana, Italy. She joined the fight against the French and the papal army alongside Garibaldi, and was left for dead in a ditch with musket balls embedded in her leg and shoulder, her left arm broken in two places by a saber. This sickness and recovery made the voices and visions clearer still: she received instructions from a Master to head to Constantinople, and from there to head for the third time in her life toward India and Tibet.

I'm fascinated by this image of her riding across the roof of the world—her features and dress and quick ability with language letting her slip past sentries to go where colonizing armies and more ostentatious travelers couldn't. I'm even more inspired by the question of what she learned once she got there. She described verses inscribed in an unknown language on the altars of Mahayana temples that were recited to her, and which she memorized and transcribed and commented on in the vast body of her work that followed. She studied this philosophy and she also studied English while in Tibet, and maybe the two tasks were connected: to learn a truth about the universe and to share it in the common language, just like Lalla.

D. T. Suzuki said of H. P. Blavatsky's writing that H. P. B. had "in some way been initiated into the deeper side of Mahayana teachings."[17] H. P. B. learned secrets from masters of many faiths and was a medium in the truest sense, a portal. She broke through heavy programming to share the belief that the narrowness of Victorian thinking, the bombast and blinkered triumphalism of colonialism, was just a childhood in a series of ages. She taught that greater knowledge and wider perspective could be found outside of colonizer philosophy and spirituality, and she helped introduce the West to the compelling idea of the potential and power generated by a bodhisattva vow: A vow to liberate all beings. A plea to stay here on Earth and not leave town for heaven or Nirvana, but for all our lives and powers to be placed in the service of others.

H. P. B. is the forgotten and discarded mother of so much of modern Western esoteric thought. She is a mother who fiercely defended her reputation for never having had sex or kids, often wore men's clothes, lived unbound by the rules of her gender, and used her body as she pleased, as a strength, as a disguise. Where other Witches choose to use sex as a conduit for power, H. P. B. used celibacy. We hope you'll feel empowered to find yourself at home anywhere you like in that spectrum, and with whoever makes you feel magical, even if that someone is you.

In Henry Steel Olcott she had a friend who believed in her. Henry Olcott had served in the US Army during the American Civil War, was later promoted to the rank of colonel, and in 1865, following the assassination of President Abraham Lincoln, assisted in the investigation of the assassination. He was a truth seeker.

H. P. B. called Henry Olcott "Maloney" and he called her "Jack," and from the first time they met he would write about her ability to manifest spiritual phenomena. They lived together in a series of rented apartments in New York City, which they decorated with taxidermized animals and images of spiritual figures. Encouraged by her, he became celibate, teetotaling, and vegetarian,[18] although she herself was unable to totally commit to the last. Together they would found the Theosophical Society, and live and study and run the society in India together from 1879 to 1885. "In 1878 H. P. Blavatsky became an American citizen, the first Russian woman ever to do so. In 1879 she and Col. Olcott moved to India, and in 1882 they established the headquarters of the Theosophical Society at Adyar, near Madras. This remains the international headquarters for the Society, which is now established in seventy countries of the world. The first major book by H. P. Blavatsky was *Isis Unveiled* . . . 'a plea for the recognition of the Hermetic philosophy, the anciently universal Wisdom-Religion.'"[19]

Isis Unveiled is a sprawling, mind-bending epic stuffed with unsourced quotes that Henry Olcott claimed she simply pulled from the air, or from her remarkable memory. It is a perfect starting point for a thousand research tunnels, highly recommended for artists and Witches to dip into, to magpie from, to follow its portals toward surprising new twists of perspective. "Blavatsky's greatest work is *The Secret Doctrine*. HPB made it clear that *The Secret Doctrine* was not written as a revelation but was rather a collection of fragments scattered throughout thousands of volumes embodying the scriptures of the great Asian and pre-Christian European religions and philosophies. Furthermore, she strongly rejected the dogmatic interpretation of any of her work. The reader is asked to study the ideas from this or any other source only in the light of common human experience and reason."[20]

This is the Witches' rallying cry: to study ideas from all sources in the light of experience and reason. This belief in a person's own right and ability to study many religions and access their own understanding of the divine helps explain in part the anger she directed toward the Christian church for keeping its followers severed by shame from their own creative power. "So little have thee first Christians (who despoiled the Jews of their Bible) understood the first four chapters of Genesis in their esoteric meaning, that they never perceived that not only was no sin intended in this disobedience, but that actually the 'Serpent' was 'the Lord God' himself who as the Ophis, the Logos, or the bearer of divine creative wisdom, taught mankind to become creators in their turn."[21]

H. P. Blavatsky was a kind of Satanist (founder and publisher of a journal called *Lucifer*[22]) who attracted millions of followers and pissed a lot of people off, and was repeatedly cast as a fraud. The taint of those accusations—even when revealed to have been orchestrated by black-mailers—lingers still.

But what if, just as an experiment, we believed her?

We don't have to take her words as scripture, she made it clear she didn't want that anyway. We could just try out believing what she tells us of her experience: of the material world moving and murmuring around her, of vivid waking dreams, of a feeling of life and conscious-ness in every object, of seeking teachers who would take her seriously and through them finding ideas that exceeded what other people knew to be possible. We can embrace her contradictions too. She certainly did. She admitted to muddying facts. It was a way of hiding in plain sight.

I wonder if her body functioned for her similarly. Some biographers insist she couldn't have traveled to Tibet because of her weight so she must have been a prostitute; others argue she couldn't have been a pros-titute for the same reason. Such perfect chauvinism, constraining what's possible from every side. Many writers spend a lot of time trying to figure out how much she weighed and when to try to answer the ques-tion of where she could have been. My guess: We wouldn't spend so much time focusing on this question about her body and what it was capable of, or as much energy dismissing her travel diaries and disparag-ing her expansive metaphysical philosophical works if she were a man.

My other guess, those first ten years on the road changed her from a girl to something more like an androgynous road warrior Witch. Dressed always in men's boots, loose robes, and heavy rings, with features that could look at home most places in the world, smoking a pound of tobacco a day and cutting it with her always-sharp knife, she is a figure of free-dom and power. This costume, this drag, this fierce selfhood was a spell that empowered her to go to new and secret places with her body and her thoughts. Protected in this way, and armed with her photographic memory for texts and a quick ear for languages, she slipped through borders and made the kinds of friends who reveal their magic to you.

There have always been heroic women and queer people. For hundreds and thousands of years, though their true histories were not often recorded, there were these travelers, warriors, leaders, priestesses, oracles.

This is what I think I love most about H. P. B.: she is an icon for our Samhain workings of the countless figures who have been out there on the unknown roads—literally and spiritually—the tens of thousands of ancestors whose names we don't know, who have helped to shepherd the infinite.

The delicate network of living beings and their whispering energies and ideas is vast. We are each a small window for that vastness to look out on the world as it is in this moment. What we see is only ever partial, even with help from guides. We suffer from network blindness, determined by our own place in it and by how we've reacted to our traumas, shutting down or keeping our heads down and powering through it. Even if we can glimpse higher planes we can still be cruel in the common ways of our time.

At Samhain let's work to be cracked open and to have our vision drawn out into the great web of perception by each other's truths. Let's use our magic and craft to become portals to each other's divinity, and to a world attuned to each other's suffering. "In magic is comfort and power. Both spring from the fertile earth of care."[23]

On Samhain last year I went for a walk early in the morning around the lake with my little kid strapped to me. For the first time, just over one year since my due date when I'd been waddling slowly around this same lake waiting for her, her skin was clear from the red burning rash that had covered her entire body her whole life until now. She looked up at me with her tough little mug, yawning and muttering herself to sleep. I was exhausted from the love and labor of care.

She almost died in our arms twice that summer. Twice she went into anaphylactic shock—at seven months old and again at eight months.

Her tiny body seized, red and gasping for air, limp and losing consciousness and turning blue; stabbed with a long needle held into her as she
screamed and vomited over and over again. The second time in her short
life that we spent the night together in the hospital she slept on me,
Marc held us from a chair pulled alongside, and I dreamt of staying
there forever, raising her in the white sterile safety of a hospital. Eating
applesauce from small plastic cups for the rest of our lives and never
facing the world again. My terror shut me down.

Even without allergies, when you have a small life in your hands,
death is suddenly everywhere. I saw it written in blood before my eyes
for weeks after she was born. I saw every possible way that her father
and I were going to fail her and hurt her play out in violent scenes on
repeat over and over, like they were painted on the inside of my eyes.

But pushed up against death, we can find life again by bringing
loving kindness to our sorrow and to our fear. Cramped in terror I said,
"Thank you and I love you" to every lurid nightmare vision. Caring for
our shadows is an alchemy.

I walked in circles around the lake, step by slow step like counting
out prayer beads, being in the beat of time, gently rocking my fear. The
baby grew stronger. We figured out what threatened her, her skin slowly
cleared, her breathing settled, and my terrified heart left the white tiles
of the hospital. Roots reached back out into the ground.

Then, on that late fall Samhain day, the trees around us were covered
in frost. Every single line outlined in crisp, glittering ice. As the Sun
rose the light caught the frost. The trees of all colors sparkled shot with
glazed light. On the road ahead of me, the yellow birch leaves which
had died in the night began, one by one, to let go of their branches. They
slipped away as the frost melted and caught the sunlight so the air all
across the road was breathing with slow falling golden leaves sparkling
in the softest possible rain of frost becoming dew. I lost my own breath
and stood under this unexpected baptism. I left the road for the trail and
found a spot where the trail opens into a natural circle in the woods. It
was cool enough in there that the ground and everything was still just
for one minute longer covered in frost and I couldn't help it even if I'd

wanted to, I turned in a slow circle and thanked the corners, thanked everything that has ever been, that May was OK and sleeping with her head against my heart.

We were blessed in that moment, sleeping May and I, with a vision of death shot through with light. Of leaves finding their resting place on strong roots. We had made it through the year, and the world was still alive with the purest beauty. In this moment I was released from the stony grip of terror, and I could start to imagine a life for us on the other side.

H. P. Blavatsky wrote, "What is imagination? Psychologists tell us that it is the plastic or creative power of the soul. . . . Pythagoras maintained it to be the remembrance of precedent spiritual, mental, and physical states."[24] She wanted us to remember that imagination is the creative power of our souls. Imagination is a memory of other possibilities, and as such it casts the world in magic. Our own inexplicable ability to imagine is the power in each of us that allows us to craft rituals and tell stories and foster communities that care for our individual and collective sorrows and open portals. She calls on us to use our magic to birth a better world. "Our voice is raised for spiritual freedom, and our plea made for enfranchisement from all tyranny."[25]

Let's end with one more story, one more Witch whose identity and contributions have been multiply erased, but who raised her voice for spiritual freedom and whose work has influenced the imagination, practices, and symbolic languages of millions of seekers. She is the maybe mixed race, probably queer woman artist behind the world's most famous tarot deck, Pamela Colman Smith.

Some accounts claim her mother was Jamaican, some suggest she was adopted. We know that Corinne Pamela Colman Smith, who was known as Pam to her family, had her birth registered on February 16, 1878, in Pimlico, in London. Her father, Charles Edward Smith, was an American merchant and her mother was Corinne Colman Smith.

The ancestry of her mother foreshadows Smith's interest in mysticism and the occult. The Colmans had been for several generations

followers of the mystic philosopher and visionary Swedenborg.
Artistic roots also lay with Smith's ancestors. Her great-grandfather
and his wife both wrote children's books and her grandfather was a
painter of the Hudson River School.[26,27]

Emanuel Swedenborg was a respected inventor and scientist who in 1741 began to have a series of intense mystical experiences, dreams, and visions, claiming that he had been called by God to reform Christianity and introduce a new church. He claimed to communicate with spirits while awake, described the structure of the spirit world, and was an early voice for equality and social reform. Swedenborg advanced an order of the universe where all people had equal standing, regardless of gender, race, or sexual orientation.

At the tail end of the nineteenth century—and now in a lot of places—these are some pretty enlightened ideas for a young woman artist to get to grow up in.

Racial and gender identity mattered to Pamela Colman Smith. She definitely played with cultural references in her dress and self-representation. She wrote, illustrated, and performed rebellious Jamaican folk stories, and owned her personal difference and diversity as she made her way around the turn-of-the-century world.[28]

Age fifteen, back in Brooklyn, Pamela enrolled at Pratt Institute in Clinton Hill, Brooklyn. The college—only about a decade old—had been opened by a self-made millionaire oil baron and was one of the first in the country to be open to all people, regardless of class, color, or gender. The school's motto was "be true to your work and your work will be true to you."[29]

At Pratt she studied art with Arthur Wesley Dow, who didn't believe in just copying nature, and he didn't believe that art should be relegated to the drawing rooms of rich people. He was an illustrator, painter, and poster artist who emphasized the artist's role as decision maker. He championed the independent instinct and will of the maker. The artist's work was to build harmonies. He considered "space art" to be visual music. He taught his students—including Georgia O'Keeffe, as well as the Overbeck Sisters of the Arts and Crafts movement—Japanese design concepts like notan, the play of light and dark to create dimension and give life to design.

The idea that both light and dark are required to give life, that our shadows give strength and dimension, is useful to remember at Samhain. Witches are artists engaged in the co-creation of a better world, a world for themselves and for the wider re-enchanting. We make harmonies, and we are powerful because we believe in our right to independent decision making. This idea emerges into public discourse in art and design, and in philosophy, and through the adventurous life and thinking of people like H. P. B. It comes through many channels and into the deft hands of Pamela Colman Smith, a young artist whose images would become the definitive imagery of the tarot and a means for us of seeing our subconscious and our magic.

She didn't graduate from Pratt. Her mother died in Jamaica, and she missed a lot of school because of bouts of illness. She suffered from migraines.

Pain—and especially the way migraine affects perception—can bring a person closer to an understanding of how thin our lived and constructed realities are. We know for sure that we are only seeing our brain's best attempt to summarize our senses when pain knocks sense reality sideways. People in chronic pain live closer to the veil between worlds.

Maybe I like to think that because constant chronic pain defined my own life from fifteen to about twenty-five. Following an injury, all my bones and muscles tried hard to build a fort around the back of my neck, causing a migraine that lasted ten years, distorting the vision in my right eye with kaleidoscopes and missing fields and auras of light, and numbing the skin down the entire left side of my body.

Here are some of the lessons I carry with me from this experience: to think about all of our repeated gestures and the systems built by our unconscious repetition. To try to see these, though they are like the air we breathe. To listen for truths beyond constructed realities, to try and thin the calcified walls between myself and the unknown. And to remember that tweaking my gestures, even in tiny ways—with movement, with ritual, with writing and song and new maps—sends waves out into systems, changes things. Gentle, joyful small action can defeat even decades of pain. Being angry that something could keep me imprisoned is not a good reason to stay there. Being grateful for every single pain-free breath I get is reasonable and multiplies. Sharing as much of my strange self, freed from the cage, as I can is common sense.

So much of the world is in pain that the stories of how we face and fight and are defeated and triumph and fight again are also part of the alchemy of care. Like maps from the underworld, they will be how we unlock new ways forward . . . even if it's just by one screaming dancing bloody two-step at a time.

Pamela wrote and illustrated *Annancy Stories* at this time of illness, death, and migraine. She passed them on as they were told to her, written with all the character of a Jamaican oral narrator. In her illustrations children sit at the feet of a Black woman teaching them, and it looks like a memory from her childhood to me. Annancy is a devilish trickster, a spider spirit, keeper of all knowledge in stories, and sometimes a cutter of tongues to keep a story secret. In the Caribbean, especially Jamaica, this spirit from Ghanaian folk religion becomes an icon of resistance. Telling his stories bought young Pamela a measure of independence and freedom, and she put on the mask and character of Annancy throughout her life, keeping the wisdom of the spider spirit close.

Her father took her to London to promote the *Annancy Stories* and to look for work for her, and he found a way to introduce her to Bram Stoker, manager of the Lyceum Theatre, who had just published a hit horror novel *Dracula*. Bram Stoker hired her to illustrate an eighteen-page souvenir brochure that he was writing for performances of the upcoming Lyceum Theatre tour. In New York, October 1899, she met Bram Stoker again, as well as Henry Irving and Ellen Terry—icons of the London theater—and talked them into letting her join the tour as one of the minor cast members. This group became her family. Ellen Terry sort of adopted her and gave her the nickname "Pixie," which she embraced for the rest of her life. Ellen Terry knew something about magic. She wrote of mesmerizing audiences, of entering into a mutual transformative trance with them.

In December 1899 Pixie's father died unexpectedly in New York. She was abroad with the theater at the time and the only family she would have now that her father was gone. So she continued the tour and then returned with them to London when it was done.

In London she made her living as an illustrator and set designer, and worked closely with Theosophist and Freemason William Butler Yeats and Bram Stoker and the Lyceum Theatre, while also writing and illustrating books of her own. Her style resonated with a visionary, romantic, modern seam in contemporary artistic practice. She independently published an artistic journal *The Green Sheaf* with much writing on dreams, including new work by W. B. Yeats. As a member of the Suffrage Atelier, a collective of professional illustrators, she also contributed artwork to fight for women's suffrage in Great Britain and donated work to the Red Cross.

In 1907 she had a major show of seventy-two drawings and water-colors in New York. She was the first painter to have an exhibit in Alfred Stieglitz's Little Galleries of the Photo-Secession, and her show marked a turning point in the success of the gallery: It was the first nonphotographic success for this space that would become famous for introducing the most avant-garde European artists of the time to America, including Henri Matisse, Auguste Rodin, Pablo Picasso, and Marcel Duchamp.

Well-known music and art critic James Gibbons Huneker, reviewing the show, wrote that "Pamela Colman Smith is a young woman with that quality rare in either sex—imagination."[30]

He also called her painting "Death in the House" "absolutely nerve shattering" and said that not even Edvard Munch "could have succeeded better in arousing a profound disquiet." He wrote that the artist belonged to the "favored choir" of William Blake and his mystics.

Back in London, Pixie hosted a weekly "at home" for artists, performing stories from the Jamaican oral tradition, and from Yeats and others. This young woman, living all alone, became a connector and a focal point for artists and thinkers. A weaver like Annancy, with enough imagination to spin out webs of story and symbol that would help to craft the world.

At this time she was living in parallel. She was a working artist who was also becoming immersed in ceremonial magic. Pixie was a member of the Golden Dawn, and then of the Independent and Rectified Rite of the Golden Dawn for about a decade.

The Golden Dawn at this time were an influential magical order that shared some origins with other European hermetic—and heretical—societies and philosophies, the Freemasons and Rosicrucians. It did differ in some pretty key ways for modern Bohemians, especially in that they welcomed women in "perfect equality" with men.

As Dennis Denisoff wrote in his history "The Hermetic Order of the Golden Dawn, 1888–1901":

> Golden Dawn members were primarily interested in magical philosophy and traditional ritual practice for the advancement of the individual's spirit. Influences included ancient Egyptian religion, the Kabbalah, Christianity, Freemasonry, paganism, theurgy, alchemy, early-modern grimoires, and Enochian magic, such as that recorded by the early-modern occultist John Dee. Magic, for the Order, was the use of methodological practices to cause changes in consciousness and/or the material world in accord with the universal will . . . The collective members of the Hermetic Order of the Golden Dawn . . . made the nineteenth century's most serious and sustained effort to re-imagine and re-engage with a prehistoric, occult tradition. In this sense it is the Order that can be seen as the major Victorian author of the often fictional, but no less influential history of occultism and natural magic.[31]

Pixie was a member at a time after secret documents of the order were left in a cab and publicized, and the order had fractured into pieces. Aleister Crowley—the queer sex magic beast of the hermetic schools—was actively making fun of the leader of the group that Pixie stuck with, A. E. Waite. A. E. Waite was dismissive of her at times and snide about her contributions, and left her name off the tarot deck when it was first published.

What he did do though was recognize the importance of the tarot and the talent of his Pixie artist friend. He made notes from his research on the symbolism of the suits and of the Major Arcana and commissioned Pixie ("a big job for very little cash" as she said) to complete the pieces of art for the deck. "I have embraced an opportunity which has been somewhat of the unexpected kind and have interested a very skillful and original artist in the proposal to design a set. Miss Pamela Colman Smith in addition to her obvious gifts, has some knowledge of tarot values; she has lent a sympathetic ear to my proposal to rectify the symbolism by reference to channels of knowledge, which are not in the open day."[32]

A. E. Waite had strong ideas about the design of the twenty-two trump cards of the Major Arcana, but he left the great emotional journey of the fifty-six cards of the Minor Arcana to the artist. Pixie had near full creative reign for the numbered cards. In all, a total of eighty images would be created, seventy-eight tarot cards plus the designs for the card back and the nameplate. Unlike almost every other deck in history until this time, each card in the Waite-Smith deck was to receive its own unique illustration.

The earliest known deck to use the structure of twenty-two Major Arcana and fifty-six Minor Arcana cards is the deck of the Sola Busca family, created by an unknown artist in Venice around 1490. The Sola Busca was the only one with an illustration for every card until Pixie's. There are layers of references to alchemical philosophy in the cards, the magic of becoming one with the universe, of dreaming the god dream. These tarot cards aren't just for fortune-telling, they contain "symbols representing actual tools and methods of psychic transformation."[33]

Images of the Sola Busca deck were acquired by the British Museum just a few years before Pixie began her project with A. E. Waite, and there are some clear references and influences. And clear points of departure. Pixie's deck, made in London just a breath before World War I, is a whole new map to a palimpsest of symbols and secrets that came before. Pixie had all the power of an artist creator. She drew her friends into the cards and her own visions of worlds beyond this one. Worlds she accessed through art and music.

In 1908 for *Strand Magazine* Pixie discussed her experience of synesthesia.

> *When I take a brush in hand and the music begins, it is like unlock-*
> *ing the door into a beautiful country. . . . There is a garden that I*
> *often see, with moonlight glistening on the vine-leaves, and drooping*
> *roses with pale petals fluttering down, tall, misty trees and purple*
> *sky, and lovers wandering there. A drawing of that garden I have*
> *shown to several people and asked them if they could play the music*
> *that I heard when I drew it. They have all, without any hesitation,*
> *played the same. I do not know the name, but—well, I know the*
> *music of that place.*[34]

In 1911 Pixie converted to Roman Catholicism, and though she claimed it was "such fun," it was certainly not an easy choice in Protestant England. It might have been lonely. She withdrew from most of her former friends at this time, and her artistic output slowed, although in 1913 she illustrated Ellen Terry's book *The Russian Ballet* and published an illustrated book *Blue Beard*. In 1914 she illustrated Eunice Fuller's work, *The Book of Friendly Giants*.

In late 1918 Pixie received a legacy from a deceased uncle. This money gave her the freedom to set up a life outside of London, in Cornwall in southwest England. "She chose that area because pixies were believed to be particularly concentrated in the region around Devon and Cornwall. She always thought herself as a pixie who really didn't fit in well among ordinary humans. She once told W. B. Yeats that she had been able to see fairies in Ireland."[35]

She may have sought out a place where she felt the company of fairies, but she kept other loving company close too.

> *Colman Smith died in 1951, in Bude, Cornwall, where she lived*
> *in a home bought with an inheritance from an uncle. The occupa-*
> *tion listed on her death certificate reads "Spinster of Independent*
> *Means." . . . [S]he was not listed as an artist and was making a*

meager living running a home for vacationing Catholic priests . . .
her estate was willed to her "flatmate" Nora Lake, a reputed spiritu-
alist and Colman Smith's likely lover; the two had been companions
for forty years. Although nothing definitive is written about the
artist's sexual predilections, she never married, was linked to no men,
and spent her time in the company of women, many of them known
queers such as the handsome Edith "Edy" Craig, a bisexual suffrag-
ist who famously lived in a ménage-à-trois with a straight couple
until her death. Craig was also the model for the Queen of Wands in
Colman Smith's tarot.[36]

Out here in the woods practicing my mostly solitary nature magic
and building castles out of books, I can easily imagine Pixie gently crafting a new personal practice inspired both by Catholicism's mysteries,
and by her love with the beautiful name and the uncanny intuitions:
Nora Lake. Balanced between the moor and the sea.

Often Pixie is characterized as dying penniless and unappreciated.
Though it is enraging that she didn't earn royalties for her work crafting
the eighty individual paintings for what would become the most popular
tarot deck of all time, I think she did live a magical life right to the end.
She lived forty years with her love and best friend, no small achievement in its own right for any of us. She had independent means and a
job where she was her own boss, caring for—and I imagine whispering
sacred and profane secrets with—old Catholic priests. In the tarot cards
she left images of her friends, of her visions, of her personal understanding of a symbolism that links our minds to each other and to the spirit
world.

She left a map that deepened our understanding beyond words, like
she was hearing a distant music and translating it for millions of seers
to come.

So she is our guide for the end. The end of the book, and for all our
imagined ends as we face them at Samhain.

As we spin toward the end of this Wheel, or before it spins around
again, I hope you will hear these words of Pixie's ringing in your head,
giving you courage, tuning you to the suffering of the world, and through

it to the song of all of us and the great transformative power of our imagining.

> *Keep an open mind to all things. Hear all the music you can, good music, for sound and form are more closely connected than we know.*
>
> *Think good thoughts of beautiful things, colors, sounds, places, not mean thoughts. When you see a lot of dirty people in a crowd, do not remember only the dirt, but the great spirit that is in them all, and the power that they represent. . . .*
>
> *Banish fear, brace your courage, place your ideal high up with the Sun, away from the dirt and squalor and ugliness around you and let that power that makes "the roar of the high-power presses" enter into your work—energy—courage—life—love."*
>
> *Use your wits, use your eyes. Perhaps you use your physical eyes too much and only see the mask.*
>
> *Find eyes within, look for the door into the unknown country.*[37]

Ritual

For a Samhain ritual, alone, or with a perfect friend, or a strange chosen family, or with your wild and delicious coven, we urge you to dress up and in doing so to become a portal.

Use ritual to find who or what you need to be infused with in this coming year. Because we are heading into the dark, a time when one year ends and the next begins; and in the interregnum, this world is thin. Its rules and laws and necessities loosen their grasp just an inch. New things can come in.

First, protect yourself. Pour a glass of some kind of offering, water is fine. Light a candle and something that makes a beautiful smoke: a dry bay leaf, rosemary, a cinnamon stick, incense.

Make a circle, even if it is out of string, on paper, or in a clearing of leaves.

Then take guidance from nonbinary, queer, Indigenous (*Wixárika*), and Latinx multidisciplinary artist, curator, educator, psychotherapist, and Witch Edgar Fabián Frías: "For this spell if I'm able to I close my eyes and then I turn inward and I say 'Divine within me' or you can say Goddess within me, Spirit within me, and then you imagine your energy moving down into the Earth and say 'Earth beneath me' and then you imagine your energy moving up into the heavens and say 'Sky above me' and then you say 'Love surround me' and you imagine this love enveloping you in this gorgeous orb of energy."[38]

Reach inside to the universe within, embrace yourself. Then reach down deep into the Earth to connect with the great currents of being. Reach up to the universe above and see the protection of love radiating on each plane. Continue this pattern of three-times reaching keeping time with your breath, and as you do, see the energies mounting like winds around you.

In your circle welcome only the energies that have your highest purpose at heart. Say it aloud: In this circle I welcome only those energies that have my highest purpose at heart.

Ask these energies—or guides or waves of inspiration or messages from your subconscious—to show you an image of themselves. This will be an image from your own symbolic language, and whether it seems like it or not, it'll have in it seeds of what you need to carry with you, in you, as you, for this crossing through the doorway, for this glimpse into the wisdom of the unknown country and for this next turn around the Sun, if we are once again to be blessed with one.

When you see something, sketch it. Pen, crayons, markers are all fine, words, symbols, stick figures are all perfect. Ask yourself what colors and materials could you use, what could it symbolize. Safe in your circle you are only receiving messages of highest love and purpose, so listen and take notes.

Next thank your guides and clear away your circle. Tuck your transmission into your heart and go spend time on a disguise that means something to you. Returning full circle to Donna Haraway's message from the Yule chapter: Play in order to be a participant in the creative magic of worlding. Play at making. Craft horns or halos out of branches and wire, layer your most dramatic scarves and gowns, paint your face in brilliant colors or stark black symbols of your own devising.

After that, what you do with this iconography you've put on is up to you. You could stay home and drink tea in front of a mirror channeling art. Make music with friends. At dusk, walk the streets. Feel the electricity of curiosity. Or wait till very late at night and go sit in a graveyard, find the gravestone of someone who seems like they would be good company, and tell them about your new self. Or, if this is available to you, just go out to a bar and dance.

Whatever you do, feel the power in the spirit you have created.

Feel the power of the spirit all around you. This is All Hallows' Eve, and all is hallowed.

We close with a Wiccan song from the Reclaiming tradition. This song is based on a blessing of love that (aside from one small change) was taught to us[39] by Amanda Yates Garcia, the Oracle of Los Angeles, who sang it in her mother's circle.

This song is sung to end a ritual, to send coven members safely home. This incantation spirals open a circle that remains always unbroken within us.

Whenever you are alone, know that this chant stitches you back into belonging.

Wherever you are, we are all with you.

INCANTATION
Our circle is open
Yet unbroken
May the peace of the GoddETC
Be ever in our hearts
Merry meet
And merry part
And merry meet again.

NOTES

Introduction

1 Migene González-Wippler, *The Complete Book of Spells, Ceremonies & Magic* (St. Paul, MN: Llewellyn Publications, 1978), xxi.

2 "Cultural Appropriation," April 7, 2020, in *Missing Witches* podcast, episode 53.

3 Pam Grossman, *Waking the Witch: Reflections on Women, Magic, and Power* (New York: Gallery Books, 2019), 8. Kindle.

4 Ipsita Roy Chakraverti, *Beloved Witch: An Autobiography* (n.p.: Harper Collins Publishers India, 2010), EPUB 2 (Adobe DRM), 486.

5 Silvia Federici, *Re-enchanting the World: Feminism and the Politics of the Commons* (Oakland, CA: PM Press, 2018), 1.

6 Amanda Yates Garcia, *Initiated: Memoir of a Witch* (New York: Grand Central Publishing, 2019), 282.

7 "Magic Is Inherently Anti-Capitalist," October 23, 2019, in *Missing Witches* podcast, episode 43.

8 Paula Gunn Allen, "Who Is Your Mother? Red Roots of White Feminism," History Is a Weapon, www.historyisaweapon.com/defcon1/allenredrootsof-whitefeminism.html.

Chapter 1

1 We can resist the normalization of the rape and murder of women in our traditions and myths while also grabbing strength from the truth in this cycle, I think.

2 Monica Sjöö, *New Age & Armageddon: The Goddess or the Gurus? Towards a Feminist Vision of the Future* (n.p.: The Women's Press, 1992), 61.

3 "A Giant Bumptious Litter: Donna Haraway on Truth, Technology, and Resisting Extinction," *Logic,* no. 9 (December 7, 2019), https://logicmag.io /nature/a-giant-bumptious-litter/.

4 Lyla June, "Reclaiming Our Indigenous European Roots," *Moon* (January 27, 2019), http://moonmagazine.org/lyla-june-reclaiming-our-indigenous -european-roots-2018-12-02/.

5   Or better yet, GodETC—see chapter 7.

6   Many versions are circulating of "The Charge of the Goddess"; we want to cite the source, so please visit the Doreen Valiente Foundation, Doreen Valiente.com, accessed June 20, 2020, www.doreenvaliente.com/Doreen -Valiente-Doreen_Valiente_Poetry-11.php.

7   Ibid.

8   Philip Heselton, *Doreen Valiente: Witch* (n.p.: Centre for Pagan Studies, 2016), 25.

9   Ibid., 40–50.

10   Sarah Waldron, "The Mother of Modern Witchcraft Was Also a Pro-Choice Spy," *Vice* (April 14, 2016), www.vice.com/en_us/article/z4jpn4/the-mother -of-modern-Witchcraft-was-also-a-pro-choice-spy.

11   Ibid.

12   Jacob Grimm, *Teutonic Mythology,* 4 vols. (Garden City, NY: Dover Publications, 1966).

13   Grimm's view is repeated by the *Online Etymology Dictionary,* s.v. "witch": "possible connection to Gothic *weihs* 'holy' and Germanic *weihan* ['consecrates'] . . . the priests of a suppressed religion naturally become magicians to its successors or opponents."

14   Ibid.

15   Edith Rose Woodford-Grimes (1887–1975) was a teacher of English literature and drama who lived alone in a house she called Theano, named for the wife of Greek philosopher Pythagoras. She was a member of the Rosicrucian Order Crotona Fellowship and of the New Forest coven, who considered themselves descendants of the historical Witch cult described by anthropologist Margaret Mead in the 1920s and 1930s. Philip Heselton, *Gerald Gardner and the Cauldron of Inspiration: An Investigation into the Sources of Gardnerian Witchcraft,* (n.p.: Holmes Pub Group, 2003).

16   Heselton, *Doreen Valiente: Witch,* 71.

17   Aleister Crowley wrote *The Gnostic Mass*—called Liber XV or "Book 15"— in 1913 and published it three times: in 1918 in *International;* in 1919 in *Equinox III, No. 1;* and in 1929 in his book *Magick in Theory and Practice.* It was privately performed while Aleister Crowley was at the Abbey of Thelema in Italy, and its first public performance was March 19, 1933, by Wilfred T. Smith and Regina Kahl in Hollywood, California, at the first Agape Lodge. Of the ritual Crowley wrote, "I wished . . . to construct a ritual through which people might enter into ecstasy as they have always done under the influence of appropriate ritual . . . I found it perfectly simple to combine the most rigidly rational conceptions of phenomena with the most exalted and

enthusiastic celebration of their sublimity." *Thelemapedia*, s.v. "The Gnostic Mass."

18 Heselton, *Doreen Valiente: Witch*, 81–82.

19 Ibid., 97.

20 Ibid., 98–100.

21 Ibid., 275.

22 Ibid., 284.

23 Ibid., 285.

24 "Doreen Valiente: A Witch Speaks," an account of a speech given at of the Pagan Federation national conference, November 22, 1997, http://freepages .rootsweb.com/~geneseeker/religions/pagan/~WICCAN/HEXCOVEN /VALIENTE.HTM.

25 Ibid.

26 Heselton, *Doreen Valiente: Witch*, 303.

27 Doreen Valiente, *The Rebirth of Witchcraft* (Ramsbury, UK: Crowood Press, 2018).

28 Rupert White, *Monica Sjöö: Life and Letters 1958–2005* (n.p.: Antenna Publications, 2018), 10.

29 Ibid., 12.

30 Ibid., 127

31 Monica Sjöö, "God Giving Birth," artcornwall.org, www.artcornwall.org /features/Monica_Sjoo_God_Giving_Birth.htm.

32 Celebrated as the "father of modern gynecology," J. Marion Sims practiced vaginal surgeries and cesarean sections dozens of times on enslaved women: Lucy, Anarcha, Betsey, and unknown others. Determined that this work would make him famous, J. Marion Sims performed thirty surgeries on Anarcha alone, all without anesthesia. Sarah Zhang, "The Surgeon Who Experimented on Slaves," *Atlantic* (April 18, 2018), www.theatlantic.com/health /archive/2018/04/j-marion-sims/558248/.

33 Sjöö, "God Giving Birth."

34 Monica Sjöö, "The Artist as Reluctant Shamanka," artcornwall.org (2004), www.artcornwall.org/features/Reluctant_shamanka_Monica_Sjoo.htm.

35 Sjöö, *New Age and Armageddon*, 10–14.

36 Audre Lorde, *A Burst of Light: and Other Essays* (Mineola, NY: Ixia Press, 2017).

37 White, *Monica Sjöö*, 168.

38 Ibid., 168.

39 Sjöö, "God Giving Birth."

40 Shai Ferraro, " 'God Giving Birth'—Connecting British Wicca with Radical Feminism and Goddess Spirituality during the 1970s–1980s: The Case Study

of Monica Sjöö," paper presented at the PAEAN [Pagan/Academic European Associates Network] Online Conference: Contemporary Pagan Culture and Witchcraft, March 26, 2014.

41 Monica Sjöö and Barbara Mor, *The Great Cosmic Mother: Rediscovering the Religion of the Earth* (San Francisco, CA: HarperSanFrancisco, 1987), xvi.

42 Pat V. T. West, "Monica Sjöö: A Feminist Artist Working to Glorify the Goddess and the Earth," *Guardian* (September 22, 2005), www.theguardian .com/news/2005/sep/23/guardianobituaries.artsobituaries1#maincontent.

43 Sjöö, *New Age and Armageddon,* 61.

44 Ibid., 64.

45 Monica Sjöö "Going to Church," accessed August 19, 2020 www.monicasjoo .net/artic/goingtochurch.htm

46 White, *Monica Sjöö,* 183.

Chapter 2

1 Audre Lorde, *A Burst of Light* (Ithaca, NY: Firebrand Books, 1988), 130.

2 Zora Neale Hurston, *Dust Tracks on a Road* (New York: Harper Perennial, 1991), e-book version.

3 Valerie Boyd, *Wrapped in Rainbows: The Life of Zora Neale Hurston* (New York: Simon and Schuster, 2003), 162.

4 Hurston, *Dust Tracks.*

5 Ibid.

6 Ibid.

7 Thadious Davis, "The Polarities of Space: Segregation and Alice Walker's Intervention in Southern Studies," in *Toward an Intellectual History of Black Women,* eds. Mia E. Bay, Farah J. Griffin, Martha S. Jones, and Barbara D. Savage (Chapel Hill, NC: University of North Carolina Press, 2015), 162.

8 Alice Walker, ed., introduction to *I Love Myself When I Am Laughing . . . and Then Again When I Am Looking Mean and Impressive: A Zora Neale Hurston Reader* (New York: Feminist Press at the City University of New York, 1979), 1–5.

9 Hurston, *Dust Tracks.*

10 Ibid.

11 Ibid.

12 "Backxwash—Most of My Experience Is a Rejection of Colonialism," October 30, 2019, in *Missing Witches* podcast, episode 45, produced by Amy Torok, https://bit.ly/39PAFTa.

13 Hurston, *Dust Tracks.*

14 Ibid.

15 Zora Neale Hurston, "How It Feels to Be Colored Me," *World Tomorrow* (1928).

16 Carla Kaplan, *Zora Neale Hurston: A Life in Letters* (New York: Anchor, 2007), 18.

17 Zora Neale Hurston, *Mules and Men* (New York: HarperCollins, 2009), 19. Kindle.

18 Hurston, *Dust Tracks*.

19 Hurston, *Mules and Men*, 229.

20 If you're not familiar with the poet June Jordan, just know that she said this: "To tell the truth is to become beautiful, to begin to love yourself, value yourself. And that's political, in its most profound way."

21 Cheryl Wall, "Living by the Word," in *Toward an Intellectual History of Black Women*, eds. Mia E. Bay, Farah J. Griffin, Martha S. Jones, and Barbara D. Savage (Chapel Hill, NC: University of North Carolina Press, 2015), 224.

22 Alice Walker, *In Search of Our Mothers' Gardens: Womanist Prose* (New York: Harcourt, 1983), 92.

23 Hurston, *Dust Tracks*.

24 "Faith Ringgold: Quilting and the Art of Optimism," *Elephant* (April 28, 2018), https://elephant.art/faith-ringgold/.

25 Curlee Raven Holton and Faith Ringgold, *Faith Ringgold: A View from the Studio* (Boston: Bunker Hill Publishing, 2004), 9.

26 Faith Ringgold, *We Flew over the Bridge* (Durham, NC, and London: Duke University Press, 2005), ix.

27 Andrew Russeth, "The Storyteller: At 85, Her Star Still Rising, Faith Ringgold Looks Back on Her Life in Art, Activism, and Education," *ARTnews* (March 1, 2016), www.artnews.com/art-news/artists/the-storyteller -faith-ringgold-5918/.

28 "Faith Ringgold: In Conversation," *Tate Talks,* streamed live on July 5, 2018, YouTube video, 1:35:55, www.youtube.com/watch?v=g5tbIjNwyrg.

29 Russeth, "The Storyteller."

30 Faith Ringgold, lecture, Distinguished W. E. B. Du Bois Lectures (Humboldt University of Berlin, April 23, 2018), www.angl.hu-berlin.de/news/conferences /distinguished-dubois-lectures.

31 Christine Kuan, "Faith Ringgold," *Oxford Art Online*, www.oxfordartonline .com/page/faith-ringgold.

32 *Encyclopedia.com,* s.v. "Faith Ringgold," www.encyclopedia.com/people /history/historians-miscellaneous-biographies/faith-ringgold.

33 bell hooks, *Yearning: Race, Gender, and Cultural Politics* (Abingdon, UK: Routledge, 2014), 21.

34 Ringgold, *We Flew,* 199.

35 Lisa Farrington, *Faith Ringgold* (San Francisco, CA: Pomegranate Press, 2004), 58.

36 bell hooks, *Belonging: A Culture of Place* (Abingdon, UK: Routledge, 2008), 153–155.

37 Faith Ringgold, *Tar Beach* (New York: Crown Publishers, 1991).

38 Holton and Ringgold, *Faith Ringgold,* 62.

39 Ibid.

40 Ringgold, *We Flew,* 96.

41 Faith Ringgold, "Anyone Can Fly" (1991).

Chapter 3

1   Tracy, "History of Cartagena, Colombia: Spanish America's Biggest Slave Port," *Atlanta Black Star,* July 4, 2015, https://atlantablackstar.com/2015 /07/04/cartagena-colombia-spanish-americas-biggest-slave-port/.

2   Nicole von Germeten, *Violent Delights, Violent Ends: Sex, Race, and Honor in Colonial Cartagena de Indias* (Albuquerque, NM: University of New Mexico Press, 2013).

3   Ibid.,122–123.

4   Ibid., 119–120.

5   Erica Lagalisse, *Occult Features of Anarchism: With Attention to the Conspiracy of Kings and the Conspiracy of the Peoples* (Oakland, CA: PM Press, 2019), 30.

6   Von Germeten, *Violent Delights,* 123.

7   Federici, *Re-enchanting the World,* 4–5.

8   Von Germeten, *Violent Delights,* 123.

9   Cecilia Vicuña and Ernesto Livon-Grosman, eds., *The Oxford Book of Latin American Poetry: A Bilingual Anthology* (Oxford, UK: Oxford University Press, 2009), 178.

10 Jerome Rothenberg, ed., *María Sabina: Selections* (Berkeley, CA: University of California Press, 2003), 164.

11 Michael Goodwin, "A Heavy Trip inside Mick Jagger's Head," *Rolling Stone,* September 3, 1970, www.rollingstone.com/music/music-news/a-heavy-trip -inside-mick-jaggers-head-184328/.

12 Heriberto Yépez, "Rereading María Sabina," Jacket, June 9, 2017, https:// jacket2.org/commentary/heriberto-y%C3%A9pez-rereading-mar%C3%ADa -sabina.

13 A *velada* is a sacred ritual, a therapy session, an act of healing, a guided trip, a song that lasts all night long.

14 Yépez, "Rereading María Sabina."

15 Brooke Gazer, "María Sabina and Magic Mushrooms," *The Eye Huatulco,* May 1, 2015, https://theeyehuatulco.com/2015/05/01/maria-sabina-and-magic-mushrooms/.

16 Yépez, "Rereading María Sabina."

17 Heriberto Yépez, "Clock Woman in the Land of Mixed Feelings: The Place of Maria Sabina in Mexican Culture," 2002, www.ubu.com/ethno/discourses/Yépez_clock.html (archived on www.rave.ca/en/community_thread/14534/).

18 The Canadian health care system hasn't kept pace with Indigenous self-government and has perpetuated health inequality for Indigenous people in Canada. There's more to be done in Canada and around the world. But we can be guided by the evidence we've already seen of the tremendous world-changing power in the idea of a right to health.

19 Yépez, "Clock Woman."

20 Álvaro Estrada, *María Sabina: Her Life and Chants* (n.p.: Ross-Erikson Publishers, 1981); video, July 21–22, 1956, by R. Gordon Wasson in Huautla de Jiménez, Oaxaca, Mexico, http://ubusound.memoryoftheworld.org/ethno/sabina/mp3/Sabina-Maria_From-The-Mushroom-Velada.Mp3.

21 Yépez, "Rereading María Sabina."

22 Michael Pollan, "The Trip Treatment: Research into Psychedelics, Shut Down for Decades, Is Now Yielding Exciting Results," *New Yorker,* February 2, 2015, www.newyorker.com/magazine/2015/02/09/trip-treatment.

23 Ibid.

24 Estrada, *María Sabina: Her Life and Chants.*

25 Maximilíano Durón, "How to Altar the World: Amalia Mesa-Bains's Art Shifts the Way We See Art History," *ARTnews,* March 27, 2018, www.artnews.com/artnews/news/icons-amalia-mesa-bains-9988/.

Chapter 4

1 Maya also said what is one of our favorite quotes, one that guides us every day as we practice this thing called life: "When you know better, you do better." There's no need to expect perfection. Just learn and grow. Know better. Do better.

2 Anna Halprin, *Returning to Health: with Dance, Movement and Imagery* (Mendocino, CA: LifeRhythm Books, 2002), 11.

3 Karen McCarthy Brown, *Mama Lola: A Vodou Priestess in Brooklyn* (Berkeley, CA: University of California Press, 2011), 9.

4 Milo Rigaud, *Secrets of Voodoo,* trans. Robert B. Cross (San Francisco, CA: City Lights Books, 2016), 7.

5 "Haiti Mobs Lynch Voodoo Priests over Cholera Fears," BBC, December 24, 2010, www.bbc.com/news/world-latin-america-12073029.

6 "Pat Robertson Says Haiti Paying for 'Pact to the Devil,'" CNN, January 13, 2010, www.cnn.com/2010/US/01/13/haiti.pat.robertson/index.html.

7 McCarthy Brown, *Mama Lola*, 295.

8 Rigaud, *Secrets of Voodoo*, 7.

9 Kim Wall and Caterina Clerici, "Vodou Is Elusive and Endangered, but It Remains the Soul of Haitian People," *Guardian*, November 7, 2015, www.theguardian.com/world/2015/nov/07/vodou-haiti-endangered-faith-soul-of-haitian-people.

10 Brown, *Mama Lola*, xvii.

11 Ibid., 17.

12 This is from a YouTube interview that has since been removed from the internet, but Karen McCarthy Brown also mentioned Mama Lola's "plenty confidence" on xvii.

13 Osunniyi Olajide Ifatunmo, "Is a 'Complete' Written Copy of the Odu Ifa?" Ooduarere.com, http://ooduarere.com/news-from-nigeria/breaking-news/complete-odu-ifa/.

14 Iyalosa Apetebii Olaomi Osunyemi Akalatunde, *Ona Agbani: The Ancient Path: Understanding and Implementing the Ways of Our Ancestors* (2002, reprint 2018), 17.

15 Ibid., 52.

16 Ibid., 53.

17 McCarthy Brown, *Mama Lola*, 221.

18 Ibid., 91.

19 Ibid., 131.

20 Ibid., 292.

21 Ibid., 224.

22 Maya Deren, *Divine Horsemen: The Living Gods of Haiti* (London: Thames & Hudson, 1953), 225.

23 Ibid., 225.

24 Ibid., 226.

25 Ibid., 227.

26 Ibid., 86.

27 McCarthy Brown, *Mama Lola*, 164.

28 Ibid., 292.

29 The legalization, validation, health, and safety of sex work is an important feminist goal.

30 McCarthy Brown, *Mama Lola*, 164.

31 Ibid., 71.

32 Ibid., 72.

33 Ibid., 74.

34 Mambo Chita Tann, *Haitian Vodou* (Woodbury, MN: Llewellyn Worldwide, 2012), 72.

35 Tara García Mathewson, "How Poverty Changes the Brain," *Atlantic*, April 19, 2017, www.theatlantic.com/education/archive/2017/04/can-brain-science -pull-families-out-of-poverty/523479/.

36 McCarthy Brown, *Mama Lola*, 75.

37 Ibid., 78.

38 Ibid., xix.

39 This interview with Brandi has since been deleted from YouTube.

40 McCarthy Brown, *Mama Lola*, 315.

41 "Tori and Dean Home Sweet Hollywood: Fright Where We Belong Part 3," streamed live on August 27, 2010, YouTube video, 9:59, www.youtube.com /watch?v=v1oD5i-2oHY.

42 McCarthy Brown, *Mama Lola*, 399.

43 This video interview with Mama Lola has since been removed from YouTube.

Chapter 5

1 Lizzo's music is a perfect soundtrack for Litha.

2 "Witches in Labs," in *Missing Witches* podcast, episode 15. Jacqui is a great friend of the pod and has appeared on episodes 15, 27, 28, and 32.

3 "The Medium of Life," April 24, 2019, in *Missing Witches* podcast, episode 27.

4 Rita Repsiene, "In Pursuit of the Goddess: How One Woman Defied the Odds to Restore the Feminist Principle," *Eurozine* (April 19, 2010), www .eurozine.com/in-pursuit-of-the-goddess/.

5 Richard D. Lyons, "Dr. Marija Gimbutas Dies at 73; Archaeologist with Feminist View," *New York Times*, February 4, 1994, www.nytimes.com/1994/02 /04/obituaries/dr-marija-gimbutas-dies-at-73-archaeologist-with-feminist -view.html.

6 Joan Marler, "A Tribute to Marija Gimbutas," *Sojourn* 2, no. 3 (1998).

7 Ibid.

8 Ibid.

9 Marija Gimbutas, *The Language of the Goddess* (New York: Harper and Row, 1989), 1.

10 Ibid., 265.

11 Ibid., 316.

12 Marler, "A Tribute to Marija Gimbutas."

13 Sjöö and Mor, *The Great Cosmic Mother,* 61.

14 Wikipedia, s.v. "Kurgan hypothesis," last modified June 20, 2020, 10:08, https://en.wikipedia.org/wiki/Kurgan_hypothesis.

15 Marija Gimbutas, *The Living Goddesses* (Berkeley, CA: University of California Press, 1999), 112.

16 Ibid., 117.

17 This interview was conducted for this book, but Vanessa also appeared on episode 35 of the *Missing Witches* podcast, September 25, 2019. Her source for this bit of knowledge was Roland Viau, *Femmes de Personne: Sexes, Genres et Pouvoirs en Iroquoisie Ancienne* (Montréal: Boreal, 2000).

18 Starr Goode, *The Goddess in Art* TV series: Interview with Marija Gimbutas, Part 1, streamed live on August 29, 2014, YouTube video, 29:28, www.youtube .com/watch?v=uxei-vuf7U8&t=1106s.

19 Ibid.

20 Ibid.

21 Gimbutas, *The Living Goddesses,* 197–211.

22 Ibid., 215.

23 Carol P. Christ, "Marija Gimbutas Triumphant: Colin Renfrew Concedes," *Feminism and Religion,* December 11, 2017, https://feminismandreligion .com/2017/12/11/marija-gimbutas-triumphant-colin-renfrew-concedes -by-carol-p-christ/.

24 Repsienne, "In Pursuit of the Goddess."

25 Marler, "A Tribute to Marija Gimbutas."

26 Layla F. Saad, *Me and White Supremacy Workbook* (self-published, 2018), 22.

27 Zsuzsanna Budapest, *My Dark Sordid Past as a Heterosexual* (n.p.: CreateSpace, 2014).

28 Ibid.

29 Ibid.

30 Zsuszanna Budapest, *Summoning the Fates: A Generational Woman's Guide to Destiny and Sacred Transformation* (Women's Spirituality Forum, 2015).

31 Ibid.

32 Ibid.

33 Ibid.

34 Budapest, *My Dark Sordid Past.*

35 Ibid.

36 Janet L. Jacobs, "The Effects of Ritual Healing on Female Victims of Abuse: A Study of Empowerment and Transformation," *Sociological Analysis* 50, no. 3 (1989): 265–279, https://academic.oup.com/socrel/article-abstract/50/3 /265/1672874.

37   Marina Pitofsky, " 'Epidemic of Violence': 2018 Is Worst for Deadly Assaults against Transgender Americans," *USA Today,* September 26, 2018, www .usatoday.com/story/news/2018/09/26/2018-deadliest-year-transgender -deaths-violence/1378001002/.

38   Cara Schulz, "Overview of the PantheaCon Gender Debate," Patheos.com, February 22, 2012, www.patheos.com/blogs/agora/2012/02/overview-of -the-pantheacon-gender-debate/.

39   Zsuzsanna Budapest, *The Holy Book of Women's Mysteries* (Oakland, CA: Wingbow Press, 1989), 110.

40   The whole text of the invitation went as follows: "This skyclad rite honors the body of each and every woman present, the beauty and grace of the feminine form in all of her infinite variety. Allow yourself to be embraced by the glori- ous love of your sisters, with voices raised in sacred song in this central ritual of Dianic tradition. Genetic women only." Sounded great until that last part. www.patheos.com/blogs/wildhunt/2012/02/pantheacon-unity-diversity -controversy.html.

41   Budapest, *The Holy Book,* xviii.

42   *Boszorkány* is the Hungarian word for "Witch." My father's hometown, Szeged, has a park called Boszorkánysziget (Island of Witches) where twelve "witches" were burned at the stake in 1728.

43   "The Medium of Life," April 24, 2019, in *Missing Witches* podcast, episode 27.

Chapter 6

1   It is worth mentioning that one week after we performed this bonfire ritual, the con man suddenly reappeared in my life in the form of bank transfers. After nearly six months of silence, he suddenly repaid me double what he had stolen. From what I can tell I am the only person he repaid. Your magic will pay its own unexpected dividends.

2   Louise Erdrich, *The Blue Jay's Dance: A Memoir of Early Motherhood* (Toronto: Harper Perennial, 1995), 103.

3   Ibid., 109.

4   Louise Erdrich, "Advice to Myself," in *Original Fire: Selected and New Poems* (London: HarperCollins, 2009), 150.

5   Aliki Barnstone, ed., *Voices of Light: Spiritual and Visionary Poems by Women from around the World from Ancient Sumeria to Now* (Boulder, CO: Shambhala, 1999), 79.

6   Lal Děd, *I, Lalla: The Poems of Lal Děd,* trans. Ranjit Hoskote (London: Pen- guin UK, 2013), ii.

7   Dean Accardi, "Embedded Mystics: Writing Lal Ded and Nund Rishi into the Kashmiri Landscape," in *Kashmir: History, Politics, Representation*, ed. Chitralekha Zutshi (Cambridge, UK: Cambridge University Press, 2017), 250.

8   Meenakshi Thakur, "Women Mystics: A Comparative Study of Lalleshwari and Julian of Norwich," St. Andrew's College, https://standrewscollege.ac.in/wp-content/uploads/2018/07/Women-Mystics.pdf.

9   *Lal Ded: Her Life and Sayings,* trans. Nil Kanth Kotru (Srinagar, Kashmir: Utpal Publications, 1989), viii.

10 Ibid.

11 Hugh Urban, "The Goddess and the Great Rite: Hindu Tantra and the Complex Origins of Modern Wicca," Academia.edu, accessed June 13, 2020, www.academia.edu/40032525/The_Goddess_and_the_Great_Rite_Hindu_Tantra_and_the_Complex_Origins_of_Modern_Wicca.

12 Ibid.

13 Sthaneshwar Timalsina, "Tantra and the West," *Science and Nonduality,* accessed June 13, 2020, www.scienceandnonduality.com/article/tantra-and-the-west.

14 Ibid.

15 Ibid.

16 Chakraverti, *Beloved Witch*, 597.

17 Silvia Federici, *Witches, Witch-Hunting, and Women* (Oakland, CA: PM Press, 2018), 4.

18 Sudipto Shome, "Code Cracked," *Hindu* (January 19, 2008).

19 Chakraverti, *Beloved Witch*, 13.

20 Ibid., 138–140.

21 Ibid., 75.

22 Ibid., 149.

23 Ibid., 156.

24 Ibid., 157.

25 Rosemary Guiley, "Isaac Newton," in *Encyclopedia of Magic and Alchemy* (New York: Infobase Publishing, 2006), 91.

26 Chakraverti, *Beloved Witch*, 78.

27 John Jay Harper, *Tranceformers: Shamans of the 21st Century* (Foresthill, CA: Reality Press, 2009), 105.

28 Chakraverti, *Beloved Witch*, 311.

29 Richard A. Lovett and Scot Hoffman, "Crystal Skulls," *National Geographic,* www.nationalgeographic.com/history/archaeology/crystal-skulls/.

30 Tim Giago, "Phony Indians," *Baltimore Sun,* 1993, www.baltimoresun.com/news/bs-xpm-1993-01-27-1993027046-story.html.

31   Chakraverti, *Beloved Witch*, 311.

32   Scott Cunningham, *Earth Power: Techniques of Natural Magic* (Woodbury, MN: Llewellyn Publications, 2013), 78.

33   Olivia Goldhill, "The Idea That Everything from Spoons to Stones Is Conscious Is Gaining Academic Credibility," *Quartz*, January 27, 2018, https://qz.com/1184574/the-idea-that-everything-from-spoons-to-stones-are-conscious-is-gaining-academic-credibility/.

34   Ibid.

35   Cunningham, *Earth Power*, 5.

36   Chakraverti, *Beloved Witch*, 296.

37   Ibid., 580.

38   Ibid., 582.

39   Ibid., 583.

40   Pawanpreet Kaur, "The Adivasi, the Colonial and the Great Indian Witch Hunt," *Sunday Guardian*, November 3, 2012, www.sunday-guardian.com/artbeat/the-adivasi-the-colonial-and-the-great-indian-witch-hunt.

41   Ipsita Roy Chakraverti, "Biography," WiccanBrigade.com.

42   Heather Greene, "Witchcraft in India: A Conversation with Ipsita Roy Chakraverti," *Wild Hunt*, September 13, 2015, https://wildhunt.org/2015/09/Witchcraft-in-india-a-conversation-with-ipsita-roy-chakraverti.html.

43   Ibid.

44   Chakraverti, *Beloved Witch*, 597.

45   Ibid., 14.

46   Ibid., 13.

47   Ibid., 356.

48   Guy L. Beck, *Sonic Theology: Hinduism and Sacred Sound* (Delhi, India: Motilal Banarsidass, 1995), 123.

49   Urban, "The Goddess and the Great Rite."

Chapter 7

1   Neil deGrasse Tyson's docuseries, *Cosmos*—see episode "The Immortals" for his brief mention of Enheduanna, then watch the whole series.

2   Betty De Shong Meador, *Inanna: Lady of Largest Heart: Poems of the Sumerian High Priestess Enheduanna* (Austin, Texas: University of Texas Press, 2001), 120.

3   Quite randomly—thank you Hollow Eve, *The Boulet Brothers' Dragula*, Season 3.

4   Meador, *Inanna*, 11.

5   "Cultural Appropriation," April 7, 2020, in *Missing Witches* podcast, episode 53.

6   Inga Muscio, *Cunt: A Declaration of Independence* (Berkeley, CA: Seal Press, 2002), xxvi.

7   Ibid., 5.

8   Meador, *Inanna,* 194.

9   The interview with Phoenix in this chapter was conducted for this book. Phoenix has, however, been on the *Missing Witches* podcast many times, episodes 53, 32, 14, 12, and 10.

10 Phoenix has also been known to end messages with "cunt wait to see you." Before the *Missing Witches* project existed, Phoenix was instrumental in my own reclamation of the word.

11 Watch the documentary *Paris Is Burning* to contextualize the importance of this "house" and the ballroom scene. Keep in mind that the film's legacy raises dubious questions; some of the film's subjects felt exploited; many feel the documentary is tainted by the white lens of director Jennie Livingston. bell hooks wrote an essay on the subject, "Is Paris Burning?"

12 Meador, *Inanna,* 57.

13 "Magic Is Inherently Anti-Capitalist," October 23, 2019, in *Missing Witches* podcast, episode 43.

14 "Douching," Womenshealth.gov.

15 Meador, *Inanna,* 141.

16 Ibid., 163.

17 Gloria Bertonis, *Stone Age Divas: Their Mystery and Their Magic* (Bloomington, IN: AuthorHouse, 2010), 72.

18 Benjamin R. Foster, *The Age of Agade: Inventing Empire in Ancient Mesopotamia* (Abingdon, UK: Routledge, 2015), 46.

19 Enheduanna, "Hymn to Inanna," 115–131.

20 Roseane Lopes, "Inanna/Ishtar—the Non-Maternal as an Archetype of Feminine Integrity," presented at the 47e Rencontre Assyriologique, Helsinki, Finland, July 2 to July 6, 2001, reprinted, www.gatewaystobabylon.com.

21 Grossman, *Waking the Witch,* 8.

22 Meador, *Inanna,* 48.

23 Chakraverti, *Beloved Witch,* 597.

24 Bernard Butler, "Pagan Queen: Jung, Individuation and the Goddess Inanna," www.gatewaystobabylon.com.

25 Meador, *Inanna,* 178–179.

26 Ibid., 181.

27 Ibid., 191.

28 This interview was conducted for this book, but Vanessa also appeared on episode 35 of the *Missing Witches* podcast, September 25, 2019.

29 Carolyn Elliott, "7 Notes on Amor Fati: A Magic of Raw Power," *Witch*, April 28, 2016, https://badwitch.es/amor-fati-notes-magic-raw-power/.

Chapter 8

1 Garcia, *Initiated*, 281.

2 Arundhati Roy, "The Pandemic Is a Portal," *Financial Times*, April 3, 2020, www.ft.com/content/10d8f5e8-74eb-11ea-95fe-fcd274e920ca.

3 RuPaul.

4 Helena Petrovna Blavatsky, *The Key to Theosophy* (Wheaton, IL: Quest Books, 1972), 24.

5 Gary Lachman, *Madame Blavatsky: The Mother of Modern Spirituality* (New York: Jeremy P. Tarcher/Penguin, 2012), 259.

6 Wikipedia, s.v. "Root Race," last modified July 13, 2020, https://en.wikipedia .org/wiki/Root_race#cite_note-FOOTNOTEBlavatsky1962Section_3-40.

7 Ibid.

8 Her ideas are also picked up by Rudolf Steiner, who changes the terminology from "root races" to "epochs" and gains great, lasting popularity.

9 Helena P. Blavatsky, *The Voice of the Silence*, rev. ed. (1899; repr. Pasadena, CA: Theosophical University Press, 2015), 50–51, www.theosociety.org/pasadena /voice/VoiceoftheSilence_eBook.pdf.

10 Lachman, *Madame Blavatsky*, x–xii.

11 Helena P. Blavatsky, *The Secret Doctrine: The Synthesis of Science, Religion and Philosophy*, vol. 1 (Woodstock, Canada: Devoted Publishing, 2018), 27.

12 Grossman, *Waking the Witch*, 22–23.

13 Charles River Editors, *The Mother of Theosophy: The Life and Legacy of H. P. Blavatsky*. Kindle.

14 Per Faxneld, *Satanic Feminism: Lucifer as the Liberator of Woman in Nineteenth-Century Culture* (Oxford, UK: Oxford University Press, 2017), 110.

15 Lachman, *Madame Blavatsky*, 50.

16 Ibid., 51–52.

17 Ibid., 262.

18 Our kiddo's allergies pushed us to veganism (almost all the way, we still eat eggs for now for her protein) and aside from our huge relief at all the ways this change transformed her health (she can breathe and isn't completely covered in a burning red rash at all times), what I mostly notice is that the weight of sadness that used to fall on me partway through every meal is gone.

Mass factory slaughter is a trauma we all learn to repress at an early age along with our trauma and terror about the loss of the natural world. Choosing to face that trauma and work our ways out of our complicity with it is a revolutionary act. "The food we eat masks so much cruelty. The fact that we can sit down and eat a piece of chicken without thinking about the horrendous conditions under which chickens are industrially bred in this country is a sign of the dangers of capitalism, how capitalism has colonized our minds. The fact that we look no further than the commodity itself, the fact that we refuse to understand the relationships that underly the commodities that we use on a daily basis. And so food is like that." *CounterPunch*, www.counterpunch .org/2014/01/24/vegan-angela-davis-connects-human-and-animal-liberation.

19 "H. P. Blavatsky and Her Writings," Theosophical Society, accessed June 14, 2020, www.theosophical.org/component/content/article/25-online-resources /online-leaflets/1796-hp-blavatsky-and-her-writings.

20 Ibid.

21 Helena P. Blavatsky, *The Secret Doctrine: Anthropogenesis* (n.p.: Theosophical Publishing Company, 1888), 215.

22 "We are about to found a magazine of our own, *Lucifer*. Don't allow yourself to be frightened: it is not the devil, into which the Catholics have falsified the name of the Morning Star, sacred to all the ancient world, of the 'bringer of light,' Phosphoros, as the Romans often called the Mother of God and Christ." Blavatsky Archives, accessed June 20, 2020, www.blavatskyarchives .com/luciferreprints.htm.

23 Yates Garcia, *Initiated*, 281.

24 Helena P. Blavatsky, *Isis Unveiled*, e-artnow.

25 Helena P. Blavatsky, *Helena P. Blavatsky Premium Collection*, e-artnow.

26 Another ancestor of Pamela Colman Smith's was "murdered with an hideous Witchcraft" in the winter of 1684. Philip Smith, "concerned about relieving the indigences of a wretched woman in the town . . . expressed herself unto him in such a manner, that he declared himself thenceforth apprehensive of receiving mischief at her hands. . . . Some of the young men in the town . . . went to give disturbance unto the woman; and all the while they were disturbing her, he was at ease, and slept as a weary man . . . Mary Webster, the woman who disturbed Philip Smith, was sent to Boston, tried for Witchcraft, and acquitted. The young men of Hadley . . . dragged her out of the house, hung her up until she was near dead, let her down, rolled her some time in the snow, and at last buried her in it, and there left her. But she survived." (Norfleet) With the benefit of contemporary perspective, it sounds like Philip Smith tried to rape a woman who rejected him; became sick with something

like syphilis, and then Philip Smith died blaming a woman who wouldn't tolerate him, only resting well when he knew she was being tortured. Much of Witch history reads like this, but the generations turn like the seasons, and down the line of those who called Witch more of us grow.

27 Stuart Kaplan, *The Artwork and Times of Pamela Colman Smith* (n.p.: U. S. Games Systems; 1st ed., 2009), 5.

28 There are all kinds of references to her from society writing at the time that try to wrap their head around her race and background, and enjoy exoticizing her in the process. In *Bohemia in London,* the author describes her as "a strange little creature, goddaughter of a Witch and sister to a fairy . . . very dark, and not thin, and when she smiled, with a smile that was peculiarly infectious, her twinkling gypsy eyes seemed to vanish altogether." Arthur Ransome, *Bohemia in London* (New York: Dodd, Mead & Company, 1907). John Butler Yeats said she looked Japanese; Irene Cooper Willis—author and barrister—described her as "dear, funny, Chinese looking little artist and painter."

29 *Pratt Institute Monthly,* vol. 7, 1899.

30 Phil Norfleet, "Alfred Stieglitz and Pamela Coleman Smith," http://pcs2051 .tripod.com/stieglitz_archive.htm.

31 Dennis Denisoff, "The Hermetic Order of the Golden Dawn, 1888–1901," *Branch,* 2013, www.branchcollective.org/?ps_articles=dennis-denisoff-the -hermetic-order-of-the-golden-dawn-1888-1901.

32 Phil Norfleet, "Creation of the Waite-Smith Tarot," http://pcs2051.tripod. com/waite-smith_tarot.htm.

33 Ralph Metzner, *Maps of Consciousness: I Ching, Tantra, Tarot, Alchemy, Astrology, Actualism* (New York: Macmillan, 1971), 58.

34 "Pictures in Music," *Strand Magazine,* July 1908: 648–652.

35 Phil Norfleet, "Retirement to Cornwall," http://pcs2051.tripod.com/.

36 Michelle Tea, "The Divine Mystery of Pamela Colman Smith," *Enchanted Living* magazine, 2017, https://enchantedlivingmagazine.com/divine -mystery-pamela-colman-smith/.

37 Pamela Colman Smith, "Should the Art Student Think?" *Craftsman,* July 1908: 417–419.

38 "Witches Found: Edgar Fabián Frías," October 2, 2019, in *Missing Witches* podcast, episode 37.

39 "Witches Found: Amanda Yates Garcia," October 16, 2019, *in Missing Witches* podcast, episode 41.

BIBLIOGRAPHY

Introduction

"Cultural Appropriation." April 7, 2020. In *Missing Witches* podcast. Episode 53. Produced by Amy Torok. https://bit.ly/2EBDdsd.

"Magic Is Inherently Anti-Capitalist." October 23, 2019. In *Missing Witches* podcast. Episode 43.

Allen, Paula Gunn. "Who Is Your Mother? Red Roots of White Feminism." *History Is a Weapon.* www.historyisaweapon.com/defcon1/allenredrootsofwhitefeminism.html.

Chakraverti, Ipsita Roy. *Beloved Witch: An Autobiography.* N.p.: HarperCollins Publishers India, 2010. EPUB 2. Adobe DRM.

Ehrenreich, Barbara and Deirdre English. *Witches, Midwives, and Nurses: A History of Women Healers.* New York: Feminist Press at the City University of New York, 1973.

Ehrenreich, Barbara. *Nickel and Dimed: On (Not) Getting By in America.* New York: Metropolitan Books, 2001.

Federici, Silvia. *Re-enchanting the World: Feminism and the Politics of the Commons.* Oakland, CA: PM Press, 2018.

——. *Witches, Witch-Hunting, and Women.* Oakland, CA: PM Press, 2018.

Grossman, Pam. *Waking the Witch: Reflections on Women, Magic, and Power.* New York: Gallery Books, June 4, 2019. Kindle.

Wippler, Migene Gonzales. *The Complete Book of Spells, Ceremonies & Magic.* St. Paul, MN: Llewellyn Publications, 1978.

Yates Garcia, Amanda. *Initiated: Memoir of a Witch.* New York: Grand Central Publishing, 2019.

Chapter 1

"A Giant Bumptious Litter: Donna Haraway on Truth, Technology, and Resisting Extinction." *Logic,* no. 9 (December 7, 2019). https://logicmag.io/nature/a-giant-bumptious-litter/.

"Doreen Valiente: A Witch Speaks." An account of a speech given at of the Pagan Federation national conference. November 22, 1997. http://freepages.rootsweb

.com/~geneseeker/religions/pagan/~WICCAN/HEXCOVEN/VALIENTE .HTM.

Ferraro, Shai. "'God Giving Birth'—Connecting British Wicca with Radical Feminism and Goddess Spirituality during the 1970s–1980s: The Case Study of Monica Sjöö." Paper presented at the PAEAN [Pagan/Academic European Associates Network] Online Conference: Contemporary Pagan Culture and Witchcraft, March 26, 2014.

Grimm, Jacob. *Teutonic Mythology*, 4 vols. Garden City, NY: Dover Publications, 1966.

Heselton, Philip. *Doreen Valiente: Witch*. N.p.: Centre for Pagan Studies, 2016.

——. *Gerald Gardner and the Cauldron of Inspiration: An Investigation into the Sources of Gardnerian Witchcraft*. N.p.: Holmes Pub Group, 2003).

June, Lyla. "Reclaiming Our Indigenous European Roots." *Moon* (January 27, 2019). http://moonmagazine.org/lyla-june-reclaiming-our-indigenous-european -roots-2018-12-02/.

Lorde, Audre. *A Burst of Light: and Other Essays*. Mineola, NY: Ixia Press, 2017.

Sjöö, Monica and Barbara Mor. The Great Cosmic Mother: Rediscovering the Religion of the Earth. San Francisco, CA: HarperSanFrancisco, 1987.

Sjöö, Monica. "God Giving Birth." artcornwall.org. www.artcornwall.org/features /Monica_Sjoo_God_Giving_Birth.htm.

——. "The Artist as Reluctant Shamanka." artcornwall (2004). www.artcornwall .org/features/Reluctant_shamanka_Monica_Sjoo.htm.

——. *New Age and Armageddon: The Goddess or the Gurus? Towards a Feminist Vision of the Future*. N.p.: The Women's Press, 1992.

Valiente, Doreen. *The Rebirth of Witchcraft*. Ramsbury, UK: Crowood Press, 2018.

Waldron, Sarah. "The Mother of Modern Witchcraft Was Also a Pro-Choice Spy." *Vice* (April 14, 2016). www.vice.com/en_us/article/z4jpn4/the-mother-of-modern -Witchcraft-was-also-a-pro-choice-spy.

West, Pat V. T. "Monica Sjöö: A Feminist Artist Working to Glorify the Goddess and the Earth." *Guardian* (September 22, 2005). www.theguardian.com /news/2005/sep/23/guardianobituaries.artsobituaries1#maincontent.

White, Rupert. *Monica Sjöö: Life and Letters 1958–2005*. N.p.: Antenna Publications, 2018.

Zhang, Sarah. "The Surgeon Who Experimented on Slaves." *Atlantic* (April 18, 2018). www.theatlantic.com/health/archive/2018/04/j-marion-sims/558248/.

Chapter 2

"African Mask Symbolism." *Archive Today*. https://archive.is/20130122145111 /http://www.essortment.com/africamasks_rnqe.htm#selection-351.55-351.77.

Boyd, Valerie. *Wrapped in Rainbows*. New York: Simon and Schuster, 2003.

Davis, Thadious. "The Polarities of Space: Segregation and Alice Walker's Intervention in Southern Studies." In *Toward an Intellectual History of Black Women*, eds. Mia E. Bay, Farah J. Griffin, Martha S. Jones, and Barbara D. Savage (Chapel Hill, NC: University of North Carolina Press, 2015), 162.

Encyclopedia.com, s.v. "Faith Ringgold." www.encyclopedia.com/people/history /historians-miscellaneous-biographies/faith-ringgold.

Farrington, Lisa. *Faith Ringgold*. San Francisco, CA: Pomegranate Press, 2004.

Graulich, Melody and Mara Witzling. "The Freedom to Say What She Pleases: A Conversation with Faith Ringgold." *NWSA Journal* 6, no. 1 (Baltimore, MD: Johns Hopkins University Press, 1994). www.faithringgold.com/wp-content /uploads/2019/03/Ringgold_NWSA-journal_-French-collection-Flag-is -Bleeding-Bitter-Nest_1994-copy.pdf.

Holton, Curlee Raven and Faith Ringgold. *Faith Ringgold: A View from the Studio*. Boston: Bunker Hill Publishing, 2004.

hooks, bell. *Yearning: Race, Gender, and Cultural Politics*. Abingdon, UK: Routledge, 2014.

Hurston, Zora Neale. *Dust Tracks on a Road*. New York: Harper Perennial, 1991. e-book.

——. *Mules and Men*. New York: HarperCollins, October 13, 2009. Kindle.

——. *Tell My Horse: Voodoo and Life in Haiti and Jamaica*. New York: Harper-Collins, 2009. Kindle.

Kaplan, Carla. *Zora Neale Hurston: A Life in Letters*. New York: Anchor, 2007.

Kuan, Christine. "Faith Ringgold," *Oxford Art Online*. www.oxfordartonline.com /page/faith-ringgold.

Lorde, Audre. *A Burst of Light*. Ithaca, NY: Firebrand Books, 1988.

Moylan, Virginia Lynn. *Zora Neale Hurston's Final Decade*. Gainesville, FL: University Press of Florida, 2011.

Ringgold, Faith. "In Conversation." *Tate Talks*, streamed live on July 5, 2018. You-Tube video, 1:35:55, www.youtube.com/watch?v=g5tbIjNwyrg.

——. Faith Ringgold Press Kit. www.faithringgold.com/press-kit/.

——. Lecture, Distinguished W. E. B. Du Bois Lectures. Humboldt University of Berlin, April 23, 2018. www.angl.hu-berlin.de/news/conferences/distinguished -dubois-lectures.

——. *Tar Beach*. New York: Crown Publishers, 1991.

——. *We Flew over the Bridge*. Durham, NC, and London: Duke University Press, 2005.

Russeth, Andrew. "The Storyteller: At 85, Her Star Still Rising, Faith Ringgold Looks Back on Her Life in Art, Activism, and Education." *ARTnews* (March 1, 2016). www.artnews.com/art-news/artists/the-storyteller-faith-ringgold-5918.

Walker, Alice, ed. *I Love Myself When I Am Laughing . . . and Then Again When I Am Looking Mean and Impressive: A Zora Neale Hurston Reader.* New York: Feminist Press at the City University of New York, 1979.

Walker, Alice. "Looking for Zora." *Ms.* (1975). www.scribd.com/doc/3275022 /Looking-for-Zora-296-313.

———. *In Search of Our Mothers' Gardens: Womanist Prose.* New York: Harcourt, 1983.

Chapter 3

Allen, John. "María Sabina: Saint Mother of the Sacred Mushrooms." Accessed June 28, 2020. https://erowid.org/plants/mushrooms/mushrooms_article6.shtml.

Aridjis, Chloe. "On María Sabina, One of Mexico's Greatest Poets." *Voices.* March 30, 2015. www.britishcouncil.org/voices-magazine/maria-sabina-one-of-mexicos -greatest-poets.

Baker, Russ. "Walt Disney, Cosmic Man!" *Who.What.Why.* January 3, 2012. https:// whowhatwhy.org/2012/01/03/walt-disney-cosmic-man/.

Dashu, Max. "Colonial Hunts: South America." In *Secret History of the Witches.* N.p.: Max Dashu, 2000. www.suppressedhistories.net/secrethistory/colhuntsouth.html.

Dawson, Alexander. "Salvador Roquet, Maria Sabina, and the Trouble with Jipis." *Hispanic American Historical Review* 95, no. 1 (February 2015): 103–133.

Durón, Maximilíano. "How to Altar the World: Amalia Mesa-Bains's Art Shifts the Way We See Art History." *ARTnews.* March 27, 2018. www.artnews.com /artnews/news/icons-amalia-mesa-bains-9988/.

Estrada, Álvaro. *María Sabina: Her Life and Chants.* N.p.: Ross-Erikson Publishers, 1981. Video, July 21–22, 1956, by R. Gordon Wasson in Huautla de Jiménez, Oaxaca, Mexico. http://ubusound.memoryoftheworld.org/ethno /sabina/mp3 /Sabina-Maria_From-The-Mushroom-Velada.Mp3.

Federici, Silvia. *Re-enchanting the World: Feminism and the Politics of the Commons.* Oakland, CA: PM Press, 2018.

Gazer, Brooke. "María Sabina and Magic Mushrooms." *Eye Huatulco.* May 1, 2015. https://theeyehuatulco.com/2015/05/01/maria-sabina-and-magic-mushrooms/.

Goodwin, Michael. "A Heavy Trip inside Mick Jagger's Head." *Rolling Stone.* September 3, 1970. www.rollingstone.com/music/music-news/a-heavy-trip-inside -mick-jaggers-head-184328/.

Lavoie, Josée G. "Medicare and the Care of First Nations, Métis and Inuit." Cambridge University Press. February 1, 2018. https://www.cambridge.org/core /journals/health-economics-policy-and-law/article/medicare-and-the-care-of -first-nations-metis-and-inuit/2CCEC7B7C8639A028F2CB037130AC4A7.

Pollan, Michael. "The Trip Treatment: Research into Psychedelics, Shut Down for Decades, Is Now Yielding Exciting Results." *New Yorker.* February 2, 2015. www.newyorker.com/magazine/2015/02/09/trip-treatment.

Rothenberg, Jerome, ed. *María Sabina: Selections*. Berkeley, CA: University of California Press, 2003.

Tracy. "History of Cartagena, Colombia: Spanish America's Biggest Slave Port." *Atlanta Black Star* (July 4, 2015). https://atlantablackstar.com/2015/07/04/cartagena-colombia-spanish-americas-biggest-slave-port/.

Vicuña, Cecilia and Ernesto Livon-Grosman, eds. The Oxford Book of Latin American Poetry: A Bilingual Anthology. Oxford, UK: Oxford University Press, 2009.

Von Germeten, Nicole. Violent Delights, Violent Ends: Sex, Race, and Honor in Colonial Cartagena de Indias (Albuquerque, NM: University of New Mexico Press, 2013).

Yépez, Heriberto. "Clock Woman in the Land of Mixed Feelings: The Place of Maria Sabina in Mexican Culture." www.ubu.com/ethno/discourses/Yépez_clock.html.

———. "Rereading María Sabina." Jacket. June 9, 2017: https://jacket2.org/commentary/heriberto-y%C3%A9pez-rereading-mar%C3%ADa-sabina.

Chapter 4

"Haiti Mobs Lynch Voodoo Priests over Cholera Fears," BBC, December 24, 2010. www.bbc.com/news/world-latin-america-12073029.

"Tori and Dean Home Sweet Hollywood: Fright Where We Belong Part 3." Streamed live on August 27, 2010. YouTube video. 9:59. www.youtube.com/watch?v=v1oD5i-2oHY.

Akalatunde, Iyalosa Apetebii Olaomi Osunyemi. *Ona Agbani: The Ancient Path: Understanding and Implementing the Ways of Our Ancestors*. 2002. Reprint 2018.

Deren, Maya. *Divine Horsemen: The Living Gods of Haiti*. London: Thames & Hudson, 1953.

Halprin, Anna. *Returning to Health: with Dance, Movement and Imagery*. Mendocino, CA: LifeRhythm Books, 2002.

Hyams, Danielle. "Vodou Was Once Blamed for the Haiti Earthquake, 10 Years Later It's Seeing a Slow Revival." *Haitian Times*. https://haitiantimes.com/2020/01/12/vodou-was-once-blamed-for-the-haiti-earthquake-10-years-later-its-seeing-a-slow-revival/.

MacFarland, Amanda. "Dance in Haiti." http://crudem.org/dance-in-haiti/.

Mathewson, Tara García. "How Poverty Changes the Brain." *Atlantic*. April 19, 2017. www.theatlantic.com/education/archive/2017/04/can-brain-science-pull-families-out-of-poverty/523479/.

McCarthy Brown, Karen. *Mama Lola: A Vodou Priestess in Brooklyn*. Berkeley, CA: University of California Press, 2011.

Olajide Ifatunmo, Osunniyi. "Is a 'Complete' Written Copy of the Odu Ifa?" Ooduarere.com. http://ooduarere.com/news-from-nigeria/breaking-news/complete-odu-ifa/.

Rigaud, Milo. *Secrets of Voodoo,* trans. Robert B. Cross. San Francisco, CA: City Lights Books, 2016.

Tann, Mambo Chita. *Haitian Vodou.* Woodbury, MN: Llewellyn Worldwide, 2012.

Chapter 5

Budapest, Zsuzsanna. *My Dark Sordid Past as a Heterosexual.* N.p.: CreateSpace, August 28, 2014.

———. *Summoning the Fates: A Generational Woman's Guide to Destiny and Sacred Transformation.* Women's Spirituality Forum. May 9, 2015.

———. *The Holy Book of Women's Mysteries.* Oakland, CA: Wingbow Press, 1989.

Christ, Carol. "Marija Gimbutas Triumphant: Colin Renfrew Concedes." *Feminism and Religion.* December 11, 2017. https://feminismandreligion.com/2017/12/11/marija-gimbutas-triumphant-colin-renfrew-concedes-by-carol-p-christ/.

Gimbutas, Marija. *The Language of the Goddess.* New York: Harper and Row, 1989.

———. *The Living Goddesses.* Berkeley, CA: University of California Press, 1999.

Goode, Starr. YouTube. www.youtube.com/channel/UCfxK1SilJGsFj0DPuFGIA_Q. www.youtube.com/watch?v=uxei-vuf7U8&. www.youtube.com/watch?v=-k34hXty4iw&.

Jacobs, Janet L. "The Effects of Ritual Healing on Female Victims of Abuse: A Study of Empowerment and Transformation." *Sociological Analysis* 50, no. 3 (1989): 265–279. https://academic.oup.com/socrel/article-abstract/50/3/265/1672874.

Lyons, Richard D. "Dr. Marija Gimbutas Dies at 73; Archaeologist with Feminist View." *New York Times,* February 4, 1994. www.nytimes.com/1994/02/04/obituaries/dr-marija-gimbutas-dies-at-73-archaeologist-with-feminist-view.html.

Marler, Joan. "A Tribute to Marija Gimbutas." *Sojourn* 2, no. 3 (1998). https://creation-designs.com/gracemillennium/sojourn/summer98/html/marler.html.

Pitofsky, Marina. "'Epidemic of Violence': 2018 Is Worst for Deadly Assaults against Transgender Americans." *USA Today.* September 26, 2018. www.usatoday.com/story/news/2018/09/26/2018-deadliest-year-transgender-deaths-violence/1378001002/.

Repsiene, Rita. "In Pursuit of the Goddess: How One Woman Defied the Odds to Restore the Feminist Principle." *Eurozine.* April 19, 2010. www.eurozine.com/in-pursuit-of-the-goddess/.

Saad, Layla F. *Me and White Supremacy Workbook.* Self-published, 2018.

Schulz, Cara. "Overview of the PantheaCon Gender Debate." Patheos.com. February 22, 2012. www.patheos.com/blogs/agora/2012/02/overview-of-the-pantheacon-gender-debate/.

Sjöö, Monica and Barbara Mor. *The Great Cosmic Mother: Rediscovering the Religion of the Earth.* San Francisco, CA: HarperSanFrancisco, 1987.

Wikipedia, s.v. "Kurgan hypothesis." Last modified June 20, 2020, https://en.wikipedia.org/wiki/Kurgan_hypothesis.

Chapter 6

Accardi, Dean. "Embedded Mystics: Writing Lal Ded and Nund Rishi into the Kashmiri Landscape." In *Kashmir: History, Politics, Representation*. ed. Chitralekha Zutshi. Cambridge, UK: Cambridge University Press, 2017.

Barnstone, Aliki, ed. *Voices of Light: Spiritual and Visionary Poems by Women from around the World from Ancient Sumeria to Now*. Boulder, CO: Shambhala, 1999.

Beck, Guy L. *Sonic Theology: Hinduism and Sacred Sound*. Delhi, India: Motilal Banarsidass, 1995.

Chakraverti, Ipsita Roy. "Biography." WiccanBrigade.com.

——. *Beloved Witch: An Autobiography*. N.p.: HarperCollins Publishers India, 2010). EPUB 2. Adobe DRM.

Cunningham, Scott. *Earth Power: Techniques of Natural Magic*. Woodbury, MN: Llewellyn Publications, 2016.

Děd, Lal. *I, Lalla: The Poems of Lal Děd*. trans. Ranjit Hoskote. London: Penguin UK, 2013.

Erdrich, Louise. "Advice to Myself." In *Original Fire: Selected and New Poems*. London: HarperCollins, 2009.

——. *The Blue Jay's Dance: A Memoir of Early Motherhood*. Toronto: Harper Perennial, 1995.

Federici, Silvia. *Witches, Witch-Hunting, and Women*. Oakland, CA: PM Press, 2018.

Giago, Tim. "Phony Indians." *Baltimore Sun* (1993). www.baltimoresun.com/news/bs-xpm-1993-01-27-1993027046-story.html.

Goldhill, Olivia. "The Idea That Everything from Spoons to Stones Is Conscious Is Gaining Academic Credibility." *Quartz* (January 27, 2018). https://qz.com/1184574/the-idea-that-everything-from-spoons-to-stones-are-conscious-is-gaining-academic-credibility/.

Greene, Heather. "Witchcraft in India: A Conversation with Ipsita Roy Chakraverti." *Wild Hunt* (September 13, 2015). https://wildhunt.org/2015/09/Witchcraft-in-india-a-conversation-with-ipsita-roy-chakraverti.html.

Guiley, Rosemary. "Isaac Newton." In *Encyclopedia of Magic and Alchemy*. New York: Infobase Publishing, 2006.

Harper, John Jay. *Tranceformers: Shamans of the 21st Century*. Foresthill, CA: Reality Press, 2009.

Kaur, Pawanpreet. "The Adivasi, the Colonial and the Great Indian Witch Hunt." *Sunday Guardian* (November 3, 2012). www.sunday-guardian.com/artbeat/the-adivasi-the-colonial-and-the-great-indian-witch-hunt.

Lal Ded: Her Life and Sayings. trans. Nil Kanth Kotru. Srinagar, Kashmir: Utpal Publications, 1989.

Lovett, Richard A. and Scot Hoffman. "Crystal Skulls." *National Geographic*. www .nationalgeographic.com/history/archaeology/crystal-skulls/.

Shome, Sudipto. "Code Cracked." *Hindu*. January 19, 2008.

Thakur, Meenakshi. "Women Mystics: A Comparative Study of Lalleshwari and Julian of Norwich." St. Andrew's College. https://standrewscollege.ac.in/wp -content/uploads/2018/07/Women-Mystics.pdf.

Urban, Hugh. "The Goddess and the Great Rite: Hindu Tantra and the Complex Origins of Modern Wicca." Academia.edu. Accessed June 13, 2020. www .academia.edu/40032525/The_Goddess_and_the_Great_Rite_Hindu_Tantra _and_the_Complex_Origins_of_Modern_Wicca.

Chapter 7

"Douching." Womenshealth.gov.

Bernard Butler. Pagan Queen: Jung, Individuation and the Goddess Inanna. www .gatewaystobabylon.com.

Elliott, Carolyn. "7 Notes on Amor Fati: A Magic of Raw Power." *Witch* (April 28, 2016). https://badwitch.es/amor-fati-notes-magic-raw-power/.

Foster, Benjamin R. *The Age of Agade: Inventing Empire in Ancient Mesopotamia*. Abingdon, UK: Routledge, 2015.

Grossman, Pam. *Waking the Witch: Reflections on Women, Magic, and Power*. New York: Gallery Books, 2019. Kindle.

Lopes, Roseane. "Inanna/Ishtar—the Non-Maternal as an Archetype of Feminine Integrity." Presented at the 47e Rencontre Assyriologique, Helsinki, Finland. July 2 to July 6, 2001. Reprinted. www.gatewaystobabylon.com.

Meador, Betty De Shong. *Inanna: Lady of Largest Heart: Poems of the Sumerian High Priestess Enheduanna*. Austin, Texas: University of Texas Press, 2001.

Muscio, Inga. *Cunt: A Declaration of Independence*. Berkeley, CA: Seal Press, 2002.

Chapter 8

"H. P. Blavatsky and Her Writings." Theosophical Society. Accessed June 14, 2020. www.theosophical.org/component/content/article/25-online-resources /online-leaflets/1796-hp-blavatsky-and-her-writings.

"Pictures in Music," *Strand Magazine* (July 1908): 648–652.

"Witches Found: Amanda Yates Garcia." October 16, 2019. In *Missing Witches* podcast. Episode 41.

"Witches Found: Edgar Fabián Frías." October 2, 2019. In *Missing Witches* podcast. Episode 37.

Bibliography

Blavatsky, Helena P. *The Secret Doctrine: Anthropogenesis.* N.p.: Theosophical Publishing Company, 1888.

———. *The Secret Doctrine: The Synthesis of Science, Religion, and Philosophy.* vol. 1. Woodstock, Canada: Devoted Publishing, 2018.

———. *The Secrets of Spirituality & Occult: The Secret Doctrine, The Key to Theosophy, The Voice of the Silence, Studies in Occultism, Isis Unveiled.* e-artnow.

———. *The Voice of the Silence.* Rev. ed. 1899; repr. Pasadena, CA: Theosophical University Press, 2015. www.theosociety.org/pasadena/voice/VoiceoftheSilence_eBook.pdf.

———. *The Key to Theosophy.* Wheaton, IL: Quest Books, 1972.

Charles River Editors. *The Mother of Theosophy: The Life and Legacy of H. P. Blavatsky.* Kindle.

Denisoff, Dennis. "The Hermetic Order of the Golden Dawn, 1888–1901." *Branch.* 2013. www.branchcollective.org/?ps_articles=dennis-denisoff-the-hermetic-order-of-the-golden-dawn-1888-1901.

Faxneld, Per. *Satanic Feminism: Lucifer as the Liberator of Woman in Nineteenth-Century Culture.* Oxford, UK: Oxford University Press, 2017.

Grossman, Pam. *Waking the Witch: Reflections on Women, Magic, and Power.* New York: Gallery Books, 2019. Kindle

Hochschartner, Jon. "Vegan Angela Davis Connects Human and Animal Liberation." January 24, 2014. *CounterPunch.* www.counterpunch.org/2014/01/24/vegan-angela-davis-connects-human-and-animal-liberation/.

Kaplan, Stuart. *The Artwork and Times of Pamela Colman Smith.* N.p.: U.S. Games Systems; 1st ed. 2009.

Lachman, Gary. *Madame Blavatsky: The Mother of Modern Spirituality.* New York: Jeremy P. Tarcher/Penguin, 2012.

Metzner, Ralph. *Maps of Consciousness: I Ching, Tantra, Tarot, Alchemy, Astrology, Actualism.* New York: Macmillan, 1971.

Norfleet, Phil. "Alfred Stieglitz and Pamela Coleman Smith." http://pcs2051.tripod.com/stieglitz_archive.htm.

———. "Creation of the Waite-Smith Tarot." http://pcs2051.tripod.com/waite-smith_tarot.htm.

———. "Retirement to Cornwall." http://pcs2051.tripod.com/.

Pratt Institute Monthly. vol. 7, 1899.

Ransome, Arthur. *Bohemia in London.* New York: Dodd, Mead & Company, 1907.

Roy, Arundhati. "The Pandemic Is a Portal." *Financial Times* (April 3, 2020). www.ft.com/content/10d8f5e8-74eb-11ea-95fe-fcd274e920ca.

Smith, Pamela Colman. "Should the Art Student Think?" *Craftsman* (July 1908): 417–419.

Tea, Michelle. "The Divine Mystery of Pamela Colman Smith." *Enchanted Living* magazine. 2017. https://enchantedlivingmagazine.com/divine-mystery-pamela -colman-smith/.

Wikipedia. s.v. "Root Race." Last modified July 13, 2020, https://en.wikipedia.org /wiki/Root_race#cite_note-FOOTNOTEBlavatsky1962Section_3-40.

Yates Garcia, Amanda. *Initiated: Memoir of a Witch*. New York: Grand Central Pub-lishing, 2019.

INDEX

A

Ad Hoc Women Artists' Committee, 68
Ain, Mireille, 116
Akalatunde, Iyalosa Apetebii Olaomi
   Osunyemi, 117–18
Allen, Paula Gunn, 7
altars, 102–4
American Civil Liberties Union, 68
Amu Mawu, 40
An, 213
androgyny, 212
Angelou, Maya, 109
Anthony, Susan B., 162, 165
anxiety, 49–50
archaeomythology, 147–48
Aridjis, Homero, 86
Art Without Walls, 68
autumn equinox, 202, 204, 226

B

Baba Yaga, 153
Backxwash, 56–57
Bamford, Christopher, 238
Bassett, Angela, 133
Baum, Lyman Frank, 239
Beaumont, Jacqui, 142, 151, 167
Belafonte, Harry, 161
Belham-Payne, John, 24, 25
Beltane, 40, 108–10, 122, 125, 134–36
Besant, Annie, 238
Beyoncé, 64
binary vs. nonbinary, 149–50
birth, giving, 29–36
Blake, Williajm, 251
Blavatsky, H. P., 234–45, 247, 249
Bletchley Park, 18–19

Boas, Franz, 58
Boyd, Valerie, 63
Brighde, 13
Brown, Karen McCarthy, 110, 116–17,
   119, 122, 127, 131–32, 134
Budapest, Z. (Zsuzsanna), 39, 142, 155–66
Butler, Bernard, 220

C

Cailleach, 13
calling the corners, 8
Campbell, Joseph, 146
Carhart-Harris, Robin, 96
Carson, Johnny, 161
Centre for Pagan Studies, 24
Chakraverti, Ipsita Roy, 4, 56, 111,
   184–96, 220
Chango, 116, 120
"The Charge of the Goddess," 17–18
Chicago, Judy, 39
Clan of Tubal Cain, 22
Clarke, Joe, 53
Cochrane, Robert, 22
Constant, Yvonne, 128, 130
Cooke, Ron, 23
coronavirus pandemic, 232–33
Craig, Edith "Edy," 255
Crowley, Aleister, 2, 21, 25, 252
crying, 51
Cullen, Countee, 59
Cunningham, Scott, 191
cunt, etymology of, 206–7

D

Dafo, 21
dancing, 108–10, 111, 123–26, 127

Darwin, Charles, 237
Davis, Angela, 56
Davis, Thadious M., 53
death, facing, 232–34, 241
Dee, John, 252
de Eguiluz, Paula (Aleluya), 80–86
de la Peña, Marisa, 3
Denisoff, Dennis, 252
Deren, Maya, 125–26
Dexter, Miriam Robbins, 153–54
Dianic Wicca, 162–64
Diogenes, 140
Disney, Walt, 89
Douglas, Tommy, 94
Dow, Arthur Wesley, 248
Drake, Nick, 99
duality, illusion of, 183, 187
Duchamp, Marcel, 251
Dunham, Katherine, 124–25
DuVal, Patrick, 61, 62
Duvalier, François (Papa Doc), 121
Dworkin, Andrea, 39
Dybing, Peter, 164
Dylan, Bob, 90

E

Edison, Thomas, 238
Ehrenreich, Barbara, 2
Einstein, Albert, 238
Elegua (Elegba), 120, 135
Elliott, Carolyn, 224
English, Deirdre, 2
Enheduanna, 203–4, 207, 209–11, 213,
    215–23, 225
Enki, 213
Enlil, 213
entheogens, 89
Eostar. See Ostara
Erdrich, Louise, 173, 177
Ersolt, Robert, 108
Ethnographic Museum of the
    Trocadéro, 69

F

Farrington, Lisa, 71
Federici, Silvia, 2, 4–5

Fitzgerald, Ella, 222
Foriero, Domingo, 59
Foster, Benjamin, 216
Franco, Affonso Arinos de Mello, 125
Frank, Anne, 226
Frías, Fabián, 256–57
Fuller, Eunice, 254

G

Gage, Matilda Joslyn, 239
Gandhi, Mohandas, 235–36, 237, 238
Garcia, Amanda Yates, 5, 232, 258
Gardner, Gerald, 2, 18, 20–21, 24–25,
    161, 182, 196
Gardnerian Wicca, 21, 22
Garibaldi, Giuseppe, 241
gender diversity, 205
George Washington Bridge, 72
Giago, Tim, 190
Gimbutas, Marija, 39, 142–55
Goddess, prehistoric images of, 148–49
Golden Dawn, 252
González-Wippler, Migene, 3
Goode, Starr, 152
Grahn, Judy, 208
Griffiths, Roland, 96
Grimm, Jacob, 20
Grof, Stanislav, 96
Grossman, Pam, 218
Groundhog Day, 48–49, 50, 51, 76
Guercken, Valentina Pavlovna, 87, 88
Guggenheim Museum, 73

H

Halprin, Anna, 110
Haraway, Donna, 14, 257
Harlem Renaissance, 58–59, 65
Hendricks, Jon, 68
Hendrix, Jimi, 99
Heselton, Philip, 19
Holiday, Billie, 102
Holmes, Athena, 57
Holton, Curlee Raven, 64, 73
hooks, bell, 70, 71
Hughes, Langston, 58, 59
Huneker, James Gibbons, 251

Hunter, WhiteFeather, 7, 59, 210
Hurston, Zora Neale, 52–53, 65, 75, 111, 133, 147

I

Ifa, 20, 113, 117–20, 134, 213
Ifatunmo, Ossunniyi Olajide, 117
Imbolc, 48–49, 51–52, 62, 68, 75–77
Inana, Phoenix, 207–8, 211, 212, 214, 219, 226
Inanna, 204, 207–8, 210–13, 217–23, 225, 226
Institute of Archaeomythology, 144
Irving, Henry, 250

J

Jacobs, Janet L., 161
Jesus, 80
Jones, Willi Posey, 65
Joplin, Janis, 99
June, Lyla, 15
Jung, Carl, 222, 237

K

Kouzen Zaka, 129

L

labor, 29–36
Lake, Nora, 255
Lal Ded, 178–83, 192
Lammas. *See* Lughnasadh
Lamoreaux, Annie, 99
Laveau, Marie, 59, 133
Lawrence, Jacob, 69
Lennon, John, 90
Lerner, Gerda, 143
Lewis, Cudjo, 52
Lincoln, Abraham, 242
Litha, 140–42, 155, 167–69
Lizzo, 141
Locke, Alain LeRoy, 58
Lopes, Roseane, 218
López, Diego, 84–85
Lorde, Audre, 50
L'Ouverture, Toussaint, 120
LSD, 96, 97, 98

Lucas, George, 146
Lugal-Ane, 220
Lughnasadh (Lammas), 172–73, 177, 181, 192, 196–98
Lwa, 116, 119, 121–24, 126, 128–30
Lyceum Theatre, 250, 251

M

Maafa, 118, 119, 134
Mabon, 202, 204, 207, 210, 212, 219, 222, 223, 225–28
Macena, Philomise (Philo), 111, 121, 122, 130
magic
    Earth and, 37–38
    shame and, 224–25
    as way of seeing and being, 7
Mama Lola, 110–13, 117, 119–24, 126–35, 241
Manbos, 111–12, 131–32
Mankiller, Wilma, 190
Marler, Joan, 144, 145
Martinez-Cruz, Paloma, 92
Marx, Karl, 237
masks, 69–71
Matisse, Henri, 69, 251
Maypole, 108–9
Meador, Betty De Shong, 202, 206, 208, 210–12, 222
menstruation, 202, 204–5, 208, 210–11
Mesa-Bains, Amalia, 102–3
Missing Witches
    meaning of, 4
    motivation for finding, 1–2
Mithra, 12
MKULTRA program, 89, 92
Molteni, Maria, 206
Moon, cycle of, 208, 210–11, 225
Mor, Barbara, 39, 148
Moses, 53
Mother's Night, 12–13, 17
Moylan, Virginia Lynn, 53
Munch, Edvard, 251
Murray, Bill, 51
Muscio, Inga, 202, 206

N

Nanna, 216, 217, 220–21
National Black Feminist Organization, 68
Nature
    belief in, 3
    completeness of, 6
    connecting with, 2
    lessons from, 7
Nehru, Jawaharlal, 238
Nettles, Islan, 163
New Age movement, 16, 36–37, 161
New Forest coven, 21
Newton, Isaac, 187
Nietzsche, Friedrich, 237
Noble, Vicki, 35
nonbinary vs. binary, 149–50

O

Obatala, 120
Ochosi, 120
Ogun, 120, 130–31
O'Keeffe, Georgia, 248
Olcott, Henry Steel, 242–43
Oliver-Lloyd, Vanessa, 151, 223
Olodumare, 119
Orisha, 120, 121, 153
Oshun, 120
Ostara (Eostar), 80, 82, 88, 94, 101–4

P

PantheaCon, 163, 165
Parsons, Gram, 99
Pasteur, Louis, 59
Picasso, Pablo, 66, 69–70, 251
Presley, Elvis, 109, 195–96
psilocybin mushrooms, 80, 86–88, 90–92, 96–100
Pythagoras, 247

R

Ragana, 153
Ramis, Harold, 51
Reagan, Claude Harley "Swiftdeer," 190
rebirth, 141–42
Renfrew, Colin, 154

Rich, Adrienne, 39
Rigaud, Milo, 112, 113
Ringgold, Faith, 52, 63–75
Robertson, Pat, 112
Rodin, Auguste, 251
The Rolling Stones, 89
Romero, George, 130
Roth, Moira, 67
Russeth, Andrew, 67

S

Saad, Layla, 156
Sabbats, 5–6, 141. *See also individual Sabbats*
Sabina, María, 80, 86–87, 89–101, 147, 238
Samhain, 232, 234, 237, 239, 245–46, 249, 255–58
Santeria, 113, 115, 118
Sargon, King, 215–16, 225
sex work, 126–27
shadow work, 50–51, 222–24, 228
Shakespeare, William, 205
shame, 208–10, 224–25
Sikoak, Jason, 205
Silbury Hill, 16, 26, 40
Sinnett, A. P., 241
Sjöö, Monica, 16, 26–28, 35–42, 43, 148
Smith, Charles Edward, 247
Smith, Corinne Colman, 247
Smith, Pamela "Pixie" Colman, 147, 234, 247–55
Society for the Study of Ancient Cultures and Civilizations, 185, 187
Sola Busca deck, 253
Sol Invictus, 12
"Solstice Carol," 44
Spelling, Tori, 133–34
spiders, 14
spring equinox, 80
Starhawk, 39, 40
Stieglitz, Alfred, 251
Stoker, Bram, 250, 251
Stonehenge, 16, 40
Suffrage Atelier, 251

summer solstice, 140
Sun Dance, 123–24
Susan B. Anthony Coven, 161, 162, 165
Suzuki, D. T., 242
Swedenborg, Emanuel, 248
symbols, power of, 145–46

T

Tailtiu, 173
Take Back the Night marches, 162–63
Tann, Chita, 129
Tantra, 179, 180, 182–84, 196
tarot, 252–53
Temple of Ur, 204, 217, 221, 225
Terry, Ellen, 250–51, 254
Theosophy, 234, 235, 238, 243
Thoreau, Henry David, 237
Thurman, Wallace, 58
Toche, Jean, 68
Tolstoy, Leo, 237
Townshend, Pete, 90
trans women, 155, 163–64
Trump, Donald, 158
Tyson, Neil deGrasse, 203

U

Urban, Hugh, 181–82, 196

V

Valiente, Doreen, 16, 17–26, 39, 181–82
Vincent, Sténio, 111
Vodou, 109–13, 116–19, 122–25, 129, 132–34
von Germeten, Nicole, 83, 85
Vonnegut, Kurt, 238

W

Waite, A. E., 252–53

Waldron, Sarah, 19
Walker, Alice, 39, 53–55, 61–62
Walker, Barbara, 207
Walker, Monefa, 228
Wall, Cheryl, 61
Wasson, Gordon, 87–89, 91, 92, 93, 96
Wheel of the Year, 3, 5–7, 108, 141
"Where We At" Black Women Artists, 68
Whitney Museum of American Art, 67
Wicca, etymology of, 20
Wilson, Alan Christie, 99
winter solstice, 5–6, 12, 17, 26, 41
Witchcraft
    activism and, 37, 56
    changing form and, 62
    as fertility cult, 25–26
Witches. *See also* Missing Witches; *individual Witches*
    as label, 63
    meaning of, 206
Witch hunts, 4, 84, 184, 193–94
WomanSpirit magazine, 39
Women Students and Artists for Black Art Liberation, 68
Woolley, Leonard, 225
worlding, 14
World War II, 18–19, 144, 174

Y

Yeats, William Butler, 251, 254
Yemaya, 120
Yépez, Heriberto, 92–93, 95, 96
Yule, 12–14, 16–17, 40–44

Z

zombies, 129–30

PHOTO CREDIT: MARC SIMARD

RISA DICKENS has an undergraduate honors baccalaureate in English Literature and a masters in Communications Studies. She helped found Worn Fashion Journal writing feminist fashion history. Since then she has worked in community building, marketing and PR in tech for over 15 years and is currently a senior community director at Yelp.

AMY TOROK is an ESL teacher, counter-culture enthusiast, professional musician and visual artist/designer with a B.A. in English Literature and a post-graduate diploma in Journalism.

Risa and Amy were on a similar track, community and event organizing in Montréal, when they met backstage at a ukulele showcase. Together they've worked their magic to create music, a coven, a podcast, and now this book.

Both Risa and Amy live tucked into the woods of Québec.

About North Atlantic Books

North Atlantic Books (NAB) is a 501(c)(3) nonprofit publisher committed to a bold exploration of the relationships between mind, body, spirit, culture, and nature. Founded in 1974, NAB aims to nurture a holistic view of the arts, sciences, humanities, and healing. To make a donation or to learn more about our books, authors, events, and newsletter, please visit www.northatlanticbooks.com.